Meyebela

Meyebela
My Bengali Girlhood

TASLIMA NASRIN

TRANSLATED BY GOPA MAJUMDAR

STEERFORTH PRESS
SOUTH ROYALTON, VERMONT

First published in French as *Enfance: au feminin* by Edition Stock, Paris, 1998
First published as *Amar Meyebela* in Bengali by Peoples Book Society, Calcutta, 1999
First published in English as *My Girlhood* by Kali for Women, New Delhi, 2002

For information about permission to reproduce
selections from this book, write to:
Steerforth Press L.C., P.O. Box 70,
South Royalton, Vermont 05068

Library of Congress Cataloging-in-Publication Data

Nāsarina, Tasalimā.
[Āmara mēyebelā. English]
My bengali girlhood / Taslima Nasrin ; Translated by Gopa Majumdar.
p. cm.
ISBN 1-58642-051-8 (alk. paper)
1. Nāsarina, Tasalimā — Childhood and youth. 2. Women authors,
Bengali — Bangladesh — Biography. 3. Authors,
Bengali — Bangladesh — Biography. I. Majumdar, Gopa. II. Title.
PK1730.3.A65 Z4613 2002
891.4'4171 — dc21

2002005767

FIRST EDITION

To my mother
who suffered all her life

CONTENTS

～ BANGLADESH ～

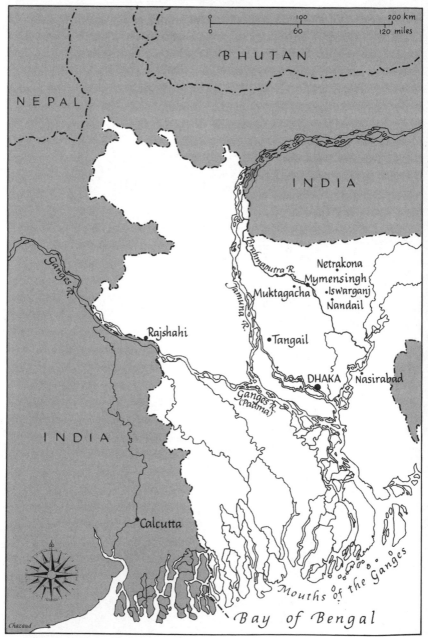

CHRONOLOGY

1947   India achieves its independence from the British Empire, leading to the creation of two states. This is known as the Partition and results in the Indian Union, with a Hindu majority, and Pakistan, with a Muslim majority. Pakistan is created out of two pieces of land that are more than 1,250 miles apart, West Pakistan and East Pakistan (which is today's Bangladesh). Culturally and linguistically the eastern part is profoundly distant from the western part.

1952   The movement in East Pakistan to have Bengali recognized as the national language takes on momentum.

1969–1971   Violent riots reveal the depth of the desire for independence.

1971   Bangladesh declares its independence on March 26. This is the beginning of the ferocious repression by the Pakistan army and guerrilla war. Indian military intervention in the country in December drives out the Pakistani troops and frees the country.

1972   Sheikh Mujibur Rahman becomes president of the new nation.

1975   Sheikh Mujibar Rahman and a large number of his family are assassinated in the military coup that takes place August 15.

~ 1 ~

The Year of the War

$\mathcal{A}$ war was about to start. Knots of wide-eyed people gathered in courtyards, in open fields, on street corners. Some just stood, questioning. Others were running, both in daylight and after dark, clutching bundles under their arms and children on their shoulders. Running, they were running away from cities to villages, from Mymensingh to Phulpur, Dhobaura, and Nandail. Rushing to the other side of the river they left behind the schools, the theater, and the shops they knew so well. They swarmed onto the rice fields, the barren lands, the forests. Even those who had never imagined they would leave packed their belongings and got out. Quickly.

Vultures began circling, the smell of rotten flesh on their beaks. The sound of bullets echoed against the restless fluttering of pigeons' wings. Some people ran as fast as their legs would take them. Others went by rail or boat. Villages were emptied, gardens deserted, pets abandoned.

One evening as dusk fell, two three-wheeled vehicles stopped at our door. We were hustled outside and began our journey to a village called Madarinagar, to the south of Panchrukhi Bazar. To cross the Brahmaputra River we had to take the ferry. But when we reached the other side half a dozen young men slipped from the shadows and blocked our way. Terrified, my sister Yasmin and I clung to Ma, staring at the guns slung over their shoulders.

So this is war, I thought, *stopping people unexpectedly and scaring them.* One, who had a thin, smooth, black mustache, peered through the open door of our vehicle. "Where d'you think you're going? If everyone leaves this town, who will be left to fight? Go back home!" Mustache ordered, his voice both nervous and firm.

Ma lifted her veil and replied with a mixture of anger and pleading, "What are you saying? The other vehicle has already gone by. My sons are in it. You must let us catch up with them."

Mustache remained unmoved. Taking his rifle from his shoulder, he struck the ground with it.

"No," he yelled. "These wheels must not move an inch forward. Go on, now, turn around." His eyes were angry. "Go back!" With a little movement I had never seen before his finger clicked something on the gun.

Putting the vehicle into reverse, our driver put us back on the ferry. No further conversation ensued until we were a little distance away. Then he lit a bidi, blew out some smelly smoke, and said, "Those boys were our very own. They weren't Punjabis. Have no fear."

All I could hear beside the roar of our vehicle's engine was the pounding of my heart. *Thud, thud, thud, thud, thud, thud* . . . as if a bullet had been shot from those six rifles and each had struck my chest. Then I heard two burkha-clad figures muttering the *sura*. And I sensed that as we passed the neighborhoods of Jubli Ghat and Golpukur Par the whole town had wrapped itself in a blanket of darkness — turned off the lights and gone to sleep.

We returned home, but Baba did not let us spend the night at home. He packed us off again in the same vehicle, this time westward to Begunbari. Yasmin and Chhotku (my little uncle) fell asleep in the three-wheeler. Ma dozed, but Grandma and I stayed awake. In her hand was a blue plastic basket, which she clutched tightly.

"What's in the basket, Grandma?"

"*Chira* and *gur*,"* she replied, coldly.

Our bidi-smoking driver eventually stopped at a house surrounded by plantains. Here, where Aunt Runu lived with her in-laws, people were carrying lanterns to the courtyard, raising them high, and staring at us.

"They are relatives from the town," said one.

"Get some water from the well," said another.

"Make them rice."

"Get some *paan*."**

"Make their bed."

"Fan them."

---

* Chira is puffed rice; gur is a brown sweet made from date palms.
** Betel leaf.

Later, we lay down on a freshly made bed. But there wasn't enough room for everyone and Chhotku, still fast asleep, placed a leg over mine. When I tried to move my own leg, Yasmin's knee dug into my stomach. Crushed between the two of them I cried plaintively, "How can I sleep without my pillow?"

Because of the prickly heat, Ma fanned all of us and, annoyed by my self-centeredness, snapped in a low voice, "Forget your pillow. Just go to sleep."

I fell silent. Curled in one corner was Grandma, her white sari covering her face, her arms, and the plastic basket with the snacks. A lantern sat on the threshold. In its dim light I could see a ghost dancing on the tin fence, its five arms and five legs spread wide. It made a hissing noise, and in terror I hid my face between my knees. "Ma, Ma, I'm scared!"

Ma made no reply. Like Chhotku, she had fallen asleep.

"Grandma! O Grandma!"

Grandma did not respond either.

Uncle Sharaf was the first to teach me about ghosts. One night, he returned home, panting and out of breath.

"I saw a female spook near the pond!" he said. His eyes were fixed on me and I wished he would look away. "It gave me such a piercing glance that I dropped everything and ran." Still shivering, he got quickly into bed and pulled the quilt over his head. So did I, lying huddled all night like a snail, afraid to move an inch or open an eye lest I see a piercing glance!

The next day he came back with a similar story. He was passing through a bamboo grove, he said, and no one was in sight. Yet he heard a nasal voice: "Why, Sharaf? Where are you off to? Stop for a second."

He sprinted home and, although it was freezing, had a quick, cold shower. Everyone stared at him, and my uncles Felu and Tutu and I sat with him until midnight. Aunt Parul fanned him, and as a special treat for a son who had just seen a ghost Grandma served him fish curry with hot rice, a pinch of salt in one corner of the plate.

As he ate, Uncle Sharaf told us about Uncle Kana, Grandma's brother. I listened intently, watching his movements and hearing his shaky voice.

"The fish Uncle Kana caught were always huge. But he could never get back home with a whole fish. One night he saw a cat following him. The fish was hanging from his shoulder. On his way home, his load suddenly felt lighter." I anticipated what he would say next. "And when he turned around, he found that half the fish had disappeared, and so had the cat. It was not a real cat at all, you see. It was a fish-spook, disguised as a cat."

After this, I began to avoid the bamboo grove that stood behind Grandma's house, not only at night, but in broad daylight as well. As soon as dusk arrived, I would hide inside, ignoring even the urgent call of nature. When I could no longer hold back, an adult carrying a lantern had to accompany me to the lavatory outside. I ran behind, keeping my eyes and ears open, went in and did what I had to do as quickly as possible.

I was about eight when we left Grandma's house and moved to our own house in Amlapara. Baba consulted his two sons about a suitable name for our new home. Noman, whom I called Dada, said, "San Souci." Kamal, whom I called Chhotda, suggested "Blue Heaven." No one asked me, but I offered a name, also.

"I like Crisenthimam," I said with great satisfaction.

Eventually Dada's choice was carved on a slab of marble and fixed on our black gate. It was a huge house, with delicately carved pillars and doors. The ceilings of the rooms were like the sky, with green iron beams supporting wooden planks that resembled railroad tracks. I could imagine a train running over them, whistling, huffing, and puffing. Close to a woodapple tree, a spiral staircase led to the roof. If I stood and looked over its carved railing, I could see the entire neighborhood. Rows of coconut and areca palms stood near the edge of a field. Our courtyard had other trees: mango, *jamun,* jackfruit, guava, woodapple, custard apple, olive, and pomegranate. Yasmin and I ran all over the house, playing *gollachhut* with our two brothers. We left behind Grandma's old house, by the side of a pond filled with Kholsey fish; left behind marble games under a banyan tree; cleaning lamp chimneys with pieces of rag smeared with ash; reading poetry with the uncles on large mats in the evenings; drinking fresh date juice and cakes of rice at dawn. But one thing traveled with me from Grandma's house, to San Souci and then to this house in Begunbari — my fear of ghosts. Uncle Sharaf's words, "Spooks and spirits go back home as soon as the night is over," were of little comfort.

In the morning, as the sun streamed in through cracks in the tin roof warming the room, I found no sign of the ghost with five legs. The only noise came from the courtyard where Ma, Grandma, and Aunt Runu's mother-in-law sat on wooden seats and talked. On this, my first visit to the country, I remembered the time I had taken a train to visit Uncle Siddique, who lived in Dhaka in a house near a huge, open field. I remembered having chanted a rhyme to the beat of the train's wheels:

> The wheels go ching-a-ching-a-ching.
> How far is Dhaka from Mymensingh?

Now, looking at the open sky, I wanted to fly high like a kite, to play hide-and-seek with the fairies in the clouds. Later, sitting on the veranda outside and brushing my teeth with powdered coal, I thought that maybe war was not such a bad thing after all. When we were still in Amlapara, our school had unexpectedly closed, and I was free to play up on our roof with my dolls all day long. When I saw an airplane in the sky I fled downstairs. Ma stuffed our ears with cotton and told us to hide under our beds. Then she sat muttering the *sura*. Soon after that, a long hole was dug in the ground in a field near our house. If a bomb fell, we would take shelter there. When the local hospital was bombed, Baba decided that the town was no longer safe. So the men — Dada, Chhotda, Uncle Sharaf, Uncle Felu, and Uncle Tutu — were packed into one vehicle and sent to Madarinagar; the rest of us were taken to Begunbari. Baba stayed behind to protect the house, vowing to leave only if the situation got worse.

Taking a deep breath, I rinsed my mouth with water drawn from the well. The smell of lemon leaves brought a smile to my face. Baba was no longer here to issue stern commands, to shout, scold, or slap. Now I could dance with the wind in the village streets. Deep shadows stretched in the woods under the trees and the vines. Dozens of broad beans swung within easy reach. I would gather them all, roast them over a slow fire, and give them away to the poor farmers. Oh, what fun! Could life possibly get any better?

"Chhotku, come on," I called. "Let's go buy some tamarind."

The suggestion made Chhotku spring to his feet. The very thought of sucking a piece of tamarind made my mouth water, and together we slipped away from the courtyard, passed under rows of plantain, and made our way to the main road through the tracks in the fields.

From nowhere, like a scarecrow our hosts' son, Hashu, appeared. He was a well-built young man with his *lungi** tucked in at the waist. In his hand was a broken branch that he used to beat the animals.

"It's all right for Chhotku to go to the shop," he exclaimed in a gruff voice. "But not you. You are a girl."

What is this peasant saying to me? I thought. "So what! I go to shops all the time," I replied contemptuously, trying to ignore the insult.

"You might be able to do that in town," he said, "but this isn't a town, is it? It's a village. Girls stay at home in villages. They don't go out."

The scarecrow crept closer. From deep within his eyes peered two gray rats.

I had heard so much about the tender green beauty of the countryside, but here I was, unable to dance among the swaying rice stalks, to go wherever my fancy took me, to get lost in distant fields and listen to the flute of a young shepherd boy. Instead, I was being scolded by a man in whose house I was a guest! A lump rose in my throat. There was nothing to do but stop, so I retraced my steps, returned to the courtyard, and sat snuggling against Ma. She was wearing a faded old sari. Her hair was loose, but her head was covered by one end of her sari. Grabbing a corner I wrapped and unwrapped it around my finger a few times before saying with a choked voice, "He wouldn't let me go!"

Ma did not reply.

I placed my hands under her chin and turned her face toward me. "That Hashu," I said, "he wouldn't let me go and buy tamarind."

"No need to eat tamarind," she snapped, jerking her face away. "All your blood will turn to water if you do."

She had said this before. In fact, she always said it, which is why I used to eat tamarind secretly on the stairs that went up to our roof. I mixed it with salt and made a paste that I placed in my mouth, bit by bit, smacking my lips and clicking my tongue. I wouldn't stop until my tongue turned white and my teeth ached from the sharp taste. Each time I cut myself I studied the wound apprehensively, wondering if water would gush out instead of blood. But no, thankfully, whenever I cut myself on a piece of glass, or by stepping on a snail, whenever I got pricked by a rosebush thorn, or fell over a broken brick in

---

* Loincloth worn by men.

the courtyard, it was always blood that trickled out, never water. Ma wiped the wound clean, dabbing it with Dettol (an antiseptic) and tying a piece of cloth over it. When she did, a triumphant smile played on my lips, I leaked blood.

So many people had lived in this house. The girls were all named after fruits — Dalim (Pomegranate), Peara (Guava), Angur (Grape), Kamala (Orange). The boys were simply called Hashu, Kashu, Bashu, and Rashu. Rashu was married to my Aunt Runu. Because war was imminent Rashu had fled; no one knew where he had gone. His mother — Aunt Runu's mother-in-law — always spoke with her mouth full. Crammed with paan, her cheeks bulged and red juice oozed out of the corners of her mouth. Her fingertips were stained with lime. Digging into her paan-box she would pick up a pinch of white powder with a clean finger, place it in a swollen cheek, and speak into Grandma's ear. "Who knows where my Rashu is? If he's dead or alive? I hear the Punjabis are killing everyone in the towns." War, I was learning, included moving around to avoid being killed. Being killed, apparently, meant you could no longer eat tamarind and nothing flowed in your veins, not even water!

Sitting on a wooden seat, Grandma's little form looked like a bundle, a bundle of white sari with a black border. It did not move. In her hand, held tightly, was that blue plastic basket filled with chira and gur. Her eyes remained perfectly still, like the rest of her body. Those same eyes had greeted Uncle Hashem, her second son, when he had knocked on her door one night.

"Why are you here so late at night? What's the matter?" she complained, raising the wick of her oil lamp and climbing down the steps that led to her front door.

"I am leaving."

He began walking in the direction of the pond, Grandma in pursuit.

"Where are you going in the middle of the night? Stop, stop, Hashem!"

"I'm going to the war," he had replied. Without stopping or looking back he continued, "And I will return only when our country is free."

"Stop, Hashem, stop!" But her stubborn child was soon totally engulfed by the darkness.

Grandma's heart beat furiously. This same heart had pumped when

7

Hashem was born; this same heart beat while she held him close in 1943, the year of the great famine; this same heart beat when she had struggled to give him warmth and to find food to keep him alive. Now she was without her son. Hashem's wife, Parul, was standing at the door, one foot on the threshold and one on the front step, sobbing loudly. Everyone said that Hashem's wife looked like a fairy. Now, it seemed to Grandma, Parul's body was glowing in the dark. She was as beautiful as the full moon. How could she take care of such a beautiful woman? Where would she hide her? Inside the house, fast asleep, lay their six-month-old daughter. How could Hashem have left his wife and child so suddenly? She knew about war. She had lived through World War II when the Japanese had bombed her town. But her household had not been torn apart like this.

Just before sunrise, Grandma took Aunt Parul to her parents and left her there. She then returned to San Souci, taking very little with her except her four sons and a blue plastic basket. She left her own house with its tin roof, and stood on our front veranda, asking her daughter and son-in-law what she should do next.

"Go to a village, Ma," advised her son-in-law. "Towns are no longer safe."

It was on the way to a village, however, that three of her sons were separated from her. Now she had only little Chhotku, who was even younger than me, her granddaughter.

Aunt Runu's mother-in-law was crying, because she did not know where her son Rashu could be found. Sitting next to her, her back to the sun, the white bundle did not speak. She knew full well where her son had gone. She knew also that if a man leaves to fight in a war, it is possible that he will never come back. Grandma's eyes did not move.

Aunt Runu's father-in-law heard that the army was making its way toward Begunbari. In a jute field only a quarter of a mile away, half a dozen severed heads had been found. While some people ran from the village others were running to look at the heads. How could a head be cut off? I wondered, but I had no interest whatsoever in finding out.

It was decided that we — the "relatives from the town" — should go to a more remote village. So in the dead of night we left once more, this time for Hashpur. Our cart was pulled by buffaloes. Kashu, Hashu's brother, sat with the driver and showed him the way. We moved slowly through a thick wood with chirping crickets, barking jackals, hooting owls, and noises I had never heard before. Suddenly the buffaloes stopped and I imagined that ghosts would pounce on us, grabbing and gobbling every human they could find. The top branches of trees were said to be their favorite perches, and on this moonless night our cart stood directly under a *sheora* tree.

Shup, shup, shup!

Were these footsteps? I curled myself into a ball and rolled closer to Ma, hiding under her as best I could. The driver whipped the buffaloes, but they would not move. "Hut," the driver called. "Hut, hut," and his whip crashed onto their backs. At long last, as suddenly as they had stopped, the two buffaloes broke into a run. Now we were swaying violently from side to side, banging our heads against the awning. Chhotku, sickly child that he was, wailed in his thin voice. Long periods of illness had robbed him of all the hair on his body — no hair on his head, no eyebrows, no eyelashes. "Hut, hut, hut!" Crash, crash! *Shup-shup, shup-shup!* With his sticklike arms, Chhotku held on to Grandma. Grandma held on, as tightly as ever, to her blue plastic basket.

Eventually our journey ended at a house where Kashu's sister, Angur, lived with her husband's family. Our cart pulled up before the house, and the driver unhitched the buffaloes and headed for a nearby field to rest. Kashu appeared, leading his "relatives from the town." As he walked, he kept glancing back. I was relieved that, unlike Hashu, no rats peered from his eyes.

Our new hosts treated us warmly. We were, after all, educated town folks accustomed to traveling by automobile, not cart. The largest room in the house was given to us. The best china and colorful glasses with a flowery pattern were brought out for our use. In the days that followed, we ate a different fish curry every day, and it was so good that when lunch was announced everyone raced to the kitchen to take a seat. As guests, we were fed first. Then came the children, followed by the men who returned from the fields. By the time the women got to eat, it was almost evening.

Beautiful quilts were spread on our beds. Our pillows had cases with the words FORGET-ME-NOT embroidered in red and blue. But there was only one pillow for each of us. Even during the war I was unable to give up my habit of clutching a pillow between my legs, so I placed my pillow there. Only then could I go to sleep and, in my dreams, float like a swan on a lake or soar like the red kite I had seen Chhotku and Kashu fly.

In this house, the girls my age wrapped their saris around their body just once. Some were already married. At dawn they let out the ducks and hens. They lit the stove, ground spices, used the *dheki* to remove the husks from the rice, and poured the rice onto a wicker basket to shake it clean.

"Want to play hopscotch?" I asked. They smiled but didn't move.

Boys were climbing trees, picking mangoes, coconuts, and other fruits, and I wanted to do the same. "If a girl climbs a tree, the tree will die," I was told. Tucking their lungis in at the waist, they began playing *ha-do-do,* and when I asked to join they replied, "No, girls don't play this game." With a towel flung on their shoulder, they went to the lake to catch fish. I followed but was told, "Girls don't fish."

"What about flying kites?" I asked.

"No, they can't fly kites, either!"

Standing straight, my hands on my hips, I demanded, "Who says they can't?"

"Can you say this quickly — kacha-gaab-paka-gaab?" one of the boys mocked. "Go on, very quickly, repeat it!" He was very dark; his body was stained with streaks of mud; his teeth were yellow.

I tried, hoping that if I could get this tongue-twister right I would be allowed to fish. A few seconds later, I realized that what I was saying was something like *kachagaabpachabaapkakapaap* — complete gibberish. Yellow Teeth sniggered, and so did the others as they went toward the lake, leaving me behind.

So there I stood staring, a city girl wearing a store-bought dress, so different from the clothes the village girls wore — dresses made of plain cloth.

In the afternoon, the women went to swim in the pond. Some were actually able to swim its length, going under the water at one end and not surfacing until they were halfway across. I, however, could only sit on the bank with my legs in the water. One, looking at my bare torso, said, "She's tall, but look, she doesn't have breasts yet!"

When I lived with Grandma, Uncle Sharaf used to swim in the fish-filled pond. He would try various strokes, then pick a lotus from the middle of the pond and return to where I was sitting and say, "Want to learn to swim?"

"Oh, yes!"

"Then eat lots of ants. Lots of 'em. They're very good for you. Help you to swim well!"

So I ate pieces of gur and handfuls of sugar crawling with ants and tried — more than once — to swim. But the water kept grabbing my legs and dragging me down. Here in Hashpur, I had seen naked children jumping into the water and swimming happily, and I, so much older, was embarrassed because all I could do was stand in waist-deep water. Like a water lily! In my imagination, however, I joined the others — crossed the pond from one end to the other on this burning hot afternoon, and enjoyed the cool water as it lapped all over my body.

It always seemed to happen that way. Whenever I let my imagination loose, Ma would send a message: "Spend too long in the water, and you'll catch a chill!" The girl from the city had to come out of the water and back onto dry land. It wasn't just dry — it was hot as a furnace!

On the dry land things were happening. The Punjabis were setting every village on fire. Some women had escaped from their burning houses and fled to Hashpur, grieving loudly and attracting everyone's attention. Hashpur was charged with tension, as if a bomb might burst any minute. There were two radios in the village — one owned by our hosts, the other in the house of Kasim Shikdar. Every evening at dusk, crowds would gather in both houses to hear the latest news.

The men sat in the courtyard, talking, arguing, smoking a hookah and passing it from hand to hand. One, a bald, fat-cheeked man wearing a green lungi, insisted, "Free Bengal Radio said that the freedom fighters will soon be here. They are on their way."

"But how could these boys tackle the army? They are too young, what do they know of fighting and wars!" countered Angur's father-in-law. He sat on a low stool, striking his bare, dark back with a towel to get rid of swarming mosquitoes. "They're supposed to have been trained in India. We've lost boys already. Too many of 'em. Zamir Ali, Turab, Jabbar, Dhonu Mia!" Running his fingers through his white goatee, he said, "In Dhaka, I hear, there's been a bloodbath. Those soldiers aren't human, I tell you, they're like animals."

Taru, a tailor in the Trishal bazaar, sighed. He couldn't see very well, walked with a heavy stick in his hand, and, although rumored to be wealthy, wore a tattered vest.

"Hmm," he would say. When he lost the sight in his left eye he had come to Hashpur to live with his son. From time to time he would disappear for about a month. No one knew where he went. But since the war had started he had remained in the village, and in the evenings he arrived to listen to the radio. When the men talked he would listen, cock his head to the right, and if he did not like something that was said he would simply say, "hmm." If a pause in the conversation followed, he would express his views, briefly and concisely.

This time, when he uttered "hmm," no one said anything. All that could be heard was the gurgling hookah. The bald, fat-cheeked man in the green lungi, sitting with his back to Taru, turned around; the tailor continued to say, "hmm."

Finally, Taru spoke. "The freedom fighters will definitely free this country. Our guerrillas are going ahead. India will send its own troops in, if need be. This country will be ours. Sheikh Mujib will run it. Ayub and Yahya will lose their control forever. You'll see!"

When he stopped, Green Lungi raised his voice. "Siraj, bring a fan here!"

The boy with the yellow teeth who had gone fishing earlier came quickly with a palm-leaf fan. No longer did he have muddy marks on his body. He had clearly had a bath and cleaned himself. Meanwhile, Green Lungi fanned himself with one hand and scratched his back with the other. The women in the house strained to hear what the men were saying in the courtyard. Grandma continued to sit on her bed, her eyes not moving. And I, fearing the army as well as the ghosts, built a nest in my heart as strong as that of a weaver bird.

Tailor Taru, as things turned out, was right. The freedom fighters did manage to free the country. On a cold winter morning we were sent to another village, Dapunia. I had been sitting on the front veranda, soaking up the sun's warmth and breathing out little clouds of steam. All of a sudden we heard loud shouts. Small children rushed out toward the main road, trying to find the source of all the noise. I could hear that the noise, whatever it was, was heading toward the house we were living in. But who could be coming to Dapunia? Was someone bringing news of more burned houses, more corpses? For the past seven days Dapunia's people had heard the deafening, continuous sound of bullets. Everyone felt anxious and apprehensive. Could the army be approaching, shouting so boisterously? It did not sound like the army and people exchanged puzzled glances. Women parted curtains, hoping to see the still-invisible source of the noise. I, of course, could easily mingle with the other children and slip out.

Then there were shouts, shouts that brought a strange thrill, and gave me goose bumps. A hundred doves suddenly took flight in my mind, spreading their wings wide. For along came a truck carrying about twenty-five young men, rifles in their hands, looking something like the soldiers who stopped our three-wheeler on the way to Madarinagar.

"Joy Bangla!" they were shouting.

These magical, mesmerizing words echoed in Dapunia's silence.

"Joy Bangla!"

As if they had spent years in a dark cave, people emerged from all parts of the village. It was as if a boat, its sails fluttering, had picked them up just as they were about to drown in an ice-cold river. They had said these words silently in their hearts, or at most had whispered them softly among themselves. But today they roared. The sheet of terror that had enveloped everyone was suddenly cast aside. I joined in, raising my arm like the others, my hand curled into a fist. "Joy Bangla!" The truck moved on through the village, and people followed behind crying victory.

I returned to the house to tell Ma, who was standing at the window. "Ma, say 'Joy Bangla!' We are free! Our country is free!" I twirled merrily as I brought the news. She was smiling, but tears streamed down her face. She brushed them away, but they kept flowing. I had never before seen such a mixture of joy and sadness on her face.

Only Grandma showed no reaction. Her eyes remained still. Long ago she seemed to have turned into a statue. Hit a stone, and it makes a sound. But hit Grandma, and she made no sound whatsoever. Why was she not smiling, showing her paan-stained teeth?

Crowds gathered in the street. People were running and shouts of "Joy Bangla" rang in the air. Yesterday there had been bullets, wailing, grief. Today there was rejoicing, laughter, and Joy Bangla! These magic words meant that no more houses would be burned, no one would be shot, no bombs would explode, no one would be caught and made to walk blindfolded. The wind would no longer carry the stench of corpses and the sky would be free of vultures. I then reasoned that we would return to our house in town, and I would again be able to sleep in my own bed, clutching my pillow. I would be able to go and wake my little dolls, all asleep in their beds.

Again I joined in the noisemaking. Was I chasing it, or was this wave of excitement chasing me? I couldn't tell, but I joined the procession now being led by Khaled. In his hand, tied to a thin bamboo rod, was a flag with a full red circle on a green background. Attached to the red circle was a piece of crushed yellow fabric. The group included every man in the village, young and old. When I noticed Chhotku carrying a similar flag, I wanted one, too. It was a totally new flag. The flag at school was also green, but it had a moon and stars on it. We had to stand before the flag and sing Pakistan's national anthem, *"Pak sar zameen saad baad."* Chhotda used to go on protest marches chanting "destroy the reign of the Ayubs" and one day he took the green flag with the moon and stars from under his mattress. When he returned that evening, he informed everyone proudly: "Today, after the march, we burned that flag!"

Khaled, still leading the group, stopped by a jackfruit tree near the road, climbed it, and held the new flag high. "This," he declared, "is the flag of Joy Bangla. From here on, this is going to be our flag. The green stands for our rice fields, the red in the middle represents the sun, and the yellow is the map of our country. We had to fight for nine months to get a new country. It's no longer East Pakistan!" He shouted, "It is to be called Joy Bangla. Everyone say it, Joy Bangla!"

The chorus was loud, joyful, noisy. Everyone seemed to be deliriously happy. Khaled climbed down from the tree. He was wearing a white lungi and a white shirt. His hair was black, his skin was black, his face marred by red pimples. His eyes were large and black, like a pair of bumblebees.

We were supposed to stay in Dapunia. However, the winds from the town had brought some good news. We learned that the violence had subsided, and life was returning to normal. Grandpa arrived soon after this news and declared, "Let's go home. Let's go home! Things are much better now," and he thrashed his arms about as if they were a pair of oars. The beard on his chin blew in the wind, moving from side to side. Before long, we were gathering our luggage and preparing to leave. Grandma had her blue plastic basket, and we had our bundles. When we reached our town, she went to her house by the pond, and Ma returned to San Souci with Yasmin and me.

But when we opened our big black gate, Baba screamed at us, "What have you done? Why did you return? The war is not over!" And, yes, we could see that the houses of many of our Hindu neighbors were still empty. Archana's house was empty, and so was

Prafulla's. Bibha's was occupied by some strangers who spoke a funny language. There was no sign of Bibha or his family. "Those people are *Biharis*,"* Baba told us. "They have occupied most of the Hindu houses."

The grass in our courtyard had grown so tall that it reached the top of my head. It was as if no one had lived in this house for a thousand years. Once, in an old and abandoned mansion in a village called Muktagachha, I had seen similar signs of decay. Walls had crumbled, exposing red bricks. Snakes were moving freely in the long, thick grass, and in the empty rooms the wind roared and whined, playing hide-and-seek with the dead. Baba, almost drowning in a sea of anxiety, sighed, "Things here are still pretty bad. The *dak* bungalow** is filled with military people." He paused and said again, "Stay the night, but tomorrow morning you've got to leave again."

We made plans to leave. Ma sent Borodada, Baba's Baba, to Grandma's, whose house was too old, its doors and windows too weak to offer any protection. So Grandma got into a rickshaw and arrived in our safe house, clutching the blue plastic basket under her burkha. As soon as dawn broke, we planned to leave for Dapunia.

Late at night, Grandma decided to do her *namaz,* and she spread her prayer mat on the floor. Propped against the wall was her blue basket. When she said her prayers, she glanced often at her basket to make sure it was all right. The basket did not move, but Grandma did. One day, while we were still in Hashpur, I had put my hand into that basket, hoping to eat some snacks. Grandma, standing on her prayer mat, hands on her knees, about to bow, could not finish. Instead, she swooped upon me and snatched the basket from my hand.

"I just want some chira!" I wailed.

"No," she snapped. "Go. Go away. Get out of here!"

But this time it was not I who disturbed her. She had almost finished her namaz when there was a terrible noise at out gate, as if a herd of wild elephants had arrived to attack our house, to swallow it like a bunch of bananas. Uncle Rashu came running. "Run, run, it's the army!" he gasped to Grandma.

Ma had just put Chhotku, Yasmin, and me to bed. She had been sitting in the same room, had taken off her heavy gold bracelets and placed them on the Koran, which she was reading.

---

*Bengali term for Indian Muslims.
**Hotel residence for government officials.

I was lying down on the straw where we spread our bedding to sleep, pulling the blanket tightly around myself. The straw, I knew, would provide warmth. Chhotku, as always, was fast asleep, for he fell asleep as soon as his head hit the pillow. It was a good thing, for on that fateful night had he awakened and cried they would have shot not only him but also Yasmin and me, who were sleeping in the same bed. Not that *I* was asleep. I was simply pretending to be asleep, traveling the land of dreams, playing with fairies, swinging on a high swing, no longer a part of this world. Pretending that I did not know that men wearing heavy boots had entered the room and were walking about, a rifle dangling from every shoulder. These men could kill anyone, anytime, casually and without a care, even as they laughed and joked among themselves. If they thought anyone in the room was awake, they would either kill them instantly or take them by force to their camp where they would be whipped and tortured with a bayonet until every bone was crushed. So little girl, never mind what those heavy boots do in your room. You must continue to sleep. Make sure your eyelids do not flutter, your limbs do not move, your fingers remain still. Your heart must not tremble — if it does, hide that tremor from these men when they lift the mosquito net and look at you, lust and desire pouring from their eyes, flames shooting out of their mouths as they speak in a language you cannot understand. Keep absolutely still when they flash a light on your face, your chest, your thighs. They must see that you are not yet fully grown, you are not even an adolescent, your breasts have not yet appeared!

It was as if a snake was slithering over my body, gliding up to my neck and coiling around it, holding it in an icy grip. I found it difficult to breathe. When the light fell on my face, my eyes nearly flew open, but I kept my eyelids still and did not allow them to flutter. Chhotku had placed a leg over mine; I let it be. One of my arms was lying on Yasmin's stomach. I did not remove it. My pillow was tucked behind my back; I let it be.

The men wearing the heavy boots were standing by my bed; one held the mosquito net with one hand, a light in the other. Their eyes and tongues — dripping with lust — swept slowly over my hair-eyes-nose-ears-neck-chest-stomach-thighs-legs-feet. The cold, slippery snake slid down the men's bodies, crawled all over me, sniffed my back, stomach, and genitals, then entered my flesh, my bones, and settled deep in the marrow.

How long had I stayed still on that awful night? I wondered. How long had the little girl pretended to be sleeping? It was as if an entire year had passed, but the flashlight had not been switched off. A decade had slipped by, but no one let the mosquito net fall. My body was growing colder, so cold that perhaps I was dying. I felt so light, as light as a feather that had just dropped from a pigeon. No longer was I lying between Yasmin and Chhotku, now both dead to the world. The north wind had swept me up to the moon, to a different land, away and out of reach of the men in boots. There, I saw an old lady sitting. "Come, come to me," she said, waving as she sat at her spinning wheel. I was thirsty, my throat was parched, and I asked for some water. "No," she said, "there is no water on the moon." What? Well, what was I going to do now? I would die of thirst. The sound of those heavy boots receded, but I could still hear them faintly. "Open your eyes, girl," said the old woman. "Why are you sweating so much on this cold winter night?" No, I was not going to open my eyes. If I did, I would only see lewd looks and dripping mouths. If I opened my eyes, I would surely see the snake! So I kept my eyes shut tight. My arm stayed on Yasmin's stomach, and Chhotku's leg remained on mine. In the distance someone was playing a flute. At this time of night, I wondered! Who would want to wake me in the middle of the night? No, I would not allow myself to awaken. I would sleep, and the others should sleep also. Close your eyes, everyone, and a cloud of sleep will take you wafting up to the moon. The old woman will say nothing. She, too, will leave her spinning wheel, lean against the cloud, and go to sleep.

A flute? No, it turned out to be the sound of a piercing wail. Ma was crying, not in our room but somewhere outside. She lay on the ground, crying where Baba had fallen flat on his face. "Don't cry, Borobu," Uncle Rashu was saying to her. "Dula-bhai is not dead. I am telling you, Borobu, he is still alive." Yes, he was alive, but only just. He had been found tied to a coconut tree. Uncle Rashu had untied him and tried to give him support. But his head had slipped from his shoulder, and Baba had fallen, facedown, onto the grass. Uncle Rashu then dragged him inside where he now lay, oozing blood from his mouth, chest, and stomach. He could barely move. Uncle Rashu was not supposed to be here. He had come to hide in some nook or corner.

When Ma heard Uncle Rashu scream, she jumped to her feet and ran from the room. She and Grandma ran into the dark courtyard, disappearing into the abandoned house next door, using the back door that normally only our sweeper used. When they reemerged, the army had gone. Baba was lying on the floor, and Grandma was searching the area around her prayer mat, muttering, "Where's my basket? Rashu, Idul, have you seen my basket?"

"They looted the whole house," Uncle Rashu answered in a low voice.

Ma went from room to room, candle in hand. She opened her cupboard — all her money was missing. The Koran was there where she had left it, but the gold bracelets were gone. So was Grandma's basket.

"So much happened so quickly!" Ma sobbed loudly. "They nearly killed Noman's father, took everything we had. Why did we ever come back to the town! Allah, what are we going to do now! I can't believe all this."

As Grandma continued to rummage everywhere for her basket, Baba began making faint noises. "Aaah . . . water! Some water," he whispered. Uncle Rashu poured water into his mouth. Only his lips moved. Uncle Rashu himself was still trembling with fear. After sending the women out, he had hidden under a bed. He knew that the soldiers were crazy about women — young, middle-aged, whatever. One simply had to look at a woman, and a stiff, hard rod would burst through his pants.

Uncle Rashu had wrapped a bedsheet around himself, so that he would look like a heap of old bedding if anyone peered under the bed. He uttered *suras* quietly, knowing that uttering *suras* just before death would strengthen one's belief in Allah. When he heard the heavy boots passing through our black gate and fading away, he came out of hiding. But he could not stop trembling. When Baba finished drinking some water, Uncle Rashu lifted his vest and, to remove fear and calm him, spat on his chest. Ma threw herself onto the floor, saying, "Disaster! Oh Allah, what a disaster! Four hundred grams of gold were in that blue basket, and twenty thousand in cash. All is gone!"

"Where did so much gold come from?" Uncle Rashu asked, his eyes growing wide.

"Every woman we know gave Ma her jewelry for safekeeping. Everyone in our family and some neighbors, too. There was Parul, Fajli, Runu, Jhunu, Soheli's mother, Sulekha's mother, and Sahab bhai's wife. They knew Ma was like Lakshmi, someone who could be trusted. So it was Ma who had taken the responsibility and guarded their property with her life. She has not slept for fear of losing it," Ma said looking at Grandma, her voice sounding strange.

The candle flickered; it was about to go out. Ma was sitting on the floor, sobbing near Baba's inert body. Uncle Rashu sighed. "Many people buried their valuables. Why did Amma have to cart all that stuff around?" Pausing, he added, "Don't worry, Borobu. The most important thing is that your lives have been spared. Your honor is safe."

But Grandma heard none of this. She continued to search under the beds and sofas, even under her prayer mat. There was no basket, but she continued to look for it.

Grandma rummaged among the bones. Thousands had been recovered from the well near the big mosque in the town and many people went to look. Some had lost their sons, others their husbands: Could these bones be theirs? Grandma picked up shinbones, ribs, arms, skulls — looking for her son. As daylight faded and darkness set in, everyone left, wiping their eyes with their handkerchiefs as they departed. Grandma, however, continued to sit, lost in a mountain of human bones, still looking for the ones that might be Hashem's.

2

My Birth, Akika, and Other Events

My mother had two sons before I was born. Thank goodness for that, or who would have carried on the family name? A girl was no good for that. A girl would add a touch of grace to a home, help her mother with household chores, and keep the men happy. After two sons, Baba wanted a daughter. His wish was granted, but the girl was born upside down. Legs first, head later.

Ma was given a small room with a tin roof next to Grandma's house by the fish-filled pond. That was where she had all her babies. She had been given that room after her marriage to Rajab Ali who, until then, had been staying in the house of an attorney. Rajab Ali did not have to pay rent, but he was required to teach his host's children. He was studying medicine, and after his marriage to Idulwara Begum he moved in with her. At first, he talked about getting his own place when his final exams were over. But he continued to live on his father-in-law's property even after he qualified as a doctor, got a job, had two sons, and his wife became pregnant a third time.

The neighbors began to talk. "Idul's husband is a *ghar-jamai!*"* they said. Ma found this remark most offensive. Her face turned purple with humiliation. Every chance she got, she told her husband, "Look, you are a doctor now and you are earning. Why don't you get your own house with your wife and children? How long will you live here, in the house of your father-in-law? People say the most unpleasant things. Do you know that?"

Sarojini, the midwife, placed rags on Ma's stomach and on top of them an earthen pot filled with red-hot coals. She moved the pot

---

*A derogatory name for men who live with their in-laws.

gently all over her belly. In intense pain, Ma clutched Sarojini's hands. Her own hands smelled of onions. There were traces of turmeric under her nails. She had just sat down in the kitchen to eat her dinner when the pain started. She got up, pushed her plate away, and went straight to her room. After that, she could do nothing but lie flat on her back and groan. Grandma began to fan her suffering daughter. "Try to bear it," the midwife said. "A woman must learn to bear pain."

It was Grandpa who ran to call Sarojini. The midwife had paid a visit to this house only three months earlier, when Grandma had given birth to Felu. Grandma always gave birth silently. No one — neither the neighbors nor anyone in the family — could tell what was going on. When the first wave of pain swept over her she simply spread a mat on the kitchen floor and lay down. Sarojini collected pieces of hot coal from the clay oven and put them in her earthen pot. When she had moved the pot on Grandma's stomach, Sarojini knew there was no need to tell her to bear the pain. She could deal with the pain simply by clenching her teeth, without uttering a single sound. After sixteen times giving birth was, to Grandma, a piece of cake. However, piece of cake or not, it was not something she wanted to do again at her age. It was all right for her married daughters or daughters-in-law to have children. They were young, it was the right time for them. But for Grandma herself, it did not appear seemly to produce a baby every year.

Sarojini said to Ma, "The warmth from these coals will ease the pain. It will help your baby to slide down. Wait for just a few more minutes, Idul. We're nearly there."

Baba returned home and took a knife and a pair of scissors from a leather case. Ma's two sons were born under Baba's supervision. This time it was going to be a girl because that's what Baba wanted. Sarojini sat near Ma's head, withdrawing into the background now that Baba was here. He placed a hand between Ma's thighs and pushed it in. A lot of turgid water gushed out. "Your water's broken. It won't be long now," said Sarojini.

Baba pushed his hand farther in, right into the womb. Beads of perspiration broke out on his forehead and his hand began to tremble. He withdrew his hand and made his way to the well, drawing a bucket of water to wash up. Grandma watched him, puzzled. Why was Rajab Ali washing his hands already? Surely it was too early to do so?

"Amma," said Baba, "Idul will have to be taken to the hospital. She cannot have her baby here."

"What!" Grandma exclaimed, surprised. "What are you saying? Why, she had the other two at home!"

"This one has turned upside down. It will be impossible to bring it out without an operation. If we don't rush her to the hospital there may be serious trouble," Baba replied, wiping his damp forehead on a sleeve.

Once her water broke, Ma began shrieking like a cow with a slit throat. The noise woke the neighbors, the whole family, even Grandma's baby, Felu.

Returning from the well, Baba discovered that the baby's leg had slipped out. "What if the baby dies on the way to the hospital?" asked Sarojini, frowning. Her words brought a crease to Baba's brow, which twisted into what looked like a pair of twin black scorpions on his forehead. He listened to the child's heartbeats with a stethoscope: *lub dup, lub du-up, lu-ub dup, lu-ub du-up, lub du-up, lu-u.* His white shirt clung to his drenched back.

Baba taught anatomy at Lytton Medical School. He showed students the different bones; cut open corpses to show the intimate details of veins, arteries, and nerves; brought out hearts, livers, and uteruses soaked in formaldehyde and displayed them on trays. It was as if he was offering his students tea and biscuits while teaching how body parts functioned. Although not an expert in obstetrics, he decided to put his hand back in. His fingers shook with uncertainty, but he found the second leg, folded at the knee, and managed to bring it out. Both legs dangled outside. The only tools he had were a small pair of scissors, a couple of knives, and a few needles and thread. How was he going to operate if he had to? Baba took off his sodden shirt and stared anxiously at the dangling legs, at his screaming wife, and at Sarojini's useless hands. If the umbilical cord wound around the baby's neck, it would choke to death. Baba's own heart was hammering in his chest; he did not dare to listen to the baby's heartbeats.

"Pull those legs, Doctor saab," Sarojini said, moving to the foot of the bed. Baba, however, did not dare. He knew from his medical books that babies usually died either because their heads were injured, or because the cord strangled them. He could not take such a big risk — surgery was essential. He would have to use forceps or do a cesarean section. He left the room quickly and said to Grandma, "Send someone to get a rickshaw. Idul must be taken to the hospital. We have no choice!"

When he came back to the room, he paced restlessly and perspired so much that his vest was now wet. Everything he knew about childbirth came back to him. If he pulled the baby's legs forward, it might expose the back. So he pulled them gently; the baby's back began to emerge.

"Push. Shut your mouth and push, with all your might. Push!" he barked at Ma. In a few moments, the baby's whole body emerged, all except the head.

"It's a girl!" shouted Sarojini. "Didn't you want a girl? You've got one now!"

But the girl's face was still out of sight. Baba had been a very bright medical student. His head was packed with knowledge. Now he began to put the theories he had learned to practical use. The baby's heart was still beating. Baba used both hands this time, one on each side of the baby's head, and loosened the umbilical cord coiled around her neck.

"Pray. Pray to God, Idul," Sarojini said to Ma.

"Think of Allah, take His name," advised Grandma, from the other side of the door.

Ma promptly started yelling, "Allah! O Allah!"

At last I arrived in this world, gasping, my heart barely beating. When I began to wail, even the sound of Ma's appeal to Allah was drowned out. Sarojini placed me in a tub and began to clean me with lukewarm water.

Aunt Runu arrived just then and snatched me away. I traveled from her hands to Aunt Jhunu's, and from there to Uncle Siddique's, who said, "My goodness, she looks like a princess! A princess is born in this house."

Dawn was just about to break; the eastern sky had started to turn bright. A wave of joy swept through the crowd gathered in the court-yard. A girl at last, after two boys. Uncle Hashem, Uncle Tutu, and Uncle Sharaf crowded around to look at their princess. Only Aunt Fajli went to Ma before taking a look at the newborn baby. "Your girl arrived on such a good and auspicious day, Borobu! It is the twelfth day of Rabi-ul-awal. Nabiji was born on this day. This girl will be most fortunate, most virtuous. You are a lucky woman, Borobu!"

Later in the morning, Grandpa went to a store and bought a bas-ketful of sweets. Before long, neighbors started pouring in to see the new arrival, the princess who had been born on the twelfth day of Rabi-ul-awal.

Often when I was older, if I asked Ma to tell me a story, she ignored my request. Instead she would say, "When I was carrying you, I slipped in the bathroom one day and fell down. As a result, you must have turned upside down. When you were born, you were placed on that round table. See how large it is? Your body filled half of it, you were so big. No one had seen such a big baby. Your grandma used to say to me, 'Keep that baby well wrapped. Put a black dot on her head, or she might catch the evil eye from someone.' Soheli's mother saw you and asked, 'How old is she? How many months?' Her eyes nearly popped out when I told her. Monu's mother couldn't get over the roundness of your head. She said, 'Even a woodapple has a few dents, but this baby's head . . . it's perfect!' "

Once, having heard this story, I placed my chin on her stomach and asked, "How is a baby born, Ma?" She was lying in her bed at the time. She removed her sari and showed me her stomach. Then she pointed and said, "Look, over here. Your father's a doctor, isn't he? He cut me open with a blade, and took out the babies."

There were white marks on her stomach. Ma pointed at each and said, "I got this mark when Noman was born. This one, after Kamal. This one's you, and that's Yasmin."

I looked at the marks and gently stroked them.

"Didn't you bleed?" I asked with eyes shut.

Ma smiled and tapped my chin. "Yes, I did. But your father stitched me up again, and I was all right."

Then she pulled me closer and held me to her breast. "Tell me, my love, if I die, will you cry for me?" she asked.

I shook my head firmly. "You won't die. If you die, I will die too."

Ma soon was going about her household chores, carrying her upside-down baby with her, even when she chopped vegetables or stuffed fuel into her clay oven, her eyes watering with the smoke. The baby slept on her lap, awakened from time to time by the smell of onion, garlic, turmeric, pepper, or the sweat on her mother's body, or by a noisy dog or crow. When Ma went to take a bath, the baby sat alone in the court-yard, in the dust, amid dry leaves, putting pieces of broken brick and other rubbish into her mouth. When her brothers came home from school they picked her up and carried her about in the courtyard.

Chhotda once placed her on the edge of the well while he stopped to tie the strings of his shorts more securely. The child had only to lean back slightly to fall into the water, but she didn't. Why should she? Why should she drown in the well, when she had gone to such enormous trouble to be born, to live? So the princess grew up, held and petted and caressed at times, ignored and neglected at others.

When I turned eleven, Ma took out her sewing machine one day and kept it whirring until two pairs of long *pajamas** were ready. A grown-up now, I must not wear shorts any longer. But that was not all. Ma told me something else, staring absently out the window. That sad and depressing afternoon she said to me: "I was not myself at that time. I cried all day. Your father had fallen in love with Razia Begum. Nearly every day when I took his shirt to wash it, I found a love letter from her in his front pocket. You were still a baby, sometimes rolling off your bed and falling down. When you cut your head I did not pay any attention. I could not concentrate on anything at all. Each night your father came home late."

Razia Begum was beautiful. Or she was according to Ma, at any rate. She had fair skin and large, dark eyes; her lips were full, and thick black hair fell to her waist. When she wore it in a bun, she looked as if she was carrying a basket on her head. Her breasts were so large that she probably found it difficult to carry them about, just as Sindhi cows find it difficult to move with heavy udders. I had never seen Razia Begum but could picture her quite easily. It seemed to me that if milked, she was sure to produce two bucketfuls. Her body was like a mountain. The earth trembled when she walked. And Ma? Ma was dark, her hair was thin, her eyes small, nose blunt, and her body as slim as the leg of a grasshopper. She was convinced Baba had tired of her. So she went around telling everyone: "I've lost everything. My life's over. Noman's father is now going to marry Chakladar's wife. Where am I going to go with my children?"

I continued to grow, even though I was neglected and dents appeared on my perfectly round head, even though I was fed stale milk, sago, and barley water. When Dada carried me about, I often sucked his little finger. And so I entered my eleventh month.

It was at this time that Baba was transferred to Pabna. Ma, in as much pain as a sinner roasting in hell, began to feel like an angel had

*Fine-quality cotton pants, worn by both sexes.

come to tell her that she was being taken to the seventh heaven. Her heart danced with joy. For many years she had dreamed of a home of her own. Now she could leave for a new place and see that dream fulfilled. Those who called her husband a ghar-jamai were silenced. The tiny, dingy room in Grandma's house by the fish-filled pond at the end of a narrow alley was left behind, as was the nightmare called Razia Begum. Ma kicked that particular horror into a dirty drain and happily left to make a fresh start.

Baba's new post was that of a prison doctor. Ma got a beautiful house within the prison compound. The prisoners helped with daily household chores; they even helped look after me. Some of them were thieves and robbers, but when they took me for a walk in the garden or carried me in their arms, the gold chain around my neck remained in place. No one touched it.

In her free time Ma did her hair, put kohl around her eyes, powdered her face, wore her sari stylishly. Here, in Pabna, there was no Razia Begum, Baba was never late coming home, love letters didn't pop out of his pocket. Soon Ma came to know her neighbors quite well, and started getting invitations to dine with them. She was respected everywhere as the doctor's wife. Ma immersed herself in a sea of joy. She tied happiness up in her *anchal** with her bunch of keys. And yet she could not totally rid herself of a vague disquiet. The reason was simple: Her husband was an extraordinarily handsome man, in addition to being a doctor. Ma was plain. She had studied up to the seventh standard and then had been married off to Baba at the age of twelve. When her first child began going to school, she demanded that she be allowed to go too. Baba agreed, and took her on his Hercules cycle every morning to drop her off. But Grandpa had strong objections. "Your job is to raise your children and stay at home," he told Ma in no uncertain terms. "And to take care of your husband. There's no need for a girl to think of education."

That was the end of it. Ma did not dare disobey her father. Baba rose higher and higher in life but Ma remained where she was, in the same dark corner, stuck at the seventh standard. All she could do was open Baba's fat medical books and leaf through them before dusting and putting them away, fully aware that compared to her husband she was totally insignificant. One day he just might leave her. It was

---

* The end of a sari.

this thought that made her turn blue with fear and prompted her to powder her dark face white, to line her small eyes with kohl to make them appear larger.

A year later, Ma's stay in seventh heaven came to an end. It was as if someone had pulled her out of her sea of happiness by her hair and had untied the knot in her anchal where she had stored all joy. She could no longer live miles away from Razia Begum for Baba had applied to be transferred back to Mymensingh. Ma was obliged to pack her bags and return to the old town, the old house. All the dreams and desires of a small and dark woman were blown away as if by a sudden dust storm.

This time, though, she did not have to stay in Grandma's house at Grandma's expense. This time Baba paid hard cash to buy a couple of rooms from Grandma. They were tucked away in the eastern corner of her courtyard. Ma now had her own home and her own kitchen but this brought little joy. She felt as if she had returned to a prison. Pabna, where she had lived inside a prison compound, had allowed her more freedom. She burst into tears as soon as she set foot in her house in Mymensingh and everybody thought they were tears of joy. Grandpa was relieved to have his daughter back home. Aunt Runu and Aunt Jhunu were delighted to see me and promptly began treating me like a new toy. They were amazed that I could now walk, talk, and run. It was almost as if they had expected me to return looking and behaving exactly as I had before I left. Baba became so busy soon after our return that it was impossible for him to imagine Ma's loneliness. He simply did not have the time. In the evenings, after doing his bit at the medical college, he began going to the Taj Pharmacy. There he sat in a tiny chamber until nine o'clock, examining patients who lifted a curtain marked DOCTOR. When I turned six I had to go to that pharmacy many times.

One day after school I threw a stone at a local street dog called Bagha, whom I had found lying in our courtyard. He had no hair and his body was covered with sores; all the boys in our area threw stones at him whenever they could. At first, he simply gave me a murderous glance but was silent. Then, when I had dusted my hands and started to climb the steps, he suddenly flew at me and sank his sharp teeth into my thigh, tearing out a chunk of flesh. I was rushed to Baba's pharmacy. On the first day he gave me three injections — two in my arms and one near my belly button. After this, I was given an injection every day for fourteen days. After each injection, Baba treated me to a plate of *rasgollas*.* I sat in a chair, my legs dangling, and ate the sweets with a spoon. Going to Baba's pharmacy in a rickshaw every evening, a light breeze playing on my hair, was something I greatly enjoyed. The pain of the needle entering my body felt no worse than the bite of an ant. I sat in the shop in Swadeshi Bazar, breathing air that smelled of medicines, and watched the patients waiting to see Baba. He felt their pulse, made them lie down, and listened to their chest and stomach through tubes stuck in his ears, then scribbled prescriptions on papers. This was a different Baba, not the same man I usually saw at night, tired and irritable after a hard day's work. After seeing this other side of him, I wanted desperately to love my father. Loving him, however, was not easy for any of us.

Sometimes, purely by chance, the "other" Baba emerged from his shell. One day after we were settled in our new home, the house full of new furniture and furnishings, Baba said to Ma, "Well, are you happy now? No one is going to call your husband a ghar-jamai anymore."

Ma, her lips colored by cheap lipstick, pouted and moved her arms, making the colorful glass bangles jingle. "So what if they don't? What's that got to do with me? They will still call me black and stupid. No education. No knowledge."

"You are a mother of three. It's the duty of a mother to take care of her children. Bring your children up properly, get them educated — that will be your reward. Besides, even if you are black and stupid, it's you I married, isn't it?" He pinched the exposed portion of her midriff.

Ma, however, failed to be reassured by his words or his show of affection. Her fear of Razia Begum returned. Every night she would stay up, waiting for Baba to come home. Crickets chirped, dogs howled, the night grew darker. Afraid that the sound of her own breathing might drown the sound of Baba's knock on the door, Ma would hold her breath. One moonless night, unable to contain herself, Ma went out, crossed the two courtyards between her new home and Grandma's, and woke her up.

"Noman's father hasn't yet come back. It's past eleven. Where could he have gone? Could he be spending the night with that woman?"

"Stop it," Grandma snapped at Ma. "Go home and go to sleep. Think of yourself and what you are going to do. What's the point of

---

* Round sweets.

crying? You think you can get that man to come back to you just by wailing and sobbing?"

Grandma's words reminded Ma of the time when Grandpa had suddenly turned up with a new bride. Grandma had wept her heart out. Unperturbed, Grandpa had begun sleeping with the other woman while Grandma slept alone in her own bed, crying into her pillow each night.

"Why do you cry so much?" Ma had asked her.

"You'll know when you grow up," Grandma had replied. "You cannot trust men. They are a bad lot."

On the particular night in question, Baba finally returned at two o'clock. Ma was still awake. "I was with a patient," Baba explained. "It was touch and go. Had to rush him to hospital. That's what delayed me."

He was delayed the next night as well. This time, Ma woke Chhotda. "Come on, get up. Come with me, just as you are," she ordered.

She set off, walking briskly toward the dark pond, holding Chhotda's hand in one hand, a flashlight in the other. They found a rickshaw on the main road, one that took them to 15 Pocha Pukur Par. An old man in a lungi, his torso bare, was sitting in a chair on the front veranda. On seeing Ma and her son he cried out sharply, "Who is it, so late at night?"

"Is this where Chakladar lives?" asked Ma.

"I am Chakladar. Who are you?" the thin, sharp voice rang out.

Ma climbed the steps and reached the veranda. "Bhai saab," she said, "is my husband here in your house? Dr. Rajab Ali?"

The ribs on Chakladar's chest — easily visible — heaved. He stood guarding his door. "No, he isn't."

Ma paid no attention. The old man was little more than a skeleton. She pushed him aside and walked in, through the living room into the bedroom. The room was dark, but in the dim light of a street lamp, Ma could see a mosquito net draped around the bed. She lifted it and switched on her flashlight. Baba was lying in that bed, Razia Begum by his side. Her breasts, like a pair of large grapefruits, were fully exposed. Baba jumped to his feet and began dressing without saying a word. Ma simply said, "Let's go."

Baba followed Ma out and got into the rickshaw with her and Chhotda. No one spoke on the way back. Chhotda just sat on Ma's lap and kept switching the flashlight on and off, on and off.

By this time, back home, I was up and crying for Ma. To keep me quiet, Dada pushed his little finger into my mouth. I began sucking it, and eventually stopped crying.

In Chhotda's hand, the flashlight was still going on and off.

Baba was born in Madarinagar, a remote village to the south of Pachrukhi Bazar in Nandail Thana. His father, Janab Ali, was a farmer. He had some land where he grew rice and kept some cattle. Young and strong, he worked hard, plowing the land with a pair of bullocks. Baba used to go with him to the rice field to do small things and learn how to be a farmer. It was assumed that, one day, he too would till the land: plant the seeds, wait for seedlings to appear, watch them grow bigger and ripen, and then harvest and store the rice. All this was taken for granted. However, one night Janab Ali's father, Zafar Ali Sarkar, who taught at the local primary school, looked at Baba over his hookah, and said:

"Janab Ali, send your boy to school."

"To school? Why? Isn't there plenty to be done at home?" asked Janab Ali, the young farmer, slapping his back with a towel to get rid of mosquitoes.

"He will get an education if he goes to school. People will respect him. He can get a job if he is educated. Look at Khushi's father. Didn't he go to school, and isn't he now working in the town? He's been buying a lot of land here, he's doing that well."

"Once," retorted Janab Ali, "we were only sharecroppers. We never had enough money for anything. Now, after many years of hard work, I have managed to buy my own land. Rajab Ali is learning the job. He will be able to join me in a few years. If we work together, we might be able to buy some more land." Janab Ali finished speaking and looked at a broken cowshed.

"Times are changing, Janab Ali. So many of our boys from the village have gone to Calcutta to study. An educated man always gets respect. If Rajab Ali goes to school, people will respect you, too. Look, he can always help in the fields, or take the cows for grazing when he gets back from school. It isn't as if I'm asking you to send him off to Calcutta."

Zafar Ali handed his hookah to his son and gently stroked his back. "Think about it."

The courtyard was bathed in moonlight. Rajab Ali was pouring salted water into the drinking troughs for the cows and looking at the older men out of the corner of his eye. His heart danced with joy.

"Rajab Ali! Where are you?" called his grandfather. Rajab Ali came running, wiping his salty hands on his lungi.

"Would you like to go to school, little boy?"

"Yes!" replied Rajab Ali, nodding vigorously.

Janab Ali said nothing. His hookah made gurgling noises.

A few days later, Zafar Ali went shopping in Pachrukhi Bazar and returned with a new white shirt, a new *dhoti,* and a copy of Vidyasagar's *Barnaparichay* (Know Your Alphabet), all for his grandson. The next morning, Rajab Ali ate a plate of rice, milked the cows, filled their troughs with hay, had a bath in the pond, and put on his new dhoti and shirt. Then he left for school, a banana leaf and a pen made from a bamboo stalk in his hand. He walked barefoot down the track through the rice fields.

The teacher taught them multiplication tables: "One ones are one." The pupils shouted: "One ones are one. Two ones are two. Three ones are three." At night, back at home, Rajab Ali turned the pages of his *Barnaparichay* impatiently, wishing he could finish reading the whole book at once. He learned how to make ink at home by pouring mustard oil on a leaf from a jackfruit tree and holding it over a burning oil lamp. The smoke from the lamp thickened and darkened the oil. He mixed it with a little water, dipped his homemade pen into it, and wrote the first letters of the alphabet on a banana leaf. He could not wait for the night to be over so he could go to school the next day. Janab Ali snapped at him: "Put that lamp out, Rajab Ali. You are wasting a lot of oil."

Zafar Ali earned five takas a month as a schoolteacher. He went back to Pachrukhi and bought a bottle of kerosene. Then he said to everyone he knew, "My grandson is now going to school. He has to study at night, so we need extra oil for his lamp. Rajab Ali will get a clerk's job in a British company one day. Mark my words."

Encouraged by his grandfather, Rajab Ali made quick progress in school. Sitting on a mat on the veranda, his legs spread out before him, he soon mastered the alphabet and moved on to Book Two, *Balyashiksha* (Lessons for Children). "Gopal is a good boy," he read, "He eats what he is given." Zafar Ali sat in the courtyard, smoking his hookah, listening to his grandson's voice as he read aloud. It was his dearest wish to send Rajab Ali to the bigger school in Chandipasha once he finished with the local primary.

In due course, Zafar Ali's dream came true. Rajab Ali began walking to the school in Chandipasha, three miles away. There he did better than most others in his class. When his matriculation results came out, his headmaster told him, "You must continue your studies. Don't stop now."

Rajab Ali didn't. At first his father refused to give him permission to go to the town. At this, the headmaster himself came to the house to speak to Janab Ali Sarkar. "Your son will become a barrister some day, or perhaps even a judge," the headmaster said. "Your entire family will benefit. Please let him go."

So Rajab Ali left his village for Mymensingh, carrying a bundle that contained two shirts, pajamas, a pair of black rubber shoes, and a bottle of mustard oil. In his pocket he had four annas. The first thing he did was look for accommodations. Someone he knew found him an attorney's house where he was allowed to stay for free in return for his services as a private tutor. He was admitted to Lytton Medical School. Then, roaming around one day in a city where he knew practically no one, Baba met Maniruddin Munshi in Notun Bazar. Munshi had a very generous heart. He owned a restaurant and fed beggars and fakirs in the street. No one paid him a penny. Did that make Baba's eyes light up? With what? Greed?

When asked this question, Ma had a ready answer. "Yes, of course it was greed. He's always been greedy. He came to the town with just a tattered old rag in his hand. My father helped him study medicine. It was because *my* father spent money on him that he became a doctor. He has totally forgotten the past. Now he gives me all the shit."

Did Baba think that if he gained Maniruddin Munshi's sympathy he would not have to use the money that came from home, money his father got by selling rice? Was that why he went to Maniruddin, to get him to pay for his medical education?

"No, no," Ma replied. "No one gave him any money from home, he brought nothing from there. If anything, he sent money to his father. To tell the truth, your father had few expenses. He did not smoke tobacco or eat paan. He had a scholarship, so his education was taken care of."

Oh, so he had his scholarship and a free room. He did not have to depend on anyone for financial help. "What about pocket money? Food?" Ma countered. "Bajan had bought a barber's shop and rented it out. Your father was given the rent that came in. After our marriage, Bajan took him to Dhaka and bought him enough cloth to make a suit. Then he kept giving him money to buy the odd meal, or whatever else he needed. The scholarship money, let me tell you, went to his father's house in the village. My father paid for his books and other expenses. Every day, your father used to touch Bajan's feet and say, "I have no one to call my own. My father lives in a village far away. He is very poor. If you don't mind, I'd like to call you Baba."

Maniruddin Munshi did not mind. On the contrary, he took Rajab Ali home, gave him a plate of rice and fish curry, stuffed some money into his pocket, and said, "Get yourself something good to eat." After this, Rajab Ali began visiting Munshi's house frequently and grew quite close to his family — so much so that, every evening, when Idulwara did her lessons with her private tutor, Rajab Ali stood outside the window and stared at her. The tutor covered the chimney of the hurricane lamp with a piece of paper, thus offering Rajab Ali, who stood in the dark, a clear view of Idulwara's face. Rajab Ali stared for as long as he could. It was clear that Idulwara was deeply interested in her studies. She read her books quickly and easily, and wrote out the history lesson she had learned by heart in a clear hand.

The proposal of marriage for this painfully thin young girl came from Rajab Ali himself, who approached Maniruddin Munshi directly. Idulwara's father saw no reason to object. Rajab Ali was good looking, had pleasant manners, and was studying medicine. Munshi agreed and, one day, invited a few neighbors and friends to witness the wedding of Rajab Ali and Idulwara. The bride was draped in a red silk sari. The guests were served *pulao* and mutton. The dark, snub-nosed girl was married to a fair, sharp-nosed boy.

After his marriage, Rajab Ali left his room in the attorney's house and moved in with his wife. They were given a small room with a tin roof. Until then, it had been occupied by young men who were allowed to stay for free and teach Idulwara. Now that she was married and was no longer required to study her tutors were asked to leave.

Rajab Ali found peace and reassurance in this house. There was a marked difference between the food he was given in the attorney's house and the food here. There, no one had taken personal care of him. Here, his mother-in-law served him *korma, kalia, dopiaza,* and other special dishes. She fanned him while he ate. Rajab Ali was desperate for the comforts of home, to be part of a family again. Now he had what he wanted. In view of the care and attention he received from his in-laws, he did not mind his wife's shortcomings. His body felt better, and so did his mind.

My two elder brothers and I were born in that small room that was vacated for him. When my brothers arrived, Grandpa stood on the steps outside and called out the *azan*. *"Alla hu Akbar!"* he cried in a voice loud enough to echo through the entire neighborhood. In my case, there was no need for the prayer because I was a girl. However, a week after my birth, my family celebrated *haittara* with some fanfare. My brothers placed candles on the walls, lighting up the whole house. Baba's friends came with various gifts, and all filled their stomachs with the good food cooked by Aaina, the cook from Grandpa's restaurant. Ma emerged from her room that day for the first time since my birth. The room was cleaned and all the clothes washed; Ma had a bath and resumed her normal life.

The haittara was followed by the *akika*. For my two brothers, a cow had been slaughtered to mark the occasion. For me, it was a goat. That was the rule: either a cow or a couple of goats for boys, and only one goat for girls. Before my akika took place, there was a big debate about a new name for the baby. Uncle Siddique said, "Usha. Let's call her Usha." Aunt Runu said, "Shobha." Aunt Jhunu wanted Papri. Throughout this debate, Dada stood near the door, silently rubbing his big toe against the threshold. He did not like any of these names. His agitation grew, and the hair on the back of his neck began rising in protest. Sadly, none of the others realized it. This was not surprising, since it was always grown-ups who chose a name for a newborn. What did a child know about names?

Dada happened to be chewing peanuts. Suddenly, he opened his mouth, parting his lips much as a crane parts its beak. His tongue began fluttering like a bamboo leaf in a storm, peanuts bits flew in every direction, and out flew words with the peanuts. At first, no one heard him. The sound of his voice was drowned by the general medley of noises: cawing crows, barking dogs, bawling babies, children shouting at play, others talking in the courtyard. Was the sound coming from Dada's throat a part of all this, or something different? It was Aunt Runu who realized that the sound was actually coming from Dada.

Promptly, she grabbed him by his shoulder and dragged him into the room, making him stand near a wooden pillar. Every eye in the room was fixed on him, on his open mouth and the chewed peanuts in it.

"Why are you crying? Has someone beaten you?" asked Aunt Runu, placing a hand under Dada's chin and tilting his head upward.

Dada wiped his streaming cheeks with a hand, gulped, and said, "My sister should be called Nasrin."

My uncles and aunts looked at one another and then they burst out laughing, as if a clown had just entered the arena. A circle was quickly formed by Uncle Siddique, Uncle Hashem, Aunt Runu, and Aunt Jhunu. Dada was made to stand in the middle.

"Why Nasrin? Where did you get that name? Who asked you to choose it?"

Dada was handed a packet of nuts. He answered, breaking open a peanut with his teeth, his eyes fixed on the nut. "There's a very pretty girl in my school whose name is Nasrin."

This time, the circle remained silent. All controlled their laughter in the hope of getting more information. "Where does this Nasrin live? Where's her home?" asked Uncle Hashem. Before Dada could reply, Uncle Siddique declared, "No, Nasrin won't do. We'll call the baby Usha." At this, Dada threw away his packet of nuts and ran out of the circle. Then he went to his room, collected some of his clothes, made up a bundle and said, "I'm leaving."

"Where do you think you're going? Stop!" Ma called him back.

"No. I'll go wherever my eyes take me," Dada answered and left the house, his little bundle on his shoulder.

My uncles and auFght he would turn back as soon as he reached the pond outside. So they broke the circle and sat comfortably on the bed, their legs dangling. But Dada did not come back.

When evening turned to night and the night got darker, Ma began to weep. Uncle Siddique and Uncle Hashem set out to look for Dada. When Grandpa heard what had happened he joined the search party. At ten o'clock, Uncle Hashem finally found the crazy boy in the woods behind Hajibari and brought him home. Ma flung her arms around her son and said, "Your sister will be given whatever name you choose, I promise!"

The next morning, Baba confirmed this. Nasrin was final. My uncles and aunts sat with long faces. How could a princess be given such an unfashionable name? Why, it had no meaning at all.

Later that day Dada returned from school and stood in the courtyard, sucking his thumb and grinning. He cast sidelong glances at those who had surrounded him the previous day. Aunt

Jhunu was picking mangoes with a long pole with a hook attached at one end.

"What other names will you give your sister, shit-pants? What will her full name be?"

"Nasrin Jahan Taslima," Dada replied, taking his thumb out and grinning from ear to ear.

Aunt Jhunu giggled. Aunt Runu was sitting in the courtyard, cutting green mangoes into tiny pieces to make *bharta*. She asked, "Do you love this girl Nasrin? The one in your school?"

Dada's grin grew broader. "Ye-es," he said.

"Would you like to marry her?"

Dada put his thumb back into his mouth, smiled shyly, and tilted his head to the right, to indicate the affirmative. The strings holding his shorts in place hung down to his knees.

Aunt Jhunu dropped the pole and tapped Dada on the head. "But that beautiful girl is not going to marry you, is she? I bet she knows that you shit in your pants in school. She must have heard!"

Dada ran indoors and found Ma. His eyes brimming with tears, he clutched her sari.

"What's the matter? Why are you crying?" she asked, stroking his head.

"Aunt Jhunu called me shit-pants."

Ma came out and told her sister, "Don't make the poor boy cry, Jhunu! His stomach's given him trouble all his life. I've had him treated, given him so many medicines, but he still has loose bowels."

A name had finally been chosen for me for my akika, but Baba postponed the ceremony. Why? Because there had not been a good crop of rice in Madarinagar that year. So he was depressed. A few months later, a good crop was harvested, but Baba was transferred to Pabna and felt depressed once more. When we returned from there, the question of my akika came up again, but two years passed before it was finally held.

On the big day my aunts decorated the entire house, drawing white *alpanas* on the floor. Then they made colorful paper chains and strung them between the pillars. Guests arrived bearing gifts: gold chains, rings, brass pitchers, the *Shobuj Shathi* (an alphabet book), dresses and shoes, a copy of the Koran, plates, bowls, and suitcases. Aaina dug big holes in the ground outside, filled them with fuel, and cooked pulao, korma, and various other dishes in huge pots and pans. The whole house was filled with the heavenly smell of his cooking. Grandpa bought great pots of yogurt and sweets, but it was Dada who was the busiest. Clad in freshly laundered clothes, new shoes on his feet, his hair parted carefully, he hovered around the guests. The minute he caught someone smiling at him affectionately, he lost no time in telling them the truth about his sister's name. It was he who had chosen it. Every other suggestion made had been rejected — not good enough.

Once the guests had gone, Ma transferred four small suitcases that had been received as gifts to the top of a wardrobe. The brass pitchers were taken to the kitchen. In the wardrobe she placed the new dresses and shoes, plates and bowls, and the Koran. The gold chains and rings were locked away in a drawer, and Ma tied the key to her anchal. The only thing left within my reach was the book *Shobuj Shathi*. Suddenly, everyone in the house became my teacher. If anyone found me leaning over my book, I was made to recite the alphabet from start to finish.

I simply repeated what the others told me. Long before I was handed a slate and a pencil to learn to write, I learned to utter the words in my book.

"Say M-a, Ma," I was told.

"M-a, Ma," I repeated.

"P-e-n, pen."

"P-e-n, pen."

"B-a-n-a-n-a, banana."

"B-a-n-a-n-a, banana."

I was no different than a mynah bird in a cage, obediently repeating everything I heard. Uncle Sharaf and Uncle Felu had not yet learned to read, but I had finished my *Shobuj Shathi*.

Soon after my akika, Grandpa sold the house to Basiruddin without telling anyone. Naturally, Grandma received an enormous shock when, one day, Basiruddin turned up to take possession. She felt as if the sky had fallen on her head. When I heard her say so, I looked up quickly and realized that it was still in place. If such a huge thing had fallen on her head, would she have survived?

No one ever learned what Grandpa did with the money. Grandma could only offer Basiruddin the most comfortable chair in the house, place tea and other refreshments before him, and say gently, "Bhai saab, if one man does something crazy, why should so many others pay for it? I have several children. Where will I take them? I am prepared to give your money back if you resell the house to me. But I can only pay in installments."

Basiruddin cleared his throat. "No, I can't accept payment in installments. But . . . very well, if you say so, I'll sell the house back to you, only if you make the whole payment in one go."

Grandma stood behind a curtain and replied, "Where will I get so much money? Please consider my position. I'm a helpless woman. Give me a few days to make arrangements."

"No, no, no," Basiruddin said firmly. "How can I give you all that time? Time isn't something I can create, is it? I have to spend what time Allah has measured out for me. If you can pay me the whole amount by the day after tomorrow, I will sell the house back to you. If not, you will have to forgive me; I must take possession."

Grandma got Uncle Sharaf to bring Basiruddin some paan. Basiruddin finished his tea, picked up a paan, helped himself to a pinch of lime, looked at the ducks and hens roaming in the courtyard, and said, "I will come back tomorrow evening."

Grandma emerged as soon as Basiruddin left. She had her own private bank inside a bamboo pole. It had been hollowed out so that she could place her savings in it. Now she broke the pole and took out all the money she had saved. Then she searched all over the house to see if any more could be found. In the end it added up to just five hundred takas.

Grandma draped her burkha around herself and left the house. She called on everyone she thought might help before reaching our place that night. Baba had just come back from the pharmacy.

"Have you heard?" Grandma exclaimed. "Now tell me what to do!"

Baba had heard. Ma had said to him as soon as he returned, "Bajan has sold the house to a man called Basiruddin. He came to take possession, but Ma told him she would buy it back. How she's going to do it, I don't know. Basiruddin wants the whole amount in a day or two. Where is Ma going to find so much money?"

However, now Baba spoke as if he had no idea what Grandma meant. "Heard what? What's happened?" he asked.

Grandma sat down on one end of the bed, Baba on the other. "Your father-in-law has sold the house," Grandma told him. Baba was wearing a lungi. He swung his legs under it. "Which house? Whose house?" he asked.

"Whose do you think?" Grandma replied, sounding exasperated. "Our house!"

"Why did he sell it?"

"How should I know? He didn't tell me, did he? He's totally mad, has no sense at all. Hasn't even told me what he did with the money."

Baba continued swinging his legs.

"I told Basiruddin I'd buy the house back . . ."

"Who's Basiruddin?" Baba interrupted.

"The man who bought the house from your father-in-law."

"Where does this Basiruddin live?" Baba wanted to know, scratching his knee.

"Somewhere in Notun Bazar. I'm not sure," Grandma told him, unfolding her handkerchief. Then she took a paan out of it and put it in her mouth.

"What does Basiruddin do?"

"I have no idea. Basiruddin came to the house . . . he wanted all the money . . . I said I'd pay in installments if he sold the house back to me." Grandma spoke haltingly.

"Very well. Pay him in installments," Baba said calmly, his tone indifferent.

"Basiruddin didn't agree. He wants just one payment, in full," Grandma explained, anxious.

"All right, then, pay him the full amount." Baba smiled sweetly.

"How? Money doesn't grow on trees, does it? How am I going to get hold of six thousand takas?" She looked helplessly at Baba. He stopped swinging his legs and called Ma.

"Idul! Make some tea. Amma, have a cup of tea."

Grandma shook her head.

"What will you have then? Have something," said Baba.

"No, I don't want anything," she said irritably.

"Come on, get some biscuits or something," Baba ordered Ma.

"No, no, no!" Grandma raised a hand to stop Ma.

After this, no one spoke for a while. Baba and Grandma continued to sit on opposite sides of the bed. Ma and I sat in the middle. Finally Grandma broke the silence. "Noman's father," she pleaded in a broken voice, "can you please lend me at least five thousand takas? If I lose my home, where will I go?"

Baba did not reply. Grandma spoke again, sounding even more pathetic: "I will pay you back, every penny, if you let me pay in installments. I'll manage that somehow, anyhow! I'll pay you every month."

Ma could not keep quiet any longer. Distressed by Baba's silence, she said, "My father did so much for your family. Now there's no one to help Ma when she is in trouble. When you went to Rajshahi to study, I had no money to buy milk for the children. It was Bajan who bought us big tins of milk. Why, we've been staying in my parents' house since our wedding!"

Grandma took off her glasses, wiped them with her sari, and replaced them. Then she said urgently, "Say something, please! Basiruddin is going to return tomorrow."

Baba remained silent. He spoke only when Grandma rose with a sigh and stepped out of the room. "Amma," he said, "I will talk to you tomorrow night."

In the end, Baba did lend her the money. True to her word, Grandma paid him back every month. It took her three years to repay the whole amount.

When Grandpa heard how she had saved the situation, he smiled happily and said, "If Khairunnisa blew on it, even a wildfire would go out!"

Grandpa was a spendthrift. He was also fond of having fun, eating well, and spreading joy and cheer among others. Of course, he could never have indulged in his passions if Grandma had not managed his household with a firm hand.

Grandpa came from Bikrampur. At the age of thirteen, he broke open his father's safe, stole what money he could find, and ran away from home. After floating around in various other towns, he ended up in Mymensingh, totally penniless. He slept in mosques at night, ate what free food they offered, and gathered beggars, fakirs, and lunatics on the streets to tell them stories about Arabia. People in the mosques occasionally gave him a little money. When he had a few pennies in his pocket, he felt like the Emperor Babar. If he saw anyone begging, he would say to him, "Where do you come from? Have you eaten today?" No beggar ever had a full stomach. Grandpa would hear the story of his life, of how he was starving, and his heart would melt. Tears of sympathy would pour down his cheeks like the monsoon rains. He would fish out the few coins he had and hand them to the beggar, saying, "Get yourself something to eat."

The new imam of the mosque near the district school noticed Grandpa. He saw that, every Friday, Grandpa would turn up with a large number of beggars and stand with them for the namaz.

The imam looked at him and felt a strong desire to make this young vagabond settle down to domestic bliss. He had a twelve-year-old daughter. It was time for her to marry. So he waited to catch Maniruddin and take him home. He got his chance one cold winter night when he found Maniruddin lying on the floor of the mosque, all curled up, without a blanket.

"Come with me, Maniruddin," the imam invited. "I will give you a proper bed and a warm quilt. You can sleep more comfortably."

Maniruddin did not move.

"Hey, get up! I can give you a hot meal. Hot rice with meat curry."

This time Maniruddin sat up. "How far is your home from here, Imam saab?" he asked, stretching lazily.

The imam kept his word. He took Maniruddin home, gave him hot rice and meat curry, a bed, and a warm quilt. Maniruddin slept until the next afternoon. He had not experienced such comfort in many years. A cruel stepmother had made him leave home, but he remembered his own mother used to feed him milk and rice and put him to bed when she was alive.

When he woke and got out of bed, he found the imam standing in the courtyard pouring water from a jug to wash his feet before doing his namaz. Maniruddin recalled that his own father had tilted the jug exactly the same way. Maniruddin took the jug from the imam's hand and poured the rest of the water himself, as if he was washing his father's feet — the father he had not seen for many, many years. The thought made him suddenly burst into tears.

"Why, what's the matter? Why are you crying?" asked the imam, taken aback.

Instead of replying Maniruddin simply covered his face with his hand and left the house. Nearly a month later, he returned with a potful of sweets and said with a smile, "Imam saab, these sweets are very good. Try one. Warm rasgollas, from Calcutta."

Everyone in the imam's house ate those sweets. Later, the imam found Maniruddin sitting in his living room. "Maniruddin, why don't you marry my daughter, Khairunnisa?" he asked.

"Marry her?" Maniruddin gave a start. "Where would I take my wife if I married?"

"Don't worry about that. I have some land and property. We'll work something out," the imam said reassuringly, placing a hand on his shoulder.

Maniruddin was in a very good mood and he quickly agreed. The imam called a *kazi** the same night, before it got too late, and had his daughter married to Maniruddin. Then he was fed rice and meat curry once more and given a warm bed. Khairunnisa married him without knowing his character or what he looked like. She herself was educated; at least she could read and write. But here she was, attached for life to a man who had no education at all. It all happened so quickly that Khairunnisa had no chance to take everything in. In fact, she had not yet even fully digested the rasgollas she had eaten earlier! The imam could have found her a far better husband, but he was convinced that Maniruddin had a very generous heart, even if he did not have a home or any money. The imam had learned one thing in his life: Nothing in the world was more desirable than a generous heart.

The imam had a son, but only in name. This son was passionately fond of forests and hunting and he traveled all over India. Every year he would return home, stay for a couple of months, and then disappear again. Having lost faith in his son the imam handed over all his property to Maniruddin before he fell ill and took to his bed. "You are like a son to me," he said to Maniruddin. That, in itself, was not a problem. Maniruddin could well have taken his son's place, but could he change himself? In less than a year he sold off half the property and gave the money to the poor. Then the government took some of the remaining land to build a boarding school. On the last bit that remained, Khairunnisa built a few rooms with tin roofs, planted some trees, and put down roots, clinging to what little she had left. Her husband's generous heart was of little use to her.

Khairunnisa had a child every year. All her children had to be fed; their mouths, like those of hungry chicks, were perpetually open. It was not enough to have a roof over their heads — who was going to provide everything else they needed? Maniruddin did not care. He went off traveling, returning home only when he ran out of money. As soon as he arrived he woke the silent household up by calling out merrily, "Where are you, Khairunnisa, give me something to eat. Come on, children, come and join me!" Without a word, Khairunnisa

---

* One who performs the Islamic marriage ceremony.

fed her husband and children. Only once did she say, "There's no food." Ma was perhaps three or four years old then. Grandpa gave a start and asked, "What did you say? No food?"

Khairunnisa sat by her cold stove on a cold wooden seat and replied in a cold voice, "No food. No rice, or *lentin*, or anything else. In the past few days I've had to pick the wild spinach that grows by the pond and boil it to feed the children."

Maniruddin said nothing in reply. In sadness, he went to bed and remained there for two days.

During that time, Khairunnisa collected the coconuts that had fallen from her trees and made some sweets with them. Then she roused her husband, saying, "Go, take these to the market and sell them. Then you can buy some groceries." Maniruddin left with a wooden box full of sweets on his head and happily started selling coconut sweets in front of the courthouse.

This went on for some time. Every day, Khairunnisa would fill the box with sweets. Maniruddin would sell them but hand over only a part of the proceeds, keeping the rest for himself. Every day, Khairunnisa would secretly save what little she could in her hollowed bamboo pole — four annas, or maybe eight. When Idulwara turned five, Khairunnisa broke her bamboo bank and handed a small bundle to her husband. It was full of money.

"Buy a shop somewhere with this money. You could start a restaurant, and sell rice and fish curry," she said.

Like an obedient child, Maniruddin started a restaurant. He bought a room and filled it with chairs and tables. He even hired a cook. Soon his restaurant proved to be a huge success. It was located right in the middle of Notun Bazar. The British were still in power. Most people disliked the British, but Maniruddin liked everyone. He chatted with whoever came to eat at his restaurant. Even thieves and other criminals became his friends. Stray dogs and cats began crowding around, slipping into the kitchen if they were hungry and helping themselves to whatever leftovers they could find. Maniruddin called in beggars and lunatics and fed them. If someone said he was hard up, Maniruddin would open his cash box and give him a fistful of money. If he saw someone coming from the market looking tired he would invite them in. "Bhai saab, where are you off to? Come in, rest for a while." People rested, and drank free glasses of lemonade. "It's not a restaurant Munshi is running, it's a free guest house," some people commented.

Khairunnisa sent her eldest son and daughter, Siddique and Idulwara, to the restaurant. It was Idulwara's duty to sweep the floor and dust the furniture. While she followed her brother in and began her work, Siddique sat with his father and ate hot *jalebis*. Both children were given a meal of rice and fish curry, and sent home before it got dark. Maniruddin himself did not return until it was quite late.

When everyone was asleep, Khairunnisa lowered the wick of her lamp and sat in its dim light, waiting for her husband. When he returned, she endured his unrestrained passion, hoping that this untamed bird would be captured and held by the lure of prosperity, physical pleasure, and affection for his children. Being a woman, Khairunnisa could not go out and look after the business. All she could do was save money in her bamboo pole. Every night, as she lay beside her husband's satisfied body, her thick black hair spread over her pillow, she tried to make him see that he had to be careful with his money. But Maniruddin had never learned to count money; he had only learned to grab fistfuls of it. Whatever else he might try to be in his life, he would never be thrifty.

In 1943 the famine started. Maniruddin saw people dying. They begged at his door for a bowlful of the starchy water that remained after the rice was cooked. He closed his restaurant and began cooking by himself — a simple meal of rice and dal and vegetables, all thrown in together — to feed the hundreds of starving. With the money he had he bought rice to keep his free kitchen going. But now rice had disappeared from the shops. Desperate, Maniruddin ran from one mosque to another, raising his hands in prayer, begging for mercy:

"We have no one but you to help us, Allah. *La ilaha illallah* — there is but one God, one Allah." Maniruddin wept like a child, his tears drenching his chest. He cried that whole year, until rice and milk powder began to fall from airplanes. Only then did anyone see him smile.

Khairunnisa did not let the famine affect her family. She had already stored some rice in her loft in case they ran short. Now she measured it out carefully every day. Her youngest child, still a babe-in-arms, lived purely on breast milk. If she had not taken charge, Maniruddin's household would have been destroyed long ago. She could not tame her husband completely, but she did make him feel attached enough to his family to return to them. Khairunnisa lived, however, in perpetual fear that the bird might fly away forever.

Everyone was so busy with the festivities on the day of my akika that nobody noticed Grandma's mother lying dead in one corner of the kitchen. After her father's death, Grandma had brought her mother to live with her. She preferred living with Khairunnisa to living with her son, the hunter, although social rules demanded that a woman be taken care of by her father in her childhood, her husband in her youth, and her son in her old age. When she was found lying cold and stiff in her bed, it was Grandpa who cried the most, rolling on the ground as though he had lost his own mother.

There was grief in this world, there was deprivation; but there was happiness, too. No one had to burn for long. In the heat of summer the rains came and washed away all pain. Aunt Jhunu stood at her window and watched the raindrops fall on the pond. The rain beat rhythmically on the tin roof. Water fell on water, as if playing a game, and the steady rhythm on the roof lifted everyone's spirits. A peacock spread its feathers and danced in every heart. Aunt Runu sang to the beat of the rain on the roof. Uncle Tutu, Uncle Sharaf, and Uncle Felu ran out into the courtyard and played in the rain. In Grandma's room her brother, Uncle Kana, sat on a low stool on the floor that still bore the white patterns of alpana, still mourning the loss of his mother. But now he forgot his grief. Peering out at the courtyard as if there was bright sunlight, he said, "Don't just sing, Runu. Dance!"

Aunt Jhunu opened her mouth to say, "You are blind, Uncle Kana. How will you see her dance?" But she did not say it. Aunt Runu tucked in her anchal at her waist, put on her anklets, and danced as she sang:

> In the blue hills,
> by the *mohua* trees,
> who plays that enchanting flute,
> again and again?
> Birds sing in the forest,
> my eyes fill with longing.

Uncle Kana kept time with his stick.

Only Baba appeared untouched by this wave of joy. He was tired and dispirited. To him, a drought was no different from a flood. The former made the rice fields crack, so nothing grew; the latter drowned everything, destroying the whole crop. Baba sent his entire salary to

Madarinagar and wrote to my grandfather, "Bajan, buy the southern land from Khushi's father as soon as possible. Do not delay. I will send you more money next month."

Baba loaned five thousand takas to Grandma to repurchase her house. Then he rented five rooms from her, in the same house, all built around a courtyard in the middle of the house. One became a living room, another a bedroom, the third became our kitchen, the fourth firewood storage, and the fifth remained empty. Most had cement floors, tin or tiled roofs, and brick walls. Some were made wholly of tin. The room Baba had bought earlier from Grandma was given to Dada and Chhotda.

To Baba, dancing, singing, or playing meant creating a lot of unnecessary noise. If he saw me playing in the rain, he caught hold of me and sent me inside and I would go cold with fear. I could always ask Ma to tell me stories and fairy tales, but I couldn't bring myself to ask something similar of Baba. If the words rose to my lips, I gulped them down. I was so scared of him that I did not dare make eye contact. He remained totally distant. Thousands of miles lay between us.

But I heard that this had not always been the case. We had been very close before Baba went to Rajshahi for further study. We had just returned from Pabna. Every evening, when Baba came home, I used to fling myself into his arms and say, "Baba, thake me fol a walk by the livel."

Every time I said that, Baba would promise to take me for a walk by the river the next day, but never did. Ma pinched my cheek affectionately when she found me in Baba's arms, and said, "Little children must not go to the riverside. There might be kidnappers. They come and catch little boys."

"So? Why should they cath me? I'm a girl," I told Ma, comfortably settled on Baba's lap. Baba would burst out laughing.

One day, I told him about a character who lurked by the river. I had heard stories about him. "Fo-ting-ting lives by the river. He had three heads, but they were chopped off. Now he talks through his feet!" I tried to frighten Baba. He paid no attention. Instead of asking me about Fo-ting-ting, he kissed my head, my forehead, and my cheeks, and said, "What are you to me, my love?"

"I'm your Ma."

This was something Baba himself had taught me to say. He kissed my cheeks again when I did it. Then he combed my loose hair with his fingers and pushed it behind my ears. I was crazy about him in those days. Nothing could keep me from him. I was his favorite child, the girl he had so badly wanted after two boys. Yet, two years later, when Baba returned from Rajshahi, having successfully obtained an advanced medical degree, I — the same girl he had left behind — failed to recognize him. I behaved as if he were a complete stranger who had forced his way into our house. He stretched his arms out for me, but I ran away. I stopped calling him Baba. In fact, I stopped speaking to him. Even today I do not address him directly.

His two years in Rajshahi ruined the closeness we once had. I could feel close with everyone in my family — Grandma, Aunt Runu, Aunt Jhunu, Uncle Hashem, Uncle Sharaf, Uncle Felu, even the unreliable Grandpa — but not Baba. Sometimes I felt it might have been better if Baba had not come back at all. We were managing quite well without him: Ma, Dada, Chhotda, and I. His return created ripples, as if a big stone had been thrown into a quiet pool. A ferocious Foting-ting had arrived and destroyed our playhouse.

Nothing could bridge the distance that crept in between us. Baba tried to get closer. "Come, Ma, come to me!" he would call, but I always stood before him like a rock, cold and lifeless. An invisible wall separated us, even when he held me close to his heart.

~ 3 ~

Growing Up

ꟷ was born at dawn on the twelfth day of Rabi-ul-awal. Such a girl ought to have said *La ilaha ilallaha Muhammadur Rasulullaha* (Allah is one, and Muhammad is His Prophet). Apparently, saints and those dear to Allah said these words as soon as they were born. Aunt Fajli had told Ma, "Look how bright her face is. And why shouldn't it be? After all, she was born on such a holy day!"

Soon, however, the sun burned the brightness of my face to a coppery brown, for I spent most of my time outdoors, running after Uncle Sharaf, Uncle Felu, and Uncle Tutu. The games started in the afternoon with something called *chor-chor*. One of us was selected to be the chor, the thief. When this chor ran and touched someone else, that other person had to take his place, stand facing the banyan tree, and count loudly to five. Then he would turn around and chase all the others in the hope of grabbing the slowest runner so that a new chor could replace him. My uncles, being older, could run much faster. I ended up being the chor most of the time. Uncle Tutu ran in a zigzag manner; I could not keep up with him. Uncle Felu ran as fast as a hare. Even if I spent all day trying to catch him, he would still elude my grasp.

When it came to marbles, my uncles again won and took everything I possessed. Uncle Sharaf kept his marbles in a glass jar. He frequently turned it upside down, spread its contents on his bed, and counted how many he had. I cast admiring glances at those bright, shining objects, but knew very well that that was all I was allowed to do. I had no right to touch them. Only once did I extend a hand toward them, and Uncle Sharaf punched me in the back.

I even lost my cigarette packs. These were required to play *chara*.

48

I collected empty cigarette packs from the roadside — Bawga, Caesar, Bristol, and Capstan. A small stone or piece of brick, referred to as a chara, was used by each player. In the courtyard, four squares were drawn on the ground. You had to stand in a square and throw your chara. Then, grabbing as many cigarettes packs as possible, you hid them under your thighs, and shouted out *"Putkir tol!"* — a challenge. The other player threw his or her chara. If my uncle's chara landed within a couple of inches of mine, I would have to hand over all the cigarette packs I was hiding or betting. If not, my uncle would have to count out the same number of packs. I always had to give away all my packs.

Playing chor-chor, marbles, and chara made my skin grow darker; the divine brightness was gone from the face. Aunt Fajli continued to hope that, one day, I would walk down the path shown by Allah.

This idea took firm root after my return one evening from Nandibari. Aunt Runu took me with her that evening when she went to visit her friend, Sharmila. Sharmila's house was old and crumbling. It looked as if it had been abandoned a long time ago, as if snakes lived in its cracked walls guarding pitchers full of gold coins. Banyan seedlings grew from those broken walls, and a certain atmosphere clung to the house. I was sure that in the dead of night a beautiful woman with jingling anklets danced on the roof. She would instantly disappear if anyone lit a lamp. There were lychee trees around the house, laden with ripe fruit. The lychees from Nandibari were reputed to be very tasty but I was afraid to pick any, since that might prompt a cobra to slide out of the broken and derelict building. An amazingly beautiful pond lay at the bottom of the steps leading up to the house. Its water was so clear that I could see the bottom of the pond. My own face floated up in the water. When the water rippled, so did my reflection, moving crazily. I was not smiling, but my face in the water smiled at me.

On that dark evening, Sharmila lit a lantern and, in its dim light, offered us a plate of sweets. I shook my head firmly and declined. "Why won't you have any?" Sharmila asked. I pursed my lips and sat in silence. The truth was that I was afraid. My old fear of snakes, ghosts, and evil spirits was choking me.

Sharmila was very beautiful. The woman who danced on the roof in the middle of the night must look like her, I thought. Perhaps the woman was Sharmila's twin, or — in a previous life — another

Sharmila. Her black hair glided down to her knees. She was alone in the house when we were there. Dressed in a white sari, she sat in a cane chair, leaning back against it. A fresh evening breeze came in through the window, lifting her hair slightly. In that dimly lit room, I could see that her eyes were black, even though she wore no kohl. They looked sad.

When Sharmila spoke, it was as if a white bird was flying down from the sky, carrying the sound of her voice on its wings. "What a sweet girl. What's your name?" she asked.

If one listened carefully, it was possible to hear the jingle of anklets when Sharmila spoke. At least, I heard the sound.

"Her name is Shobha," Aunt Runu replied.

"Have some sweets, Shobha," she said with a smile.

I wanted to tell her my name was not Shobha, but I could not speak. It was true that Shobha was a nicer name than Nasrin, but it was not mine. I felt uncomfortable when anyone called me Shobha; it made me feel like a liar and a thief, as if I had stolen somebody else's name and was trying to pass it off as mine.

All of a sudden, completely out of the blue, it seemed to me that the woman sitting in front of us was not the real Sharmila at all. She was her dead twin, or the Sharmila from another life. The sweet scent of jasmine bathed the room. There were no flowers in sight, nor did jasmine grow in the garden, so where was the scent coming from? Sharmila's body? Perhaps.

I clutched Aunt Runu's hand. "Let's go home!" I implored.

The light from the lantern grew fainter, and then suddenly went out, but Sharmila's glowing body lit up the room. Glowing and spreading that sweet smell, Sharmila said, "The moon is going to rise soon. We can sit in bright moonlight and sing, 'On this moonlit night, all have gone to the forest.' You will sing, too." Her laughter rang out, making a sharp, tinkling sound. I snuggled closer to Aunt Runu and spoke hoarsely: "Let's go, let's go home."

On our way back, I noticed something strange. The same moon that was over Sharmila's house traveled with us, flying across the sky, right up to our own house. "Look, look!" I said to Aunt Runu, "the moon is coming with us!" Aunt Runu did not seem at all surprised. As soon as we reached home I said to Ma, "Do you know, Ma, that the moon traveled with us wherever we went? It came here, all the way from Nandibari!"

"What did you eat in Sharmila's house?" she asked, showing no surprise.

"She ate absolutely nothing," Aunt Runu replied proudly. "It's a Hindu household, isn't it? So she did not eat even a morsel."

A few days after my visit to Sharmila's house Ma mentioned this to Aunt Fajli. "Fajli, why do you think my daughter does not eat in the Hindu's house or let me put a dot on her forehead? Is it because she was born on an auspicious day?"

Aunt Fajli was a frequent visitor to Grandma's house. She crossed the woods near Hajibari to come over to our place. As soon as she arrived, she took off the burkha that covered her body and went out first to the courtyard, then to the kitchen. She lifted the lid of every pot she could find to see what had been, or was being, cooked. No matter what she found — fried *hilsa*,* or fish *koftas* — she wrinkled her nose as if every dish smelled bad, or as if none of them was to her liking. When she sat down to eat, Grandma chose the best piece of fish and put it on her plate. She was always served rice from the middle of a pan, never from the top or the bottom. Aubergines fried in batter were also specially selected, so that she got none of the ones that were slightly burned or squashed. Grandma also gave her a handful of fried onions to go with the aubergines. But Aunt Fajli's nose remained wrinkled when she ate, as if she was forcing herself to swallow all that rubbish out of politeness, as if a visit to this house was depriving her of the wonderfully delicious food she would have eaten at her father-in-law's, where she lived, but what could she do, it *was* pretty late in the afternoon, so she was obliged to eat here. At least, this is how it seemed to me. In addition to wrinkling her nose, Aunt Fajli made various comments as she ate: "Who has cooked the spinach? It's gritty." Or, "Didn't you put garam masala in the meat curry?" Or, "You should have used more oil when you fried this fish."

That day, when Ma told her about my not eating with the Hindus and not wearing a dot, Aunt Fajli had complained that there was not enough garlic in the curried pigeon. At this, Grandma had dropped four cloves of garlic on Aunt Fajli's plate and said, "See if it tastes any better!" Aunt Fajli had given Grandma a tight little smile. "What did you do that for, Ma? Raw garlic will not mix well with the gravy, will it? No, I'm just thankful that the meat was soft and well cooked. Allah

---

* A species of shad.

has said one must not make a fuss over one's food, that eating something light and simple, just to satisfy hunger, is enough. The Prophet himself was a small eater."

A few curly tendrils of hair hung over Aunt Fajli's fair forehead. She looked as beautiful as the goddess Durga. When Ma made that comment about me, Aunt Fajli had finished her lunch and was lying in bed, chewing a paan. She declared, in the presence of everyone else who was resting after their meal: "Didn't I tell you this girl would grow up to be virtuous? She does not eat in the house of a Hindu and she refuses to wear a dot on her forehead because that's what Hindus do. No one ever told her or taught her to behave like this, did they? So how did she learn? Allah must have told her. That's the truth, you mark my words. When she was a baby, she used to smile so sweetly in her sleep. I'm sure she played with angels in her dreams. Borobu is a lucky woman."

Aunt Fajli thought Ma lucky. Others might have agreed with her, but Ma herself remained convinced that she was most unfortunate. She had longed for an education, but that had proved impossible, even though she was known to be a good student. In accordance with Grandpa's wishes, she went to school draped in a burkha, which made the other girls smirk when they saw her. Her school days came to an end when she got married. On her last day there, her teachers clicked their tongues in sympathy and said, You certainly had the brains, and you might have finished a bachelor's and master's degree. See if you can continue studying after marriage. After her wedding, Ma had made just one demand: I want to go back to school. Baba had no objection, so Ma was able to return to school at the same time that she admitted Dada to one. Grandpa objected. Even so, she could not forget her dream. When Baba went to Rajshahi for his own studies, Ma enrolled in school without telling anyone. Dada was then in the seventh standard in the district school. Ma was admitted to the seventh standard in Mahakali Vidyalaya, a school for girls. Her teachers knew that she was married and had children, but kept it a secret from the other students so that Ma could mix with the younger girls and sit with them in class. In the quarterly exams, Ma scored the highest marks. Sadly, her secret was unearthed by her family. Before her final exams, Grandpa spoke to her again, repeating what he had said before: There was no need for women to be educated. Your job is to stay at home and take care of your children. He convinced Baba, who said as much in a letter from Rajshahi. And with that, invisible shackles were placed on Ma's feet. Her carefully nurtured dream was shattered once more.

If she was truly fortunate, why did Grandpa steal into her room one day, look around quickly to make sure there was no one about, and fish out a small container wrapped in paper? He placed it in Ma's right hand and closed her fingers over it, so that no one could see.

"Hide it away," he whispered, for even walls had ears, "and apply it to your face every night."

Grandpa had put given her a potion that was supposed to make her complexion fairer, so that she would seem attractive to Baba, so that he would not leave her and the children. Ma used it every night but her complexion did not change. If anything, her eyes looked sunken, dark rings formed under them, and her nose remained as blunt as ever. So what, she told herself. She might not be pretty, but she was gifted. She could cook and sew, couldn't she? But was that good enough? Weren't there women — a large number of them — who were far better than her at cooking and sewing? Never mind, Ma told herself. She might not have beauty or talent, but she was at least a healthy, normal human being. Not lame, or blind, or mad. Soheli's mother had a daughter who was completely insane; when they married her off the truth was carefully concealed from the bridegroom and his family. Surely the world would grant Ma a status better and higher than that madwoman, in spite of all her drawbacks?

But Ma sometimes did feel as if she was going mad. Household responsibilities failed to satisfy her. When Baba was working in Rajshahi, she left Dada and Chhotda with Grandma and went to visit him alone. The thought that Baba might not love her terrified her. When Grandpa gave her that potion to improve her complexion, Ma's fears increased. As a child, she used to stand alone under a date palm and cry every time Grandpa bought a red dress for her and a blue one for Aunt Fajli. When Baba went shopping he would ask the man in the shop to show him saris for a dark girl. When they were given to her, Ma did not cry, but she was afraid, and the fear never left her.

On the way to Rajshahi, that fear reared its ugly head, but Ma tried to suppress it. She had never left Mymensingh on her own before. So what, she said to herself, why shouldn't she leave now? After all, she was going to her own husband, the father of her two children, the same man who had offered his prayers before a priest and accepted her as his wife. She was not going off for an illicit liaison with another man; she had every right to go where she was going. It's true that Baba hadn't asked her to visit, but she felt an intense longing for him. Baba had left her a drum full of rice and money for household expenses. But Ma had no interest in household chores. Rice and food were not everything in life. Even a painfully thin, simple, and stupid (according to Baba) woman has a heart, and that heart was in turmoil. But who was going to see it, who was to understand? Certainly no one in her family.

Baba's job was transferable and he could be posted anywhere in the country. Ever since his arrival in Rajshahi he had been trying to return to Mymensingh, but his bosses paid no attention. Suddenly, like a bolt out of the blue, his wife turned up at his door. Her lips were scarlet, her face white with powder. In her hand was a leather suitcase that contained colorful saris, the potion Grandpa had given her, and another little container holding a powder.

Baba started, as if he had seen a ghost. "You! Why are you here? How did you come? Who brought you here?"

"I came alone," Ma replied, forcing a smile.

"Alone? All the way? How is that possible? How are the children?" Baba asked, all in one breath.

"They are well. How are you? You don't write. Have you forgotten me?" Ma choked on the last few words. Her eyes brimmed over.

Baba paced restlessly for a while before sitting down in an old iron chair. It was a part of the furniture provided in his doctor's quarters.

"Have you gone mad? You left two small children at home!" he accused.

"Nothing will happen to the children. They'll be well looked after," Ma said, and slowly began edging closer to Baba.

"Have you still got the money I left with you?" Baba asked with a frown.

"No, I ran out. Bajan and Miabhai had to buy milk for the children," Ma said as she laid a hand on the arm of Baba's chair. She exuded a sweet smell.

"If you had told me I would have brought enough money with me the next time I came home. You must go back to Mymensingh tomorrow." Baba rose abruptly from his chair, thrusting his hands into his pockets.

"Who cooks for you? What do you eat? You've lost weight." Ma placed a soft hand on Baba's back. It had the same sweet smell.

Baba did not reply. His thick dark eyebrows remained twisted in a frown. He was tired and annoyed.

Years later, when Baba returned to Rajshahi to do a two-year condensed course, he said to Ma before he left: "For heaven's sake, don't leave the children and go off somewhere!" Ma cried her heart out. Baba cleared his throat and added, "I am leaving enough money. I will come back in six months and give you some more."

After he left, he wrote very rarely. The few letters that he did write went like this:

> How are Noman, Kamal, Nasrin? If you run out of rice, get your father to go to the wholesale market in Notun Bazar and buy some more. Keep an eye on Noman and Kamal's studies. Tell them to pay attention to their lessons. Next month, I will send you the money to repay the loan you took from Sulekha's mother. Don't waste any money, and don't buy what you don't really need. Take care. Rajab Ali

The language in Ma's letters was entirely different. She had, after all, been raised in the city. What's more, after their wedding she had seen two or three Hindi movies with Baba. Having seen Dilip Kumar and Madhubala on the silver screen, she had no difficulty in filling a whole page with her neat writing:

> My dearest love, how are you? When will you come back to me? I don't like living without you. I writhe like a hunted bird, shot by an arrow. Please come and take me away. We can live together happily with our children. You will come back from Rajshahi with a higher degree. I have told everyone I am so proud of you. I know I am not worthy of you. I haven't got the kind of knowledge and intellect that you have. But that does not matter. I may have nothing else, but I have you. You are my happiness, my peace. I want nothing else in this world.

In reply, Baba wrote:

> Do not spend more than a couple of takas on groceries every day. If you run short of money, get your provisions

on credit from Monu Mia's shop. Keep track of everything you buy.

Ma did not bother to note things down in her accounts book — she
just didn't feel like it. She kept a little money tied in a knot in her anchal.
If any of her children wanted to buy savories, or ice cream, she untied
the knot and took out the necessary amount. The next morning, she
would send Dada to buy some hot snacks from a sweets shop for our
breakfast. Some days there was cooking oil in our house, but no salt; Ma
would borrow some from Grandma. When darkness fell, we discovered
that while our lamp had its cotton wick in place, there was no kerosene.
Sulekha's mother from next door had to lend us enough to last the night.

One day, Chhotda went out to buy groceries with money Ma had
given him. Hours passed, but there was no sign of him. Ma could not
even light the stove. Finally Uncle Hashem went to look for him and
caught him at the main crossing. Why was he sitting there? Because
he had no money. What happened? He had taken the money out of
his pocket, thinking it was some old, useless piece of paper, and
dropped it along the way.

Two years later, when Baba returned from Rajshahi after getting
his degree, everyone in the house found him far more distant. I was
only four at the time, but even I refused to go to him. He and Ma
seemed to have little to say to each other, apart from discussing the
shopping for the house. Ma slowly gave up creaming her face and
wearing makeup, and began handing long lists to Baba: mustard oil:
200 gms; onions: 1 kg; salt: 300 gms; masoor dal: 500 gms. Baba read
her lists, went to the market, and came back with a bag of groceries.
Ma cooked, and served Baba his lunch in the afternoon; at night, his
dinner awaited his return, his plate covered with a lid.

When Baba came home for the night, he washed his hands and feet
with water drawn from the well, ate his dinner, belched, and went to
bed. He was too tired and irritable to do anything else. This was due
in part to the weight of his responsibilities. He had not only to think
of his wife and children but also of his home in Madarinagar. Never,
it seemed, did he allow himself to forget that he was the son of a poor
farmer.

After Zafar Ali Sarkar's death, no one in Madarinagar showed the
least interest in sending two of Baba's younger brothers — Riazuddin

and Iman Ali — to school. My grandfather had made them work in the fields. Baba wanted to pay for the education of his two youngest brothers, Aman-ud-daula and Motin Mia; he dreamed of bringing them to town and educating them there, thus taking Zafar Ali Sarkar's place in the family. He had a lot of dreams for Madarinagar as well. Riazuddin and Iman Ali helped nurture those dreams by frequently visiting their brother in town, wearing green lungis and rubber shoes.

"We should buy the land to the north of the pond. Khushi's father is going to sell it. If we don't buy it now, someone else is bound to grab it."

"Bajan says two extra pairs of oxen will help a lot."

These remarks took Baba back to his childhood, when he used to take the cows out to graze, and stare at the open, green rice fields stretching to the distant horizon. He handed over a great deal of money to Riazuddin, and said: "All right, buy the land." Later he would give more money, to buy the oxen.

Ma did not fail to notice this generous gesture. As soon as she learned that Baba had parted with a lot of money to buy extra land, she drew up a long shopping list and gave it to her husband.

1. Two saris to wear at home
2. Petticoat (white)
3. Blouse (red)
4. A pair of sandals (Bata company)
5. Earrings (long, dangling ones)
6. Glass bangles
7. Soap
8. Scented hair oil (Jabakusum)
9. Bar of 570 soap to wash clothes
10. Soda

Baba raised his eyebrows as he read. "What's this? I bought you a new sari only two months ago!" he said.

"That's now torn," Ma replied coldly. "I wear that one sari, and I do all the housework — cooking, and cleaning, and washing, and scrubbing. A sari isn't made of jute, is it?"

"Show me where it's torn!" Baba demanded, frowning heavily.

Ma's sari truly had a small tear in it. At Baba's words, she ripped it apart and showed him the long gash. Her eyes remained still, like the eyes of a statue. A painful lump hurt her throat.

"Why do you need scented hair oil? I just bought a bottle of coconut oil! That should be sufficient," Baba went on.

"That? Oh, that was used up ages ago."

Baba peeled off his spectacles in one swift motion. "Bring me the bottle!"

"I've thrown it away," Ma replied indifferently.

Baba put his spectacles back on, looked at the list again, and said: "Here's a taka to buy a bar of soap to wash clothes. No need to buy anything else." Baba left, placing a taka on a table. Ma did not touch it; it remained where it was. Every time she looked at that taka, Ma felt as if she was an outcast in her own home.

When Aunt Fajli called her a lucky woman, Ma thought about her life, all the past events, and she just couldn't agree. So what if her daughter was born on the twelfth day of Rabi-ul-awal? What difference did that make? Ma sighed. "Don't talk of *my* luck, Fajli. I am not destined to be happy."

Aunt Fajli laid a hand on Ma's back. "Think of Allah. Take His name. You'll find peace. Tell your husband to do namaz."

Ma glanced at Aunt Fajli's fair hand and said, "My husband calls me a black owl every day. Will taking Allah's name make my skin any less dark?"

"Borobu!" Aunt Fajli quickly raised her heavy body and spoke reprovingly. "The color of our skin is something Allah has given us. We must be happy with whatever we have."

At last Ma felt as if she had been offered a straw to grasp, just when she thought she was drowning. Allah was responsible for the color of one's skin. If anyone jeered at her because of her dark complexion, it amounted to mocking Allah Himself.

Before I turned five Ma had had two miscarriages and was pregnant again. Baba was transferred to Ishwarganj. Once more Ma had to move with her husband, three children, and baggage. Grandma had just given birth to Chhotku. In that house it was not unusual for mother and daughter to be pregnant at the same time.

In Ishwarganj, Baba's hospital gave him a jeep. He used it to drop my brothers off at school every morning on his way to work. I was still too young to go to school. Ma taught me rhymes at home.

A few days before Ma had her fourth child Baba took his jeep to Mymensingh and brought Aunt Jhunu to Ishwarganj. She got out of the jeep wearing a freshly ironed *salwar-kamiz.** She was very happy that day and began chatting with my brothers at once, as if so much had happened back home in the six months we had been gone that she would need more than six years to finish telling them about it. Aunt Jhunu was only a year and a half older than Dada. She began telling him about her new tutor, Rashu, who had recently started and apparently stared at her throughout the lessons, his mouth hanging open like a fish. It was almost midnight by the time she finished describing how Rashu looked.

Within a short time, Aunt Jhunu had our house spick-and-span. Everything was in place. When Baba saw it, he said, "Teach your sister how to take care of a house!" Ma smiled a little bitterly at this, saying, "In his eyes, I can never do anything right, anyway."

Baba dragged Aunt Jhunu onto his lap and tickled her stomach, saying, "You are growing more beautiful every day. Whoever marries you will be a very lucky man!"

Aunt Jhunu covered her face with her *urna*** and wriggled out of his grasp. Her ears and nose were red with embarrassment. Baba's jokes with Aunt Fajli were more intimate. He would pull her by the hand and make her sit on his bed. Then he would say, "Hello you beauty, please come to me, give me peace and joy. I could die for you, d'you know that?"

Aunt Fajli would giggle: "You are very naughty, Dula-bhai!"

Brothers-in-law were allowed to joke, even use sexual innuendos, with their sisters-in-law. No one objected. Still, Ma felt that Baba crossed all limits. He just could not stop himself from pawing a woman if she had fair skin — be it Ma's own sister or Chakladar's wife.

Six days after Aunt Jhunu's arrival, Ma's pains started. Baba was informed and he arrived from the hospital with his medical bag and a nurse at noon.

"This time I want a boy," he declared. The house was reeking with the smell of Dettol and reverberating with Ma's screams. Aunt Jhunu was standing outside the closed door to Ma's room, peering in through a small hole. She had stuffed her mouth with a handkerchief and was laughing. I stood behind her, asking, "How is a baby born?"

---

*Salwar are loose-fitting pants worn by women; *kamiz* is a tuniclike top.
**A piece of cloth that women wear over the kamiz to cover their head and chest.

My heart was thumping. Aunt Jhunu removed her eye from the small hole from time to time, her face red with laughter, but all she said was, "How? I cannot tell you." Why? I wondered innocently.

She was still laughing when we heard the baby cry. Since I could not reach the hole in the door, Aunt Jhunu raised me in her arms so that I could look in. It was only for a few seconds, but I saw Baba standing there, his blood on his gloves. The nurse was washing the baby in a tub. I started trembling. What had Baba done with all those knives and scissors? Had he cut open Ma's stomach? Was that why she was bleeding and crying in pain? Aunt Jhunu was waiting to see the baby, clutching little quilts Grandma had sent with her. As soon as Baba opened the door and came out she asked eagerly, "What is it, Dula-bhai? A boy or a girl?"

Baba replied, "Didn't get what I wanted. It's a girl."

"Dark or fair?" Aunt Jhunu wanted to know.

"What do you think?" Baba snapped. "What can a dark woman produce? Surely not a fair-skinned baby! Anyway, I have heaps to do at the hospital. I'm going back."

Baba left. We wrapped the baby in a quilt and picked her up. She was then massaged with mustard oil and put to bed. There she lay, her little head on a little pillow, her tiny body on a small quilt, her bed covered by a small mosquito net. We tucked it in, and sat by her bed, ready with a feeding bottle shaped like a boat. Ma continued to moan. Dada and Chhotda returned from school and stared, completely round-eyed, at the baby.

When Baba came back at night it was Aunt Jhunu who served him his dinner, after which he went to bed straightaway. The baby began crying, which made him snap, "Shut up, everyone! Let me sleep." Aunt Jhunu picked up the baby, said, "*Sh-sh,* don't cry, baby," softly into the baby's ear, and changed her nappy. Then she gave her a little drink.

I lay in my bed and heard the noises in the house that night, its air heavy with sadness. I felt very sorry for everyone — Baba, Ma, the baby, Aunt Jhunu, even myself.

From Ishwarganj, Baba was transferred back to Mymensingh, then to Thakurgaon, and back again. All this took eighteen months. On our return from Thakurgaon to the house we had known all our lives, Baba announced that from now on we were all to remain in that house, even if he was transferred somewhere else. If he were ordered to go, he would go alone, not with his entire family. Moving from one place to another was adversely affecting Dada and Chhotda's education.

By this time I had grown quite tall. There was some talk of sending me to school. Ma spent her days with my baby sister, feeding and bathing her, massaging her with mustard oil and placing her in the sun. Baba had decided to call her Yasmin, to rhyme with Nasrin. When dusk fell, Dada sat with me in front of a hurricane lamp to help me with my lessons. I was fully capable of reading rhymes and poems, little stories for children, and *Tagore for the Young*. I could read fluently, but when Dada began testing my knowledge, I got quite confused.

"When was Rabindranath Tagore born?" Dada would ask. "Spell the word *momentous*." Or, "Who wrote the poem 'Kajla Didi'?"

I was scared of Dada's questions. If my answer was wrong he would either give me a slap or call the whole family to make fun of me. One day before we moved to Ishwarganj, Dada had decided to act as my teacher and told me to spell the words out loud as I read from my book. At that time, although I could both spell and read, I was more interested in the pictures that accompanied the words. At Dada's command, I took out a book called *So Many Pictures, So Many Words,* and began reading: "T-u-r-m-e-r-i-c."

"All right. That's the spelling. What's the word?" Dada asked. I looked at the picture. It looked like ginger to me. "Ginger," I replied.

The next word was "H-i-l-s-a." I looked at the picture and said confidently, "Fish."

My thirteen-year-old teacher was not happy with this. He called Ma, Grandma, Aunt Runu, Aunt Jhunu, Uncle Hashem, Uncle Tutu, and whoever else was at home. When they were all seated around me, he said, "Listen everyone. See how she reads. Go on, read that first word again."

I failed to understand why it was necessary to call everyone. There was nothing remarkable about reading from a book, I did it every day. Perhaps I had read so well that Dada wanted them all to applaud. That was why he had called them. If I read well, Aunt Runu would dance with me in her arms, Uncle Tutu would give me a sweet, and Grandma would give me a big guava from her tree. So I read as loudly and clearly as I could, moving my finger along each letter: "T-u-r-m-e-r-i-c." Then I looked at the picture and said, "Ginger." At once, everyone roared with laughter. Aunt Jhunu had to sit down, still laughing, her urna slipping from her shoulder. Aunt Runu was giggling helplessly.

"Ha, ha, ha, ha!" guffawed Dada and Uncle Tutu. Even Ma and Grandma couldn't stop laughing. I stared at their faces, a smile slowly appearing on my own, for laughter is infectious. It was as if a little play was enacted, one in which I was the only actor on the stage. Everyone else was in the audience. Grandma was the first to speak. "That word you just spelled is turmeric," she said with a smile. "It may look like ginger in that picture, but that's the wrong word!"

It was the pictures that I remembered; I was not in the least interested in the words. The truth was that I read the pictures. Long before I started to draw the letters of the alphabet, I learned to draw trees, flowers, a river, and a boat. When we were in Thakurgaon, Chhotda had taken me to kindergarten, enrolled me, and pushed me into a classroom. I screamed the roof down. In order to calm me, the teacher placed me on his knee and sang, *"Khoya khoya chaand, khula aasman."* When my howling ceased, he made me sit with the other children, saying, "Boys and girls, draw me a pitcher, will you?"

I drew a pitcher in two or three swift strokes. Then I made a garland of leaves and flowers around it. The other children in my class stopped drawing and bent over mine. On my very first day in that school, I became famous. The teacher picked me up, raised me high, and proclaimed: "Look at this little girl. One day, she will become a great artist."

Dada sat down to teach me and said, "Do you know the poet Nazrul's marching song? *Chol, chol, chol?* You do? All right, recite it for me."

I began,

> Drums beat high in the sky
> the anxious earth waits below
> youth of this radiant dawn
> march on!

Before I could proceed any further, Dada interrupted: "What does *radiant* mean?"

I remained silent. Dada hit me hard with a lead pencil, rapping my fingers sharply. "What's the point in learning a poem by heart, you idiot, unless you learn what it means?"

After Dada suddenly decided to be my teacher, I spent the entire evening getting thrashed. He struck my hand with a pencil, smacked my cheek, and punched me in the back. This went on until Ma called us to dinner. On other days, I would sit with my uncles in Grandma's courtyard and read aloud as if I was in a classroom, which was considered necessary so that the adults could hear us and be sure that we were studying. We read by hurricane lamps, one lamp for two of us. Uncle Sharaf and I read rhymes. Uncle Felu could only manage simple words like *Ma, pen, banana*. Uncle Tutu read whole sentences: "A storm came raging. Tin roofs of houses went flying everywhere. Trees were uprooted. People slipped and fell down." Uncle Tutu read these lines and laughed. His whole body, from the hair on his head to the nails on his toes, shook with laughter. Uncle Felu and Uncle Sharaf joined in. I sat looking puzzled. If people lost their roofs in a raging storm, then slipped and fell, surely that was very sad; why were they laughing? Eventually Grandma heard them and shouted from her room: "Why do I hear laughter when you are supposed to be studying?" But Uncle Tutu did this every evening. He just *had* to read his story about the storm.

We were called to the kitchen to have dinner at eight o'clock. We sat on wooden seats and ate rice with dal and fish curry. No matter what we ate, we had to end every meal with a large bowl of milk. Since Yasmin slept with Ma and Baba in their bed, I had to sleep in Grandma's house. Three cots were joined and placed side by side. Mattresses and sheets were spread out and, in that long, large bed, I slept with Uncle Sharaf, Uncle Felu, Grandpa, and Grandma.

Two months after we returned from Thakurgaon, Grandpa took Uncle Sharaf, Uncle Felu, and me to Rajbari School and registered us there. Uncle Sharaf and I went to the second standard, Uncle Felu to the first. Grandpa bought us three black umbrellas, and had our names written in white on each. Every morning we ate rice mixed with ghee and sugar and left for school, holding our umbrellas over our heads. The school provided lunch. On our return in the afternoon, we had more rice and went to play in a field adjacent to the house. When dusk fell, we had to return home, wash our dirty, dusty hands and feet at the well, light the lamps, and sit down with our books.

My life was spent in two different courtyards — one was ours, the other was Grandma's. My books and papers were scattered in both houses, as were my clothes and shoes. Sometimes I ate in one kitchen, sometimes in the other. Those days joy and sorrow came and went quickly and frequently, as if they were next-door neighbors. Since I had started going to school my spirits had lifted and I realized that I could be in a good mood all day if I was given a colorful tin plate at lunch. Some of the plates had fruit or flowers painted on them, while the others were plain. When the bell rang for lunch, one of the girls in my class would place a plate on every desk. A little later, a staff member came and served us lunch — either bread, eggs and a banana, or *khichuri,* a concoction of rice and dal cooked together.

Poppy, a good student who sat in the front row, always chose a plate with a design for herself. (Her mother and aunt taught in the same school.) I could never take liberties like Poppy. I sat in the last row; I wasn't smart; I always hung my head. Only rarely, by some lucky chance, did I get a flowery plate. When I did, my eyes remained fixed on the painting, not on the food.

The school building had once belonged to King Shashikanto. He had left the building, and so had the queen, the prince, and princess. The empty rooms were filled with tables and chairs, benches and stools. There was a sprawling old banyan tree in the compound and a beautiful white statue of Meerabai in front of the house. Also within the compound was a pond, its water as dark and deep as the eyes of a swan. Steps made of white marble went down to the water. Another flight of stairs ran down from the main building and spread into the garden.

The building's doors were so high that our gatekeeper could not touch the top of their frames, even with a long stick. The ceiling could well have been the open sky. The windows had colorful panes with patterns painted on them. When I entered the school, I truly felt like a princess. But that was as far as it went. In my classroom, when I had to face a roomful of children, I felt very lonely, very foolish. I was too shy to stand in front of the blackboard, to raise my voice and recite a poem so that all might hear. In fear I hung my head and looked down, my voice practically disappeared, and the words that came out sounded quite meaningless. I was hit on the head with an eraser and packed off to sit in the back row.

I was certainly not well known in this school, not like Poppy, who was as beautiful as a fairy. Even in drawing class my hands trembled no matter what we were asked to draw — an elephant, a horse, a river, or a boat. Poppy's drawings earned her full marks. I simply came to be known as the niece of that naughty boy, Sharaf.

One evening after school, Sharaf and Nasim, one of Sharaf's class-mates, were caught, their hands tied behind their backs, their eyes blindfolded, and they were made to stand on the stairs where they were severely caned. Then they were beaten. Nasim had pinched some money from his father's pocket and given it to Sharaf. In return, Sharaf gave Nasim a magnet. Uncle Felu and I had to stand in the garden with all the other children, all with frightened faces, to watch this scene. That evening we returned home without Uncle Sharaf, who was locked up in school. When Grandpa heard what had happened he brought his son back but tied him to a pillar and beat him again.

In my school, some girls put fern leaves in their books and called them *vidyapatta,* leaves of knowledge. I did the same, but even so, when I was called to do a sum on the blackboard, or asked to recite a particular poem, my head hung low and the words dropped from my mouth and scattered on the dusty floor. The poem in question was one that I knew well and described a scene by a small river. But I could not utter the words. I could see the river, the tall grass on its banks, the shepherd boys crossing it — if only I could be asked to draw the scene! Even though my hands would tremble from nervousness, I knew I could draw, do something. Instead I stood mute and heard the loud laughter that rang out when the teacher boxed my ears. When the bell rang and gym class began, all the others ran to the playing field, leaving me behind. No one asked me to join their game. I sat in a corner of the stairs of the main building, lonely and miserable. It seemed as if the whole school had decided not to speak to me. Perhaps I should not speak to myself, either, I thought.

Back at home, I still felt lonely, although the house was full of people. Uncle Sharaf and the others included me in their games only when they could not find anyone else. I could not run like them, or play marbles, or fly kites. They climbed trees, then came down to go for a swim. I stood under a date palm and watched their noisy antics. Dada no longer played cricket. He had developed a new passion: photography. A friend had loaned him a camera, and Dada went to the riverside and the park, dressed in trendy tight trousers and shoes. Here he took photos from different angles. Then he made an album to paste his pictures in. I was allowed to look at his album from a distance but not to touch it. Everyone was busy with their own hobbies and no one had any time for me. I was given the job of cleaning the glass chimneys of all the lanterns each evening with a piece of rag smeared with ash, lighting the wicks, and placing the lamps in all the rooms. Actually, I volunteered to do this job, for this gave me the opportunity to suspend a lamp from each arm and pretend I was selling ice cream. As I passed from one room to another, I called out: "Mala-a-i ice cre-e-e-eam!"

Aunt Runu was the first to stop me. "Come here, ice creamwala, here's some money. Give me an ice cream!"

I was thrilled. I stopped, pretended to take the money, opened the top of the lamp, and brought out an ice cream. The whole thing was make-believe, but it was my own game. There was no question of winning or losing. Uncle Sharaf and Uncle Felu found nothing of interest in my game. "You should play with Chhotku," they advised me. Chhotku was then two and a half years old.

I continued to grow, but almost without any purpose, without gaining knowledge or showing any sign of intelligence. I was shy and slow. Uncle Sharaf and Uncle Felu progressed from chor-chor to football and cricket, but I remained stuck with the same old games. Now I played with Chhotku and other children younger than me. I still cut round pieces of paper and pretended to roast them over hurricane lamps, as if they were breads. When asked to write out multiplication tables, I drew with colored pencils, filling pieces of paper with pictures: a hut made with hemp stalks, banana trees behind it, the sky behind the trees, a bird in the sky, a red sun, a river by the hut, a boat in that river, a boatman at its stern, and a young woman wearing a bright red sari going to the river to fetch water, a pitcher under her arm,

Aunt Fajli failed to understand why a girl born on the twelfth day of Rabi-ul-awal should be so interested in drawing. "Why do you draw human figures?" she asked, "Can you give them life?" I could only stare dumbly at my aunt. This made absolutely no sense to me. Why should I need to give life to a human figure? Wasn't drawing one enough? I could only stare dumbly at my aunt. But if I was doing something objectionable, so was Ma. She had found more letters from Razia Begum in Baba's shirt pockets. She could no longer think straight. She stopped eating, bathing, doing her hair, or even dressing properly. Her sari slipped from her shoulder and swept the floor — she paid no attention. She turned away from all her duties and sat in a room, the door locked. One day, Soheli's mother turned up, saw her, and said, "Look, if you do nothing but mope at home and pine for your husband, it's not going to do you any good. You need a distraction. Come with me." So saying, she got Ma dressed, combed her hair, and took her to see a film at Alaka, the local cinema.

That was the beginning. Soheli's mother did this a few more times, but soon Ma started going out on her own, without waiting for company. She would simply get into a rickshaw, go to the cinema, and stand in a crowded foyer to buy a ticket. Inside the theater, she munched peanuts as she watched the film. This was my mother, my dark and plain mother, draped in a disheveled sari, cheap sandals on her feet. Clothes and jewelry no longer interested her. Baba had some gold jewelry pieces made for his wife and two daughters. Ma would leave them lying in the bathroom, in the kitchen, or under her pillow. She did not care if they were lost. She began going out without bothering to take her burkha. She who had been wearing a burkha since the age of twelve. Now, when she rushed out, she sometimes did not even wear matching slippers. She couldn't care less. The only thing she cared about was the hero Uttam Kumar. Of him, she dreamed every night, putting a garland around her neck, her eyes sparkling with passion.

I had never been to the cinema. I had seen a bioscope, however, for one winter afternoon a man arrived at our playing field with a wooden box. You peered through a hole in the box to see the moving pictures that came and went in a flash. The man sang a song explaining what the pictures meant. Shortly afterward, before the memories of this bioscope faded from my mind, we heard some exciting news. In the field next to Sahabuddin's house a government-produced educational film was going to be shown. As soon as it got dark, all the children in our neighborhood ran to the field and took their seats — bricks laid out on the ground. The film was shown on a large screen. I saw people walk, run, and move their lips. Then I returned home, without having made heads or tails of the film.

"What has this girl got instead of brains in her head?" commented my uncles. "Cow dung?"

Perhaps my head *was* filled with nothing but cow dung. Otherwise, why hadn't I told everyone about what took place on that fateful day? I could have, but I didn't. In a house full of people, no one realized what happened. No one saw, no one heard. It was August 16, 1967. Only two days earlier, Pakistan's independence day had been celebrated. I returned from school, and was waiting for Ma to come back and give me something to eat.

A reading session was in progress in Grandma's room. This was nothing new. Uncle Kana was sitting on a low stool, leaning against a pillar; Grandma was lying on her bed, chewing a paan. Aunt Jhunu was half lying; Uncle Hashem was seated in one chair, legs crossed. He was fanning himself, and Aunt Runu, resting her chest against a pillow, was reading aloud from *The Bandit Behram*. Such a scene was quite common at the end of a long, hot afternoon after everyone had had a short nap. Aunt Runu read, and everyone else listened. There was some chuckling, some appreciation, an occasional comment such as, "What nonsense!" I was standing at the door, because children were not allowed to go into the room and disturb the proceedings. Uncle Hashem said to me, "Go on, go out in the field and play."

I had no wish to go. I was very hungry, but Ma had locked the cabinet where the food was kept and gone out. So I went back to Grandma's courtyard, making my way from there to the empty courtyard in our own house, past the well and the coconut tree that stood next to it. I was sitting on the front step, alone, legs stretched out, cheek against my hand, when Uncle Sharaf turned up. Who knows what brought him there — perhaps a cricket ball had landed in our courtyard or he had left his marbles outside. He was taller than me by nearly a foot. His brown eyes darted restlessly from one thing to another — the leaves on the trees, the doors to our rooms, the black cat in our yard, and the empty chair in our living room. He was wearing a sleeveless vest and white shorts.

"Where's Borobu?" he asked. "Not here," I replied, shaking my head, my hand still on my cheek.

"Where has she gone?" Uncle Sharaf asked urgently, as if he needed to see Ma at once. Then he sat down next to me, and slapped my back. "What are you doing, sitting here all by yourself?"

"Nothing," I replied morosely.

"When is Borobu coming back?" Uncle Sharaf went on. I did not reply. He then removed my hand from my cheek and said more gently, "Don't sit clutching your cheek like that. It's unlucky."

I wanted to say, "I am starving," but I did not. Instead, I said, "Hey, you don't know where Ma has gone, do you?" I moved a bit closer and added, "Promise you won't tell?"

"All right, I won't. Where has she gone?"

"Promise?"

"Promise."

"Truly?"

"Truly."

"Swear in the name of Allah?"

"Look, what is this? Stop this nonsense and tell me." Uncle Sharaf sounded impatient.

"No, you have to swear. Swear to Allah — say *Allahr kasam!*"

It was my belief then that if anyone said Allahr kasam, they would not dare go back on their word.

Uncle Sharaf looked suitably grave. "Very well. Allahr kasam."

Reassured, I whispered into his ear: "Ma has gone to see a film!"

The news did not appear to surprise Uncle Sharaf. "I see," he said very casually, as if Ma had simply gone to the bathroom or to the house next door. She was not supposed to go to the cinema at all. Grandpa had forbidden her, because watching a film was sinful.

"Listen, woman, if you step out of the house once more, you'll be in very big trouble," he had threatened.

But Ma had gone out, ignoring his threat. Uncle Sharaf was unperturbed. "I saw a film yesterday myself!" he informed me coolly.

"You? You went to the cinema?" I asked, totally amazed.

"Yes!" he replied, his eyes dancing.

"What if Grandpa finds out?" I asked timidly.

"Come on, I'll show you something interesting," said Uncle Sharaf. He suddenly rose to his feet and began walking toward the room at the far end of the house, beyond Dada and Chhotda's room in the southern corner of our courtyard. It was made of tin and painted black. I followed him. There were two doors to the room. The front one was locked. The door at the rear was bolted but could be opened, if one knew how. No sound from the main house carried this far. The silence was eerie. An old broad-bean creeper spread over a large area behind the room, together with other wild plants, vines, and dead leaves. I had never before come to this part of the house because of my fear of snakes. Chhotda had once seen a snake here, although it was said to be nonpoisonous. I walked behind Uncle Sharaf, but before stepping into the thick growth of wild plants, said, "Uncle Sharaf, there are snakes in this jungle."

"Pooh, don't be afraid. What an idiot you are, a perfect coward. Come with me. I'll show you this funny thing, no one knows about it." He proceeded to walk into the bushes as if he knew for sure that every snake in the vicinity was asleep in its hole.

"Tell me what it is," I said, after hesitating for a few moments.

"If I tell you now, it will spoil the surprise."

We got to the rear door. Uncle Sharaf slipped a finger inside and unbolted it. I ran through the bushes and joined him. Curiosity got the better of me that day. The lure of this secret and interesting thing was so strong that I did not mind taking my life in my hands and passing through a snake-infested area.

The smell of dead rats hit me as soon as we stepped into the room. I could hear other rats scurrying about. One side of the room was crammed with firewood and on the other stood a wooden cot. I felt quite scared but did not admit it, in case Uncle Sharaf called me an idiot and a coward again. He was a very brave young man, one who roamed alone all over town, even went to the riverside. I really admired his courage. Hiding my fear as best as I could, and bursting with curiosity, I asked: "Does Fo-ting-ting live by the riverside, Uncle Sharaf?"

He sat down on the bed, his legs dangling. "No," he said.

"Will you take me there one day?" I pleaded earnestly.

"Won't you be scared?" Uncle Sharaf inquired, poking my tummy.

"No," I replied bravely.

"You will. You are a big coward." Uncle Sharaf cuffed me.

"No, no. I don't feel scared anymore, believe me. I am grown up now," I declared, telling myself that if I could cross those bushes crawling with snakes, I would not be afraid of other horrors.

"I don't believe you," Uncle Sharaf said, kicking the door shut.

I clutched his hand. "I swear I won't. Really, truly. Allahr kasam!"

"This is a good place. There's no one around. No one can tell where we are," said Uncle Sharaf, changing the subject.

I knew he liked hiding and doing things in secret. Once he had called out to me from behind the kitchen and said, "You want a smoke?" He took out a box of matches and a thin, reedy stalk of a jute plant. Lighting one end of the stalk he had put the other into his mouth and inhaled, as if he was smoking a cigarette. Then he had blown out a cloud of smoke, passed the stalk to me, and said, "Have a go." I did exactly what I had seen him do.

"You won't tell anyone, will you?" he had asked.

"No." I had shaken my head, coughing.

Uncle Sharaf was like that. He did not care what anyone said to him or whether he was punished for any mischief. He did what he wanted to, behind everyone's back.

"What did you do with the money Nasim gave you?" I now asked him. It was something I was dying to know.

"I've buried it in the ground," he confessed, without even bothering to make me promise not to tell.

I was flattered. In this lonely, isolated little spot, Uncle Sharaf had agreed to take me to the riverside, and told me about his hidden treasure — something no one else knew about. I could no longer think of myself simply as a young girl with cow dung in her head. I began to feel important.

"In the ground? Where? Somewhere in this house?" I whispered.

"Yes. When I'm older, I'll buy a ship with that money."

"A ship? Will you let me travel in it?"

My heart jumped with joy. I could see a huge ship, sailing along a river and making its way to the sea. With me in it, watching the silver water lapping against its sides, glistening in the sun. I had seen such a picture on a calendar produced by a pharmaceutical company.

Uncle Sharaf's eyes danced again. This time, he did not have a jute stalk in his hand or a matchbox, just a strange smile on his lips.

I could not understand what it meant.

"Time to show you that thing," he said abruptly and without the slightest warning, pulled me down on the cot. All I was wearing was some frilly shorts. Uncle Sharaf pulled those too.

I was aghast. Pulling them up again hastily, I said, "Why are you taking my clothes off? Show me what you said you would."

Uncle Sharaf laughed and threw himself down on me. Then, with one hand he removed my shorts once more, and with the other took off his own, pressing his willie hard against my body. My chest felt heavy; I could not breathe. I tried to push him away. "What are you doing, Uncle Sharaf? Let me go!" I shrieked, pushing with all my might. But I could not move him an inch.

"Didn't I tell you I would show you something interesting? This is it!" He was still grinning, and biting his lower lip. "Do you know what this is called? It's called fucking. Everyone in this world does it. Your parents do, and mine."

Uncle Sharaf pushed himself harder against me. It looked so ugly to me, I covered my eyes with my hands.

Suddenly, a rat scurried across the floor. The noise made Uncle Sharaf jump off the cot. I did not lose a second. Pulling my shorts up I ran out of the room as fast as I could, with not a thought to spare about the snakes in the bushes. My heart thudded crazily, as if a hundred rats were jumping in my chest.

Uncle Sharaf called after me in a threatening voice: "Don't tell anyone about this. If you do, I will kill you!"

~ 4 ~

Ma

Che local boys marched in procession down the main road, shouting *"Lar ke lenge Pakistan / Beer mujahid nau jawan, / Kobul moder jaan poraan, / Aante hobey pak Quran."* (They'll fight to get Pakistan, / brave, young men of the motherland, / They'll lay their lives down every one / To ensure the writ of the Holy Koran.)

When she heard those boys, Ma stopped playing hopscotch, jumped up, and said, *"Lar ke lenge Pakistan!"* without really understanding what the words meant. Then, one day, she heard that the British had left India and the Muslims had obtained a new country called Pakistan. The local boys marched down the street again, dancing with joy and chanting, *"Pakistan zindabad!"* Long live Pakistan!

The creation of Pakistan in 1947 did nothing to alter Ma's life. Her elder brother, Siddique, continued to go to the Naseerabad Madrasa, just as he had before. Sultan Ustadji came to their house to teach her the Koran, also as before. Ma couldn't see what difference it made to have a new country. Her Bajan still went to the mosque five times a day for namaz — anyway, no one had ever stopped him. So why was everyone going mad about bringing in a "new" Koran?

The only difference between the past and the present was that her friend Amala and her family had left. They sold their land and all their property at throwaway prices and, with tears in their eyes, went over to Hindustan. Amala and Ma had been best friends. Anyone would have been heartbroken to lose a friend like that. Ma certainly was — but she could do nothing to make Amala come back or to stop others from leaving. Soon her school was emptied. Not a Hindu girl in sight. A handful of Muslims sat in the empty classrooms and read the new chapter in their history books: Pakistan Is Our Country.

"Qaid-e-azam Muhammad Ali Jinnah is the father of our nation." They were made to learn the words by heart.

Other books changed, too. Instead of the poetry of Satyendranath Dutta and Jatindramohan Bagchi, poems by Ghulam Mustafa and Bande Ali Mia were now taught. Rabindranath Tagore was replaced by Kazi Nazrul Islam. Ma, however, continued to sing the old songs she had learned from Amala's sister, and life went on as usual, filled with little joys and sorrows. She still swam in their pond, pushing aside the plants and vines that grew in the water. She still ate fish curry and rice and sat on a wooden stool, exactly as she had always done. A country's name might change, but how could its people? Instead of the British, you now saw men from Lahore on the streets. Ma called them foreigners.

In her own little world, her dolls lay quietly in their beds. Only Amala's doll, who was married to one of Ma's, looked sad. A special grief clung to the secret recesses of Ma's heart.

She was forced into marriage before she could fully outgrow her dolls. Afterward, she would ask Baba to take her to fairs and buy her a doll. However, her passion for dolls ended when a real baby was born.

In 1952 protesters marched, demanding that Bengali be made the national language of East Pakistan. Some Urdu speakers shot at them. This really puzzled Ma. "If Muslims are going to attack fellow Muslims, what's the point of having a separate nation?" she wondered. The protesters had a list of six demands. They marched down the same street, but their slogans had changed. Instead of "We'll fight to get Pakistan," they now shouted, "The state language we demand is Bengali, not Urdu," and "Urdu-speaking rulers should be hanged together!"

How strange, thought Ma, the whole character of these marches had changed before her very eyes, but she was still where she had always been — at the end of a narrow alley, sitting near a fish-filled pond.

On my way to buy provisions at Monumia's shop I often saw a tall, thin boy on our street. He occupied a small tin room under a *boroi* tree, which had the sweetest fruit in the area. Behind the tin room was a much larger house where his mother and siblings lived. It was customary to let a grown-up boy use a room outside the main house. Dada and Chhotda had a similar arrangement. One day, Chhotda happened to mention that the tall boy was called Mintu, and was

Chhotda's friend Khokon's elder brother. Khokon and Chhotda were really close friends, so close that they fell in love at the same time with the same girl.

Mintu struck me as being very lonely. I often saw him wearing a thin shirt and a blue lungi, walking alone or standing at his door, whistling absently. The boroi tree was so laden with ripe fruit that my mouth watered and I stopped for a while every time I passed it. My heart longed to gather up the fruit that had fallen to the ground, but I was afraid Mintu would box my ears if he caught me. I swallowed the temptation and went home. Anyone else from the neighborhood would always speak to me, even if it was just to say, "Where are you off to? Mind the traffic." But Mintu never said a word; he only looked at me. Maybe he was shy. On quiet afternoons he spoke to himself. On moonlit nights he lay alone under the *kamini* tree, surrounded by its beautiful smell.

In 1969, I was taken out of Rajbari and put into Vidyamoyee School, in the middle of town. To its right was Ganginar par, to the left Notun Bazar. This school was farther than the previous one and I had to go by rickshaw, paying the driver four annas each way. Every morning Baba counted out eight annas and gave them to Ma. She kept the money tied in her anchal until ten o'clock — school started at half-past. On the way there I saw that the whole town looked as if someone had knocked it down and scattered it through the streets. Often I would see stones and bricks, or the trunks of chopped-down trees. Policemen stood at street corners. Chhotda frequently played truant and joined protest marches. When he did, he always came home late. Baba paced the courtyard. Ma stood at our front door with a lantern in her hand. Chhotda had been told not to go on these marches but he was not an obedient child, not like Dada. Chhotda was much more difficult to control. He slipped out whenever he got the chance.

It was January 24 and the boys were marching again. I had been hearing them since early morning. For some unknown reason a large number of crows had gathered in the sky, cawing incessantly. Why were they doing that? And why were so many people running toward the marchers? What had happened? Ma left the kitchen and ran out as she was, barefoot, her hair hanging loose, her sari disheveled, her hands smelling of onions and smeared with spices. She ran to Mukul's house, on the main road, opposite the railroad crossing and the signaler's booth. From their open veranda she could see that everyone was running toward the railway tracks, going past the district school and the sweets shop that stood beyond it. Ma and a few other women stopped some of the boys, and soon the veranda in Mukul's house was filled with teenagers — Faruk, Rafiq, Chandan, and others. All had been hit by bullets. Buckets of water were brought from in, along with a bottle of Dettol and cotton. Ma and the others washed their wounds, dabbed them with Dettol, and tied bandages made from strips torn from their saris. Some of the boys were put on rickshaws and sent straight to the hospital.

Baba returned in the afternoon. Without a word to anyone he went to Mintu's house. Ma and I followed Baba. Others from the neighborhood also turned up. I saw Baba look sorrowfully at Mintu's mother and then at the empty tin room. "What is it? Has something happened to Mintu?" His mother clutched Baba's hand and wailed. She had already heard the news. Mintu was leading the march, he had been shot by the police, and the boys had taken him to the hospital. Baba sighed deeply but did not speak. Mintu's sister, Monu, was crying loudly. The crows continued their racket. Mintu's mother fainted. The other women, who had returned from Mukul's house, poured water on her head to make her come around. Between sobs, Monu was saying to Ma, "Idul apa, I am going to kill those who killed my brother!" She kept trying to leave the house; Ma had to hold her back. How could Monu kill those murderers? They had guns. How could anyone face them empty-handed?

Some of the neighbors were standing next to Mintu's room, talking about what had happened. The marchers had just passed the veterinary hospital when, without the slightest warning, the police opened fire. The boys had started running in the opposite direction, all except for Mintu. More people arrived at Mintu's house. Khokon, Bachchu, and Humayun, his three brothers, had to push their way in. Then Mintu was brought home on a bier, covered with a white sheet.

I stood under the boroi tree and watched that covered body. He had been a shy and quiet young boy. That morning, only a few hours ago, he had been seen standing outside his room, looking restless. When his mother called him in for breakfast, he said he was going out for a short while but would be back soon. His mother had left his breakfast in the kitchen, covered with a plate. It was still in the kitchen, exactly where it had been left, when Mintu was brought back to the house.

The ground under the tree was thick with fruit that had fallen from its branches. It was the best, the sweetest boroi in the whole area, but that day I did not feel like picking up a single fruit. There was no one around to box my ears, but even so I felt no desire to help myself. I had just seen my own mother stroking Mintu's mother's head, tears pouring down her cheeks. She was saying, "Don't cry. So many boys have sworn by Mintu's blood that, one day, they will definitely take revenge. Things will change. Please, please don't cry."

When Mintu returned home as a corpse, all the neighbors cried, not just his own family. I had no idea that people had loved that thin lonely boy quite so much. Chhotda, I noticed, was not speaking. He had taken part in the same march. In fact, he was standing to the right of Mintu when the bullet hit. It had passed Chhotda, then struck Mintu's chest. Instead of Mintu, it could well have been he who was shot dead that day.

Mintu was buried in the cemetery in Akua. I had never seen so much grief in our neighborhood. The adults stood by the road in small groups and spoke in low voices. Children did not go out to play. It was as if the entire neighborhood had decided not to eat, or laugh, or play, or sleep.

A few days later, Sheikh Mujib came to visit Mintu's family. Such a lot of people turned up to see him! Chhotda said, "Oh, if only *I* had died that day there would have been a crowd in our house. Sheikh Mujib would have come *here!*" He sounded truly sorry. I had never before heard anyone express such profound regret at not being dead.

I, too, went to look at Sheikh Mujib. It was not easy in that crowd. At first, I stood on tiptoe. That didn't work. I placed one brick on top of another and stood on top of them. I still couldn't see him. So I climbed a wall — a relatively low wall first, then a higher one, ignoring the risk of slipping and breaking my leg. I could see Sheikh Mujib at last. Tall, wearing a black jacket and glasses, he looked a little like Shahabuddin, who lived in our area. But no one ever crowded round to see Shahabuddin! Sheikh Mujib seemed to have flown down straight from heaven. He was different from all other men. To comfort Mintu's mother, he gently stroked her head. Under the boroi tree, fresh sweet fruit was lying on the ground, but I felt no desire to eat.

It did not take us long to get back to normal. Human nature is like that — people cannot carry the weight of grief for very long. Within a month children went back to the field to play, men returned from grocery stores with heavy shopping bags, women were busy in their kitchens. Like the others, I resumed my routine, spreading a mat in the courtyard when dusk fell and doing my lessons by the light of a hurricane lamp. It was only when I went past the cemetery on the way to school that I walked with my hands clenched and my head bowed. Ma had told me to do this. But I did something else without being told. If I saw flowers anywhere — no matter in whose garden or on whose trees — I picked them and placed them on Mintu's grave. I believed that Mintu could smell those flowers.

Ma thought that the new Pakistan was so fragile that it would very likely break up again. People were singing a different tune, openly abusing Ayub Khan. Young men were still demonstrating, demanding self-rule for East Pakistan. The government frequently placed the whole country under curfew, calling for a blackout. At night everyone had to put out all lights and sit in the dark. Every ruler was the same, thought Ma. The West Pakistan rulers were as ruthless as the British. East Pakistan's products and possessions were all being sent to West Pakistan, just as the British had stripped India of her wealth and taken shiploads of loot to their country. Ma felt nothing for Pakistan. It could break into little fragments, it could go to the dogs, she didn't care. All she cared about was her children — she didn't want any of them to die in a march. If she could live somewhere safe with all her children, she would be happy. That was all she asked. If she had had an education, she could have found a job, and given her indifferent husband his freedom or perhaps found freedom for herself. Once she did go to Dhaka by rail, accompanied by Chhotda, to look for a job. She had heard there were plenty of jobs in Dhaka; one simply had to reach out and grab one. She went to a hospital to ask if she might work there as a nurse. "You don't become a nurse just like that!" the authorities told her. "You need proper qualifications, a certificate from a nursing school." Ma returned home, disappointed. On seeing her, Baba snarled, "Why do some people have to go looking for trouble?"

Ma could not bear to let Chhotda out of her sight. What if he, like Mintu, was shot dead? Her heart ached for the child she had been unable to wean until he was nearly six years old. In the end, she had taken Grandma's advice. "Try neem leaves," Grandma had said. "Make a paste and apply it to your breasts. Only then will he stop."

So Ma crushed neem leaves, made a paste, and smeared it on her nipples in the hope that its bitter taste would discourage her son. It worked.

Chhotda was slow to learn how to talk properly. Even at two, he could only say, "Ba-aa ba-aa" for "Baba." When he was taken to a school to be admitted to the sixth standard, the headmaster asked him just one question: "Can you spell the word *hippopotamus?*" Chhotda said, "Hip-pot, tam-pop, pot-mas," and finally gave up, running out of breath. Luckily the headmaster knew Baba, so he was admitted despite that stammering performance. Once, Baba bought him a geometry box — one that contained pencils and a ruler, compass, and protractor — and a watch, and said, "If you do well in your studies, you'll get a cycle." Chhotda lost the watch on the third day and began offering the compass to anyone who wanted to remove a piece of meat stuck between their teeth. Having seen Dada teach me, one day he was seized by the desire to do the same. He opened a book and said to me, "Can you read these words?"

"Nast, nast, how many eggs? One, two, three . . ."

Dada interrupted, staring at him in surprise. "Stop!" he said, "what are you saying? That's not 'nast,' it's 'ants'!"

Even after Chhotda grew physically and was clearly no longer a child, Ma continued to think of him as her baby. She was afraid he might turn out to be a complete idiot, good for nothing, but it was Dada who grew up to be a quiet and meek young boy who couldn't say boo to a goose. Chhotda was just the opposite. His teachers complained that he was lacking in discipline.

"What is this I hear?" asked Baba one day, dragging his son by his ear into his room. "Don't you obey the rules?"

"Yes, I do, I do!" Chhotda snorted angrily.

"Really? You mean your teachers are all liars?"

"Yes," Chhotda replied nonchalantly.

Baba gave him a resounding slap. "Why did you break the school radio?" he asked.

Chhotda bristled. "I was lis-listening to the ra-ra-radio, and this boy tried to t-t-take it away from me, so I broke it."

"Wonderful! What wonderful logic. I ought to salute my son! I work so hard day and night simply so that my children get an education and grow up to be good human beings. But if they are not going to do that, why should I bother?"

Baba made Chhotda sit at his desk. "It's his mother who has spoiled him!" he muttered.

In our house, whenever someone was beaten, they were later rewarded. The day after Chhotda was slapped by Baba, Ma took some money from him and bought her son a cricket bat and ball. He began using both, but it turned out that hitting the furniture in our house gave him far greater pleasure than hitting the ball.

After she learned about Chhotda's involvement with protest marches, Ma began to pester Baba to buy their son a guitar. If he developed an interest in music, perhaps he would stop participating in marches and rallies. Baba eventually gave in and parted with enough money to buy Chhotda a Hawaiian guitar. Dada did not fail to notice Ma's partiality toward her younger son. "Tell Baba to buy me a violin," he said to Ma.

"Tell him yourself," Ma said irritably. "Haven't you got a tongue to speak?"

Dada's face fell. He did not have the courage to ask Baba for a violin. So he retired to his room and continued to tap his desk in rhythm with the song "Say good-bye, Ma / I wanna go there to kill myself hanging / whole world would see me smiling." To be honest, Dada only knew one song, a tune that he had learned from Ma when he was four years old.

Chhotda, on the other hand, learned to play *sa-re-ga-ma* on his guitar and picked up popular film music quickly. Every month Ma had to ask Baba for money for the guitar teacher and every month, before he coughed up the money, Baba asked, "Have you found out how he is doing in his studies? Or do you think he can have a good life purely by playing his guitar? I've hired tutors for him — math, English, and science. Does he go to them regularly? Do you have any idea? How long does he stay up at night to study? Sulekha's brothers study till ten o'clock."

When he finally found the money to pay the guitar teacher, Baba always threw it, either on the table, or the bed, or the floor, but for the other three teachers he went and handed them their salaries personally.

Ma simply failed to understand how Baba's mind worked. She was convinced that no one in the world had such a complex character. Sometimes, it seemed as if Baba lived only for his family and gave all he had for the welfare of his children. At other times, it seemed as if he didn't care and lived with them only because people might talk if he didn't. The truth, Ma thought, was that he was devoted to Razia Begum. But then one day Baba made her feel that when he worked hard, it was for his family in Madarinagar. This happened around the time he invited his brother, Aman-ud-daula, to come and live with us. Baba returned early from his chamber that day with two kilos of lamb instead of one and said to Ma, "Cook this meat well, make sure it's roasted with lots of onion, and don't forget to cook vegetables. Instead of simple dal, make some spicy gravy dal."

That night, Baba called both his sons and said, "How are you doing in your studies? Do you go to your tutors regularly?"

Dada hung his head, and rubbed his big toe on the floor. "Yes, I do," he replied.

"Which do you do more — play or study?" Baba went on.

Dada gave him the answer he knew Baba wanted to hear: "Study."

"What does a man with education get to do?"

"Ride in a motorcar," Dada replied, staring at the floor.

"And you? What about you?" Baba turned to Chhotda, "What do you think an educated man achieves in life?"

"R-r-ride in a motorcar," Chhotda answered promptly.

They were all referring to an old Bengali saying that implied that only a man with education would prosper in life. But Baba was an educated man and he did not ride a motorcar! The only vehicle he ever rode in was a cycle rickshaw. These words rose to my lips, but I gulped them down, as usual.

"Hmm," Baba continued. "Someone is visiting our house. His name is Aman-ud-daula. He is your uncle. What is he to you?"

Chhotda leaned against a pillar, and replied, "He is our uncle."

"Yes, that's right." Baba pulled Chhotda away from the pillar and made him stand up straight. "This is the correct way to stand. Keep your back straight . . . And you!" He suddenly noticed me and beckoned. "Have *you* seen your uncle? My brother?" I nodded yes, that I had seen him.

"Very well. Go on, go back to your studies, all of you. Dinner will be ready soon. When you go to eat, make sure your uncle joins you. He is part of the family, very close to all of us. Do you understand?"

Dada nodded obediently. "Yes, we understand!"

The room that was used to store firewood was given to Uncle Aman. Baba removed all the wood, had the room cleaned, and put in a bed, a table, and a chair. Then he took his brother to a college in town, had him enrolled, and informed everyone at home that from now on he would live with us. Baba would pay all his expenses.

"You have your own family. How will you manage the extra expense?" Ma asked.

"I'll have to, somehow. He is my own brother, after all. I can hardly ignore my responsibilities. Besides, his being here will help you, too. He can do most of the grocery shopping."

"Noman and Kamal are now old enough to do my shopping for me," Ma replied coldly.

The next day, Baba bought her a printed cotton sari. Ma ate a paan that day, made sure her lips looked red, then put on her new sari and sat close to Baba. "This is a very good-quality sari," she told him.

Instead of commenting on her appearance, Baba asked anxiously, "Has Aman eaten anything?"

Ma felt a sharp stab of disappointment. Was that the reason Baba had bought her a gift? Simply to ensure that she would take good care of his brother? That's what people did for their servants! Gave them the occasional gift to keep them happy so that they did their work and served their master faithfully. Was Ma no more than a servant in this house? That was how she felt. Baba did not seem to care at all about her personal happiness. About a week after Uncle Aman's arrival, Ma said to Baba, "Sulekha is getting married. You and I have been invited to her wedding. Let's go."

"No," said Baba. When Ma insisted, he got cross. "Look, here's some money. Buy her a present and you can go alone, okay?"

This was the kind of man Ma lived with. People saw her as a doctor's wife, her life full of joy and happiness. Only Ma knew how the scent of another woman wafted up from her husband's body and blew away her dreams and desires. Only she knew that, even after she swallowed her pride, buried her shame, and offered herself to her husband, he turned away from her in bed and slept on his side. What kept Ma company during her sleepless nights were her own long, deep sighs.

Eventually, Ma took Chhotda with her to Sulekha's wedding, but she felt very lonely when she returned. The house was full of people but that did nothing to lift Ma's spirits. Baba returned that night, humming under his breath, his lips red with paan juice. He did not touch the meal that was waiting for him.

"Why won't you eat anything? Who has fed you tonight? Another woman?" Ma fired her questions as soon as he entered.

"A patient invited me to dinner tonight," Baba smiled.

"A patient? Man or woman?" Ma asked, squeezing herself into one corner of the bed.

"A patient is a patient. How does it matter whether it's a man or not?" Baba snapped.

"Ah ha, you think I can't see through your clever little ploys? Razia Begum was your patient, wasn't she? Didn't I pick you up from her bed? Well, didn't I? You think you can fool me, can get away with anything and do what you want, just because I am a simple woman!" Ma exclaimed.

Baba lay down beside her and said, "Do what I want? I wish I could!"

The next morning, he woke to the sound of Chhotda playing a song on his guitar: "Have you ever seen how life is defeated? / Burned by grief, drenched by tears, it is destroyed inch by inch." Baba jumped out of bed and began singing the next line: "The pages of a newspaper give us all the news / But no one knows what's written on the pages of our lives."

Ma entered the room at this moment, a plate of bread and poached eggs in her hand. She stared at Baba, totally taken aback. He startled her further by saying, "Kamal plays quite well, I must say. That song describes my feelings exactly. Have you heard it?"

Before leaving for the hospital that day, Baba called Chhotda. "Who teaches you the guitar? The month's almost over — don't you need money to pay him? How much is it?"

Then he opened his wallet and gave Chhotda the necessary amount. Chhotda's whole face lit up. "Music alone isn't going to get you anywhere, you know. You *have* to do your studies. What you must have is a routine. Eat when it's time to eat. Study when it's time to study. And play your guitar when it's time for music."

Baba had come to the city from a remote village but he had become a doctor and was quite successful. So why did he think that a sad song that spoke of grief and failure was appropriate for him? Why did he like it so much? Ma simply couldn't understand. Nothing Baba did ever made any sense. What was he made of? One moment he seemed cold and lifeless, the next moment he was a man with deep, strong feelings. She was completely confused.

That night, before Baba returned, Ma dressed with special care.

She wore her sari in a more fashionable style and made her lips red with paan juice. When Baba sat down to eat, Ma fanned him and said to me, "Go and sleep in your Grandma's house tonight."

Normally I would have jumped at the chance to sleep in Grandma's house. Ma knew that, so she was extremely surprised when I stayed where I was, making no attempt to move.

"Go," she said again, "to Grandma's house."

I shook my head. "No," I said.

Ma turned around and looked at me. "What? You won't go?"

"No," I repeated, more clearly and firmly.

"What's the matter with you? Has anyone said anything? Tutu? Sharaf? Felu?"

"No," I said again, scratching the wooden railing that ran around our bed.

"Well, if no one has said anything, why won't you go?" Ma pushed me toward the door.

I held the door firmly and refused to budge. Before me loomed the dark courtyard.

"I can't cope with this girl anymore!" Ma complained. "She doesn't listen to anything I say. I tell her to stay inside, and she wants to go out and play. Play, play, play . . . that's all she ever does. And then when she gets beaten, she comes whining back. Look how thin she is. She eats so little, like a bird. When she was small, three of us had to hold her down to make her drink her milk. Even now she always makes a fuss. Won't have any milk or eggs. Do you see how stubborn she's become? Here I am telling her to go to her grandma, but she won't!"

I continued to stand at the door, rooted to the spot. Ma moved closer, laid a hand on my back, and said more gently, "Go on. Your uncles will tell you stories. Take your ribbon. Jhunu will tie your hair for you."

Still I stood like a statue. "Leave it," said Baba, "if she doesn't want to go, let her be."

"Stubborn!" Ma muttered. "And impudent!"

Ma clearly thought I was peculiar. If a visitor came to our house, I would run and hide behind her. Ma could never understand why I was so shy, so timid, so hesitant to do anything. I spoke very little. When I wanted to tell a story, I had to search for the right words, but I was always ready to hear one. I had heard so many from so many different people, but I couldn't tell one myself, not clearly and coherently, anyway.

It was the same with reading. I devoured everything that came my way. I had already finished several books of fairy tales — *The Frog Prince, Tales from Grandma,* and others — but no matter what or how much I read I couldn't bring myself to open up and express my thoughts. I should have been able to explain why I would not go to Grandma's house, why I had rejected even that most tempting prospect of hearing my uncles' stories. But I said nothing. No one could ever make me talk. If anyone hit me or scolded me, I simply stared back vacantly. My ears were boxed, I was slapped, pushed, and punched every day, but I did not speak. In fact, I couldn't even cry openly.

I was born on the twelfth day of Rabi-ul-awal. I had shown a great deal of promise and raised people's expectations, but the way I turned out caused much disappointment. Perhaps I should have been religious, but I showed no interest in learning Arabic. During my lessons, all I could think of was when I might be able to read another fairy tale, draw a picture, run out to the railroad tracks, or play in the open field. I had been warned many times that drawing human figures was a bad thing, it was sinful — *draw a human figure only if you can give it life* — but I never did lose my great enthusiasm for drawing figures of men and women.

Ma went to Aunt Fajli's house and brought back a piece of paper. On it the Prophet Muhammad's shoes were drawn in red, over which was printed a verse sent to him by Allah. Ma called it Naal Sharif. It was placed inside a medallion and hung around my neck. The hope was that it would remove all irrational fears from my mind.

— 5 —

Snakes

I did not know why I loved drawing human figures even though I knew it was sinful to do so. Every time Ma saw me drawing a man or a woman, she said, "Draw plants, or trees or flowers, there's no harm in that. Don't draw living things; don't draw humans. You can't give them life, can you? Only Allah can do that."

One day I could not help saying, "You said it's all right to draw trees. Aren't trees living things?" The words slipped out before I could stop myself. Ma pursed her lips and continued to braid her hair, tying it with a tassel. "Stop being impertinent and do as you're told."

I was supposed to do what I was told simply because that's what Ma said. If she told me to eat shit, I would have to do it — that's how it was. Why did everyone make such a fuss over giving life to something I had drawn? I was simply *drawing* a human figure, not creating one. Ma refused to see the difference. She tried to win arguments by force, perhaps simply because she was my mother. Her word had to be law.

Despite all her warnings, I had drawn a man, not because I wished to be difficult but because it was necessary. I had originally drawn a boat. Since a boat was a lifeless object, no one had any problem with that. The problem arose when I put a boatman in it. How could a boat sail on the river all on its own? It did not seem right. I just had to put in a boatman with an oar in his hand. My cousin Humaira came to visit Grandma and saw the drawing. After she left, having expressed shock and horror at my action, Ma snatched away all my colored pencils and said, "Stop this nonsense with sketching and drawing. Pay more attention to your studies."

I was not one to burst into tears. I just withdrew into myself.

Ma lay on her bed by an open window and loosened her sari blouse to ease the discomfort of prickly heat. She thought nothing of snatching my pencils away. It was as if she had picked up some rubbish from our courtyard and thrown it into a dustbin. The whole thing was as trivial and insignificant as that.

"Read more loudly, I can't hear you!" Ma shouted. I started, coming out of my reverie. But there was a hard lump in my throat; my voice had disappeared. How could I read loudly? I failed to obey Ma's command.

That same night, however, Ma stroked my head gently and said, "Come, my dear, stand with me. Let's do our namaz together." Her tender touch melted my heart, and my pain was blown away by a soft, southerly breeze. My mother was like that. One minute she would scold and perhaps even beat me; the next minute she was full of affection. Once she hit Dada with a cane. Later that day, she massaged his aching back with mustard oil.

"If you do your namaz," Ma told me, "Allah will love you. He will give you whatever you want."

Whatever I want? What could be better than that? So I followed what Ma was doing. I knelt, then rose to my feet, joining my palms sideways in prayer. I closed my eyes and spoke to Allah silently. It was said that Allah could hear everything; there was no need to utter the words aloud. *Dear Allah,* I asked, *please give me two chum-chums.* I finished my namaz and opened my eyes. There were no *chum-chums,* my favorite sweets, anywhere in sight. Puzzled, I searched under the prayer mat, but they were not there, either. Afterward, I said to Ma, feeling very close to tears, "Allah didn't give me what I wanted!"

"You could not have prayed hard enough, with all your heart. That's why you didn't get what you wanted," Ma explained.

After this, I stood frequently with Ma to do namaz at night, and prayed very hard for various things — a mechanical car, a jar full of marbles, a balloon with a whistle attached to it — but I did not get any of those things. I couldn't possibly pray any harder. Perhaps I was being punished for some sin. At any rate, I began to think of myself as a sinner. When Uncle Sharaf took me to that empty room and stripped me naked, was that somehow *my* fault, *my* sin? Was that why Allah hated me? Perhaps.

My heart felt very heavy. That night, when Ma asked me to go and sleep in Grandma's house, I did not go. The thought of sleeping with my uncles frightened me. But, of course, Ma had no idea about how I felt. Only a few days after that horrible incident, Uncle Sharaf had wanted me to join him by the pond. He had a magnet, he said, he was going to perform more tricks. I did not go. He tapped my head and went away.

Uncle Tutu had taken up acting. He had learned some lines from a play called *Siraj-ud-daula* and acted them out almost every evening in his room, behind closed doors. His audience consisted of all the children in the house, who clapped enthusiastically when he finished. Sometimes I poked my head in, but if I found the room in darkness, I didn't enter. I had no wish to go into a dark room, *any* dark room, again.

Sometimes, on moonlit nights, Uncle Kana sat out in the courtyard and told us how he lost his sight one day when he went deer hunting. When that particular story was over, Uncle Kana told us many others. I sat very close to Ma, so close that she was forced to say, "Don't cling to me like that. It's so hot — move away!" But I did not stir. Ma herself moved away from me. At once, I began to feel scared and insecure, afraid that someone might pull down my shorts again.

When Ma left me alone to go to the cinema, I said to her, "Don't go, Ma. I feel scared."

"Don't be silly!" Ma snapped. "The house is full of people. Why should you feel scared?"

She left me with Grandma, who remained in the kitchen all day. I sat morosely on the threshold. Grandma shooed me out like a stray dog: "Go away, get out of here. I'm busy and you're in the way."

I knew that when the sunlight falling on the steps moved lower down it would be time for Ma to come back. *Go on,* I said silently to the sun, *move quickly, get down from the top steps.* The sun took its own sweet time to move — it shifted ever so slowly!

Stray dogs roamed in the yard, and so did black cats. Crows and ravens cawed in the trees. Hawkers cried at the door — men who took old clothes and shoes in exchange for sweets, men who carried wooden boxes with shiny glass lids. Through the glass one could see stacks of ribbons, glass bangles, and other jewelry. Aunt Jhunu was drawn like a magnet toward this particular hawker, eagerly inspecting glass bangles and earrings whenever he came and sat under the neem tree.

Gypsy women came, too, with baskets of bangles on their heads. Then came a man selling cotton candy — the pink, fluffy candy simply melted in the mouth — and a man with a bear, and another with monkeys that danced and did little tricks. The *chanachurwala* came wearing a red costume and a tall hat. He jingled a stick with bells attached at one end and sang: *"Hee-eyee chanachur gar-r-r-um!"* His song made Aunt Runu and Aunt Jhunu rush out of the house to buy packets of the hot, savory snack. Other hawkers arrived to sell other edibles. Sometimes I saw Uncle Sharaf go into the house with a packet of warm, roasted peanuts in his hand. Uncle Felu would carry an ice cream. Mouth watering, standing alone by the well, I stared at them helplessly.

One day I saw a gypsy woman enter the house, a basket on her head. She was a snake charmer. My uncles had called her in to see her perform. She set the basket down in the yard and then sat down herself. My uncles and aunts stood around her. Grandma watched from the kitchen door. Snakes started slithering out of her basket — a black snake, a yellow one, a cobra, and then a huge python. The woman put the others back in the basket, and allowed the python to slither all over the courtyard. I had never seen anything so horrific. I left the spot where I was standing near the well and ran to Phulbahari, our servant, who was smoking a bidi on the little veranda attached to our kitchen. "Phulbahari, I'm terrified!" I cried.

A glowing white smile flashed on Phulbahari's dark face. "What's there to be afraid of? Those snakes aren't poisonous. The snake charmers got rid of their poison sacs."

Still, I continued to feel afraid, even after the gypsy woman left. I was afraid to step into the courtyard or out into the field because a snake might appear at my feet. Lying in bed at night I could imagine a snake sitting coiled under my bed, then slowly climbing up, crawling on my pillow, all over my body. Sometimes I even dreamed of snakes. In my dreams, hundreds of snakes surrounded me with raised hoods, and I found myself alone, totally alone, standing by the railroad tracks, or in the middle of the main road, or by a pond under a tree, or a closed, confined room — I couldn't tell which. There was no noise anywhere except for the sound of hissing snakes. I began shouting, "Ma! Ma!" But there was no sign of her in that world of snakes. I could do nothing but withdraw into myself, folding my arms and legs, curling myself into a ball, pushing myself further and further into it, until I woke to the sound of my own thudding heart.

Fear of snakes and fear of men had me petrified in those days. And there was Ma, telling me to go and sleep with my uncles! I simply could not bring myself to tell her what Uncle Sharaf had done. Someone had stitched my lips with invisible thread.

While I went about hiding my fears, wearing a special medallion around my neck, changes were being made to our home. After renting five rooms from Grandma, Baba bought some new furniture. A dinner table and chairs were placed in our kitchen where we ate our meals, three times a day, just like the English sahibs. Baba was very fond of Western styles. His shoes were smart; they squeaked when he walked. The Baba who used to wear pajamas and a long, loose shirt, the one who rode a Hercules cycle, was changing rapidly. Now he tucked his shirt into his trousers, wore a tie, and at times even put on a jacket over his shirt. Why should the new Baba — now a sahib — eat on the floor, sitting on a wooden stool or a mat? For our living room he had bought a cane settee. We even studied at desks, though the practice of sitting together with my uncles on the same mat, sharing the light from the same lamp, had not ceased altogether.

One day, I was lying alone in my room staring out of the window when a sudden commotion brought me running to Grandma's court-yard. As soon as I got there, Uncle Felu told me what had happened. Aunt Jhunu's gold earrings had been stolen. No one knew who the culprit was. People were looking at each other suspiciously.

Aunt Jhunu pulled me into a room and whispered, "If you have taken them, give them back. I won't tell anyone."

I shook my head. But, suddenly, Aunt Jhunu's suspicion began to make me doubt myself. Perhaps I *had* stolen her earrings. Perhaps I had buried them somewhere. My heart jumped when I caught anyone looking at me. We were going to try "magic rice" to find the thief. Everyone was supposed to eat special rice that had a magic spell on it. The thief would start throwing up at once and would vomit blood as final evidence of his or her guilt.

Khatibuddin, the imam of the mosque in Akua, arrived to put the spell on a bowl of rice. He muttered something to himself and blew on the rice. Instantly, it acquired special magical properties. Everyone was given a handful to eat. People chewed, and looked at each other to see who would start vomiting blood. I trembled as I chewed the rice, feeling as if I was going to be sick at once. If I threw up, everyone would crouch over my vomit to inspect it and find traces of blood. Then they would break every branch off every tree, drag me to the muddy courtyard, and then throw me down and beat me mercilessly.

I would have to dig up Aunt Jhunu's earrings from somewhere. Where had I buried them? Under a coconut tree, or the steps near the storeroom where we kept the firewood? Were they behind the lavatory in the outhouse? They had to be there somewhere. When I caught Aunt Jhunu's eye, I began to feel guilty; I looked at myself through *her* eyes. I ceased to exist as myself.

Only three people did not eat the magic rice — Grandpa, Uncle Sharaf, and Phulbahari. Grandpa and Uncle Sharaf were not home. Phulbahari refused, point-blank, to eat a single grain. She set her dark jaw, tucked her anchal firmly in at the waist, and said, "I did not steal those earrings; I will not eat that rice. That fellow who's supposed to have put a spell on it is a number-one crook. I have worked in his house, and I know jolly well what he's like. A man like *him* blows on that rice, and you expect *me* to put it in my mouth? Never, not on your life!"

Phulbahari spat on the ground. Nothing and no one could persuade her to do as she was told.

"Why are you calling the imam a crook? It's sinful!" Ma scolded her.

Phulbahari paid no attention. She held herself erect. Her body was smooth, dark, slim, and straight, like a well-oiled bamboo rod. Her face was pockmarked. Her lips were dark because she smoked bidis, always keeping one tucked behind her ear when she ground spices, mopped the floor, or swept the yard. When she was done, she would lean against the wall in the kitchen and light her bidi.

Her refusal to eat the rice convinced everyone that she was the thief. All right, they said, forget the rice. Let's try the "moving bowl." This suggestion came from Aunt Runu. This test could be performed only by Jabeda Khatun, Uncle Kana's wife. One part of the muddy yard was smoothed and a bronze bowl placed on it. It would start moving if someone whose zodiac sign was Libra placed his or her hands on it and stop only when it reached the thief.

Jabeda Khatun was born under the sign of Libra. She placed her hands on the bowl, and sure enough, it began moving under her touch, going from the yard to a room, crossing a corner of the veranda and, finally, stopping in the kitchen, right under Phulbahari's buttocks. She was leaning over the grinding stone at the time, crushing spices. Everyone in the house followed the bowl into the kitchen.

"Phulbahari!" called Uncle Hashem sternly. "Let's have those earrings."

Phulbahari sprang to her feet, hissing like a cobra. Cheap, golden earrings glinted from her ears.

"I did not steal. You think I am the thief just because I am poor. Well, let me tell you, a poor person isn't always a thief. If I *was* one, I'd probably be better off; I wouldn't even try to work hard at making an honest living. Your stupid bowl has it all wrong."

No one was prepared to believe her. Grandma said, "Phulbahari, hand those earrings over. Tell us where you put them. We'll take them out ourselves."

Phulbahari stood, holding her hands away from her body. They were covered with turmeric. She curled her dark, chapped, bidi-stained lips and replied, "One of you must have stolen those earrings. It wasn't me."

Before she could finish speaking, Ma pounced upon her and grabbed her by her hair. Then she dragged her out in the courtyard, under a mango tree. Phulbahari slipped, although she tried hard to keep her feet on firm ground. Uncle Tutu brought a half-burned log from the kitchen and began beating her severely. She fell. Her bidi dropped from behind her ear and was crushed under her. She rolled all over the yard, shouting, "Phulbahari does not steal!"

She lost her job and was sent packing the same day. She went out limping. I watched her go, sure that she had not stolen Aunt Jhunu's earrings. She was right. The bowl had gotten it all wrong.

The very next day, Phulbahari was replaced by Toi-toi, a middle-aged woman from a nearby slum. Toi-toi was not her real name. Her real name was Noorjahan, and she kept a few ducks, which stayed in and around a pond all day. When Noorjahan returned home in the evening she called out to them, "Aai, aai, toi, toi!" At the sound of her voice her ducks came out of the pond, quacking, and followed her home. One lazy evening Uncle Tutu happened to be standing by the pond, watching at dusk, when he heard Noorjahan's call. He promptly started calling her Toi-toi. The name stuck, and everyone — with the exception of Grandma — started calling her by that name.

Toi-toi, alias Noorjahan, alias Alek and Khalek's mother, began working as a part-time maid. She was short, and her teeth were stained with paan juice. She ground spices, washed dirty dishes, swept the house, and cooked in our separate kitchen. She was paid five takas a month and was fed once a day. Finding a woman to do small jobs in the house, on either a temporary or permanent basis, was not a problem. The slum, only a few steps from our house, was full of women looking for work. One could just reach out and grab them. If one woman left, another easily took her place. Toi-toi replaced Phulbahari, and then *she* was told to go because she shirked her work. How did she do that? Well, she often left the house before dark in a hurry to go back home, back to Alek and Khalek, and her six pairs of ducks.

"Toi-toi doesn't want to work," Ma complained to Grandma. "I had to make dinner all on my own. I must have live-in help. It's hard to manage without it."

Grandma said, "Give her a few more days. Noorjahan is an honest woman; she's not given to stealing." But her words had no effect on Ma. She sacked Toi-toi after just a couple of weeks, handing her half her wages, two and a half takas. "I've paid you for all the days that you've worked. Here's the money; you can check for yourself. I will get someone else to do my work."

Toi-toi left. No one felt the slightest regret at her departure.

The day Toi-toi left, Ma had to work alone in the kitchen, lighting the oven, peeling the vegetables, cleaning and cutting the fish and meat before starting dinner. When it came to lighting the oven, Ma could not find the box of matches. This was a job always done by either Phulbahari or Toi-toi. Only they knew where the matches were kept.

"Go and get a match from Aman-ud-daula," Ma said to me. She knew Uncle Aman would have a box of matches since she had seen him smoking cigarettes.

I opened the door and went into the room. Uncle was lying in his bed. He looked like my father — curly hair, sharp nose, large eyes, thick dark eyebrows, fair complexion. If Baba could be pressed under the bricks and flattened somewhat, and his height reduced, he would look like Uncle Aman.

The room, I could see, looked completely different. There was no firewood, no rats. A picture in a frame hung on the tin wall. It was of Uncle Aman himself. His hair in the picture looked wavy, and on his feet were fancy shoes. To the right of this picture was a calendar with a woman's face on it. On a clotheshorse lay his clothes, unfolded.

"Uncle," I said looking at the calendar, "Ma is asking for matches."

"What is your Ma going to do with matches?" he inquired, getting out of bed and rubbing the hair on his bare chest.

"She'll light the oven. Then she'll cook."

"But I haven't got any matches!" Uncle Aman told me.

At these words, I turned around and took a step to walk out of the room. Uncle dragged me inside. "Wait, wait, take your matches. I've got some," he said, grinning.

Suddenly, as if by magic, a matchbox appeared in his hand. I stretched mine to take it, but Uncle Aman moved his own hand away. I tried again; he moved it once more. One minute I could see the matchbox, and the next minute it was gone. It was a bit like watching a glowworm: a flash of light one moment, darkness the next. To get my hands on the matchbox I moved nearer to Uncle Aman. He pulled me to him. Then, instead of giving me the matches, he started tickling me under my arms and on my stomach, laying me flat on his bed. I shrank like a snail. He picked up my tense, curled-up body and threw it in the air. He caught me as I fell, his hand sliding down my body, stopping at my panties. Then he began pulling my panties down. I tried to roll off the bed. My feet were on the floor, my back still on the bed, my panties near my knees, my knees neither on the floor nor on the bed. Around my neck hung the medallion of Naal Sharif.

Uncle lifted his lungi. I saw a big snake raise its head between his legs, poised for attack. I went numb with fear, but to my greater horror, the snake did attack, in that little place between my thighs — once, twice, thrice. I remained totally petrified. Staring into my wide eyes, Uncle said, "Would you like a candy? Tomorrow, I will buy you candy. Look, here's the matchbox. Take it. And listen, sweetheart, don't tell anyone that you have seen my cock and I have seen your little sweet pussy. It's bad to talk about such things. You must tell no one."

I left his room, the box of matches in my hand. I ached between my thighs; I felt like I had to pee, but saw my panties were already wet. I had no idea what this game was called, this business of stripping me naked. Nor could I guess why Uncle Sharaf and Uncle Aman wanted to climb on top of me. Uncle Aman had told me not to tell anyone else. I started to think he was right. It was not something one talked about. Suddenly, at the age of seven, I was filled with a new awareness. Whatever had happened was shameful, and it would not be right to talk about it. It had to be kept a secret.

Even today, I sometimes wonder why I did not tell anyone about those two incidents. Was it because I did not want people to think badly of my uncles? Was I in charge of protecting their good name? I had read in a book that one had to respect everyone who was older.

Was it because my uncles were older than me and, for that reason alone, worthy of my respect? Or was it because I had believed them to be good people and did not want that belief shattered? As if what had happened was just not true, was a lie from start to finish, no more than a nightmare? Or maybe those men only *looked* like my uncles, but were really different men, enemies from some distant past! Who told me to hide my pain and suffer in silence? Was I afraid that, if I talked about it, no one would believe me, that they would dismiss my allegations, say that I was possessed by some evil spirit, or that I was either a liar or totally mad? Would they hit my hand instead of kissing me and holding me close? Or could it be that no one seemed to be my own, there was no one to hold me if I cried my heart out. I was not that close to Ma, even though she was my whole world. I lived under her protection. She was like a tree — I sat in its shade when I was tired. She was like a deep, clear pond; I drank its water when I was thirsty. She had given me life; she nurtured it. If I could not turn even to her at a moment like this, who else could help me?

After that, I felt myself split in two. One half went out with all the other children, played games, and ran around. The other half sat alone and depressed by the pond, or the train tracks, or on the steps by our door. Alone, even in the middle of a crowd. Thousands of miles separated this lonely girl from all the others. When she stretched her arm, she could not touch anyone, not even her mother. When she tried, her hands only grasped emptiness.

～ 6 ～

The Peer's House I

Toward the end of 1969 we left Grandma's house in Akua, the house in a narrow alley by the pond filled with Kholsey fish. We said good-bye to the banyan tree, the neem, the date and areca palms that surrounded the house. We left all that — Baba, Ma, Dada, Chhotda, Yasmin, and I — and moved to a new, large house in Amlapara. Here, one had only to press a switch and a light would come on, or a fan would start spinning. The rooms were huge; the verandas had big, strong pillars. It was as if we had chanced upon an empty palace and moved into it. The windows of the house were colorful, and their red, blue, yellow, and purple panes were taller than me. Thirty-eight steps descended from the main building to the courtyard. There were niches in the wall, like the niches one sees in the walls of temples. Baba later had those covered up, and he removed the steps and replaced them with a long veranda, like the corridors that run through school buildings. Baba knew a wealthy man, M. A. Kahhar, whose house in Amlapara had walls without niches and a long passageway. I guessed that Baba was trying, by demolishing some parts and building others, to create something similar in his own house. Baba was easily impressed by rich people, thinking everything about them was wonderful, even their tasteless, shapeless verandas. One could never tell what Baba might do next. Out of the blue, bags of cement and sand and lots of bricks would arrive at the house. It was clear that some construction was about to start, but impossible to tell what it would be until it was finished. No one ever knew what went on in Baba's mind.

Our house was higher than any other in the area and I felt I could touch the wide blue sky simply by standing on the roof and stretching out my arm. The day before our furniture and the other family members arrived, Chhotda and I spent the night in the empty house. Chhotda brought his guitar and played quite late into the night. I lay on the yellow cover that usually wrapped the guitar, listening to the echoes that bounced off the walls. If I shouted "Chhotda," the word would be repeated as many as seven times, as if seven little princes were hiding behind seven different walls, mimicking me.

The trees that stood around the house were primarily coconut and areca palms. There were thirty flowering plants and fruit trees in the courtyard. I couldn't believe we were living in such a big house. A few things happened after we moved in. First, there was a burglary. Someone removed the iron grille from a window, crept into the house, and stole some money and jewelry. Second, Ma saw Baba and Razia Begum together in a rickshaw going past the Alaka cinema. Third, Dada and his friends brought out a magazine called *Pata,* which contained a mixture of poems, stories, and puzzles. In it, Dada had written a poem, "The Rainbow," and published it under my name — Nasrin Jahan Taslima — although when I was enrolled in Vidyamoyee School, Aunt Jhunu had shortened my name to Taslima Nasrin.

"In the next issue, I will print another poem under your name," Dada told me.

"In that case, I will write it myself!" I said happily.

Dada snorted. "You? You can't write a poem, or anything else!"

At once, a cloud of depression engulfed me. I collected all the jamun that I could gather in my skirt and ran to the roof. The juice from the fruit left purple patches on my skirt but all I could think of was poetry.

After that day, every time Dada left the house I opened his drawer and avidly read his notebook of poems. Oh, if only I could write like that!

After moving to the new house, Baba bought a tape recorder from someone who had just returned from Germany. It weighed a ton. Dada showed it to all his friends, saying, "It's made in Germany." Like many of our countrymen, Dada was very impressed by Hitler, overwhelmed by his valor — and this object from Hitler's country impressed him greatly.*

His friends gaped at the machine. They had only seen gramo-

---

* Because Hitler and the Germans were enemies of the British during World War II they were admired by nationalists on the Indian subcontinent. This sentiment lingered.

phones made by His Master's Voice. This was something totally new. It had two discs that went around and around; a tape ran from one to the other. Having seen what the machine could do, people returned to make recordings. Narayan Sanyal read his one-act play, Pintu played his guitar, and Mahboob sang songs by Nazrul. Every sound was captured by the tapes. I watched the proceedings from a distance, standing at the door, clutching the curtain. I was not allowed to get any closer, not even to watch, let alone touch anything. Dada recited poems by Tagore and Nazrul in his deep voice and taped those, too. Almost overnight, he became well known throughout the town. He played songs by Hemanta Mukhopadhyay, Satinath Bhaduri, and Manna Dey. Dada and Chhotda spent most of their time draped over that machine. I longed to touch it, but Dada said, "Don't lay a finger on anything. Just look from a distance!"

When he went out, however, I did touch it. If Yasmin expressed a similar wish, I said, "Don't come near. Stay where you are!" Obediently, she stopped some distance away. I pressed a few keys and the machine started playing a song. Then I lay on the bed, one leg resting on other, and listened to the music. I felt a strong desire to become Dada.

After the burglary, a new rule was introduced in our house. We were told to keep all the doors and windows closed, even if it was boiling hot. Baba had the broken window fixed and placed three more rods across it. They were long and heavy, like the ones used in prisons. The rooms now were very dark. Even during the day, we had to switch on the lights to eat or study. Like rats, we crept about in those dark, damp rooms.

Ever since she had seen Razia Begum with Baba, Ma had taken to her bed. She took her clothes and other belongings from Baba's room, moved to a different room, and simply lay there all day, looking pale. She stopped cooking, washing, bathing, even eating. Seeing her, you would think she was seriously ill. Her hair was dry and disheveled, and she didn't bother to oil or comb it. She was covered with prickly heat from head to toe, and her clothes clung to her damp, sweating body. She was silent all day, but as soon as Baba returned home, she began wailing in a thin, sharp voice. "There he is! He's spent the whole day with that other woman! Did you buy such a big house just to marry her and bring her here?"

Baba made no reply, as if he had not heard. The sounds that wafted through the air might have been no more than a cat meowing, or logs crackling in the fire. Baba acted like he was totally unaware of Ma standing in front of him, whining incessantly. He walked about the house, moving from his room to the courtyard, asking after his children, the domestic help, even the cats and dogs. Then he called Moni to give him his dinner. Moni had been brought from the slum behind Grandma's house to help with our housework. After eating his food, Baba belched, stood before a mirror, and combed his hair, having first massaged it with mustard oil. Then he went out again.

Ma shouted after him: "Don't forget you are a doctor today only because my father helped you out. You'd have remained what you were, a stupid farmer's son. You married me for money, didn't you? Now you think you've got money of your own, so you can leave me and have fun with someone else's wife. Allah will destroy you one day, mark my words, all this merrymaking will have to stop. Then I'd like to see what you do with your arrogance! I am cursing you here and now: If you have eaten my father's salt, Allah will punish you for causing me such pain. You and everyone in your family will get leprosy. They'll be finished, all of them!"

Ma was convinced that Baba would return home that night or the following morning with Razia Begum in tow as his second wife. No one dared go anywhere near Ma during one of her outbursts. But one day, before I could stop myself, the words slipped out of my mouth: "Why do you shout so much? This isn't a neighborhood like Akua, you know."

Ma swooped down on me instantly, grabbing me by the hair. She gave it such a sharp tug that the chair I was sitting on overturned and I crashed against the wall. Ma spun me around like a top. Then she slapped me hard on both cheeks and spoke in a harsh, rasping voice. "What did you say, you stupid girl? Your father's a bastard, and you are no better. Has your father ever done anything for you? And yet you take his side! But of course you would; you have the same blood, don't you, bitch? The blood of the devil himself! You've been making my life an absolute hell ever since you were born, you little monster. I've had bad luck. Why didn't I stuff your mouth with salt and kill you when you were born?"

Ma continued in the same vein, bitterly regretting that she had allowed me to live. My eyes filled with tears, but she didn't look at me, not even once.

Ma's language gradually became more and more obscene, the prickly heat on her body spread, and deep, dark circles formed under her eyes. She started cursing not just Baba but everyone else in the house as well. Her children were her enemies. The servants were vipers. When Moni served her lunch in her room, Ma threw the plate out into the courtyard, fearing a conspiracy to poison her. If any of my uncles or aunts came to visit us from Grandma's house, Ma sat with them in her room, graphically describing how she had seen Baba and Razia Begum snuggling against each other in a rickshaw. Then she whined and moaned some more.

This was how we all began to pass our days, listening to Ma yelling at Baba, throwing not just words but whatever she could at him. Baba did not respond at all. As soon as Ma started attacking him we bent over our desks, pretending we had neither seen nor heard anything. I would usually start doing complicated math. The advantage was that one was allowed to scribble figures in the margin, scratch them out, then scribble again. It looked as if I was grappling with the most difficult of sums. What no one knew, except me, was that in my imagination I was traveling well beyond the complexities of mathematics, sitting in an open field by a quiet pool on a cool, cloudy afternoon and watching seagulls flying in the sky. I drew the scene in my notebook but would quickly scratch it out if I heard footsteps. Baba didn't know about it, nor did Ma.

Life fell into a routine until, one day, things went too far. Baba had only just returned home when Ma started again: "There he is, my enemy. He's done what he wanted to do with that other one, and now he's back. Womanizer! Bloody lout!"

Baba had not yet had a chance to wash his hands or change from his shirt and trousers into a lungi. All he had done was loosen his tie. Without waiting another second he rushed into Ma's room, saying, "Who do you think you are, woman? What do you think you're doing? You live in *my* house, eat *my* food, and you think you can say whatever you like to me?"

His roaring voice took my breath away. My pen, poised over the margin, trembled, as did the fingers that were curled around it. Then I heard Ma scream. I jumped up from my chair and ran to stand at the door to Ma's room. What I saw was horrible. Baba sprang on Ma, just as a tiger attacks its prey. (I had never actually seen a tiger jump on another animal but I was sure that this is how it happened.) He caught Ma's hair, threw her to the floor, and kicked her chest and stomach. On his feet were strong, sturdy shoes from Bata.

Ma tried to roll under the bed but failed. I was joined at the door by Dada, Chhotda, even Yasmin. Like small mice we watched in silence as blood started pouring from Ma's nose and mouth and she screamed in pain, "He's killing me! Help! Save me!"

None of us dared to step forward. Ma continued to groan; the floor was flooded with her urine.

"Will you keep saying those filthy things? Will you? I really will kill you today!" Baba gasped, speaking between short breaths.

"No! Let me go. I'll never say anything again. Please let me go, I beg of you!" Ma pleaded with folded hands, tears streaming down her face, sitting half naked on the wet floor.

Baba shooed us out of the way and stormed into his own room. Ma spent the night lying on the floor, crying. I wanted to sit with her, stroke her back, and say, *Don't cry anymore, Ma. One day I will wipe out your humiliation. I will take revenge, one day, I promise!* But I couldn't find the courage to speak. I sat bent over my math notebook till midnight, then went to bed on an empty stomach. Sleepless, I dreamed of leaving the house forever, going somewhere far away, to a cleaner, purer life.

After this incident, Uncle Hashem caught Baba on the street one day, thrashed him black and blue, and threw him into the house like a sack of sand. "If you lay a hand on my sister once more," he threatened, "I will get the dogs to eat your corpse!"

Strong as steel though he was, Baba had to spend a week in bed. Moni took his meals into his room every day. He called me to his side morning and night, saying, "You must study hard, little girl."

On the last day, after which he would resume a normal life, he called me in to see him. It was a holiday. "You must memorize every word that's written in your books, like a parrot. You must come first in your class. The girls who stand first now and do better than you, don't they eat what you do? So why shouldn't you be in their place? Is your brain any smaller than theirs? Is it?"

I stood facing Baba and said, "No."

To tell the truth, I had often thought my brain *was* smaller than other people's, but I said what I knew Baba wanted to hear. It was the safest thing to do.

Then Baba asked gently, "My love, can you run your fingers through my hair?"

I stood behind the bed and placed my fingers in Baba's hair. They didn't feel like my fingers. In fact, *I* didn't feel like myself. It was someone else standing here. I stared indifferently out of the open door and watched the sun playing on the tank in the courtyard. The water glistened. I felt like throwing myself into it and swimming, thrashing my arms and legs as hard as I could. But how far could I go in a tank that was only two and a half feet wide? I'd have to stay, right here, by that tank under the guava tree whose top branches caught the full glare of the sun; stay here in this house where I had to silently obey commands issued by others. My fingers moved through Baba's hair like a mouse that has been caught and injured by a cat.

"My love!" Baba called.

"Ji!" I responded.

(This was something Ma had taught me. If someone older addressed me, I was supposed to say, "Ji!" If, instead, I said "yes?" or "what?" it would be most disrespectful. Ma was not in the least impressed by my manners. On Eid,* all the youngsters were expected to touch the feet of every grown-up in the family. I never could. Ma would push me into Baba's room, but I stood like a statue on the threshold, unable to touch anyone's feet, even Baba's or Ma's.)

"Pull my hair, please. Pull it hard!" Baba beseeched.

He had thick, curly, black hair. When I tried pulling it hard, bits of dried blood came up from the roots and struck to my fingers. It looked like dark sand. Suddenly I felt afraid. Was Baba going to die? What would happen if he died right here on this bed, flat on his back? I'd keep pulling his hair, and suddenly find that he was no longer breathing. I might keep standing by his bed until nightfall, but Baba would not say, "That's enough, dear. Go and do your studies now. You must do well in school and grow up to be a worthy human being."

The sun moved from the tank and climbed on top of the guava tree. Baba started snoring. There was hardly any point in stroking the hair of someone who was snoring, So I tiptoed out of the room and found Ma standing outside with a glass of lemonade in her hand. She spoke in a low voice so that no one but me could hear her. "Go," she said, "give this lemonade to your father."

"Baba has fallen asleep," I whispered. Ma handed me the glass anyway. "Never mind," she said. "He can drink it when he wakes up. He likes lemonade very much."

---

*Religious festivals.

102

I was a girl who obeyed commands without asking questions, so I went back and placed the glass on the side table by Baba's bed. Ma was wearing a red-printed sari. Her hair, tied into a loose knot, was covered with her anchal. She cast a sympathetic glance at Baba from the door, then coolly walked into the room, stood by his bed, and began stroking his hair.

I seized this chance to disappear. Up on the roof, I stood biting a guava and watched the other neighborhood girls in the courtyard of the house next door playing gollachhut. We could never play at our house, at least not while Baba was around. When he was home everyone had to be within calling distance. I hadn't yet taken the last bite of my guava when I heard Baba call me. I ran down immediately and presented myself once more to carry out his instructions.

"Who has sent this lemonade?" he asked, his voice harsh and raucous.

"Ma," I replied, lowering my eyes.

"Why? Did I ask for it?" Baba was now sitting up on his bed, his legs dangling. It sounded like his hands were itching to slap me on both cheeks. I remained silent.

"Take that lemonade and throw it out;" he said curtly.

I did as I was told without uttering a word; I turned the glass upside down under the guava tree. Baba went on ranting: "No one should come into my room. Tell everyone that I don't wish to see them or eat anything they have made. I know very well they are planning to poison me. I don't want any of my enemies living in my house!"

Still I remained silent.

The next day, Aunt Fajli came to our house to comfort Ma. She held her close, stroked her gently, and said with tears in her eyes: "Borobu, stop thinking of this mundane world. Stop going to the movies. Don't do what's sinful. Forget all this, even your husband and children, and think of the path shown by Allah. That is the only way to find peace."

From that day on, Ma gave up going to the movies and walked on Allah's path instead. That path led to Noumahal where Aunt Fajli lived in her father-in-law's house. Her father-in-law's name was Amirullah. He was Muslim, although he was not Bengali, and had been a teacher in a religious school. After the Partition, he moved from Medenipur in India to East Bengal. Then he cleared a bit of the jungle at Hajibari in Noumahal, built a single-story house, and began living there permanently. He worked for a while for the municipal corporation, then left his job and began reading from the Koran and the hadith for the benefit of his neighbors. They, in turn, paid him a fee known as *hadia,* since it was understood that whoever spoke of Allah and the Prophet's advice had to be paid. Allah would be pleased and reserve a place in heaven for those who served Him.

Aunt Fajli's arrival in Amirullah's household was as sudden and dramatic as the falling of a meteorite. A professional matchmaker had been appointed to look for a bride for Amirullah's son, Musa. The matchmaker went from one house to another, and eventually reached Grandma's. There, sitting on a metal chair in the courtyard, he decided he had come to the end of his journey. There was no need to visit another house.

After he heard a description of Aunt Fajli's beauty from the matchmaker, Amirullah went to Grandma's house the very next day, clutching a pot of rasgollas in one hand and his son, Musa, with the other. Why had he come, people wondered, what did he want? He wanted Fajilatunnisa. But she was in school. Most people in the house looked through the cracks in the tin walls and stared at the two strange men dressed in white robes and speaking a different language.

Fajilatunnisa returned from school and found that a couple of strangers were seated in the front room. Their eager eyes immediately swept over her, from head to foot, ogling freely and frankly. Deeply embarrassed, Aunt Fajli ran out of the house. But Amirullah's eyes were dazzled by her. He had never seen a girl quite so beautiful. He folded his hands and looked at Grandpa. "If you agree," he entreated, "we can arrange a marriage right now, this very minute. Then we can think of a celebration, invite guests, and send your daughter off to her new home."

Grandma was standing behind the curtain. She did not like the idea at all and gestured to Grandpa to come inside. Grandpa saw the gesture but decided to ignore it, for he knew what she was going to say. She never acted impulsively. She had no wish to force her young daughter into marriage. The poor girl had only just returned from school and had no idea what was going on. But Grandpa paid no attention and gave his approval. "Yes, yes, of course. If you are so keen on this marriage, how can I refuse? You are such a learned and cultured man!"

Aunt Fajli was hunted down, captured, and brought back home. A red sari was draped around her, and she was made to sit down and get married. Uncle Siddique sat outside under a custard-apple tree feeling totally dejected. He used to help his sister with her lessons. In another three years, she would have passed her matriculation and could have gone to college. Instead, look what was happening! Grandpa, having decided a woman did not need to study, was marrying her off. No one dared protest.

Overjoyed and triumphant, Amirullah did not drink his tea or eat any of the biscuits placed before him. He did not waste a second, but chanted the necessary prayers, got Grandpa to accept six hundred takas as *kabin,* and heard the bride and groom, sitting in separate rooms, agree to this marriage. Trying to make the best of a bad situation, Grandma said, "At least get him to raise kabin more than six hundred takas."

"Don't be stupid!" Grandpa scolded. "One doesn't bargain or argue over money with someone as knowledgeable and refined as Amirullah."

A few days later, the wedding was celebrated with fanfare. Lots of guests were invited to a sumptuous meal. Then Aunt Fajli got into a *palki* and left for her new home, weeping copiously. Uncle Siddique also cried openly and unashamedly.

Three years later, he himself was forced into marriage by Grandpa. He and Grandpa happened to be traveling, and when Grandpa saw a very fair girl called Halima in a village he had his son married without informing or consulting anyone at home. Halima was fair, but quite large and, having been brought up in a village, quite rustic in her ways. Grandma sobbed noisily when the trio returned home. Uncle Siddique was the brightest of all her children — she had hoped that one day he would study law and become a barrister or a judge.

Soon after Uncle Siddique's sudden marriage Grandpa chopped down the custard-apple tree with a single blow of his ax. It was his belief that an evil spirit lived in it and it might just attack and possess the new bride. Of course, all these things happened long before I was born.

Aunt Fajli was well known for her habit of roaming the neighborhood, visiting every house. She knew everyone in the area. But Amirullah changed her so completely that this same girl began draping herself in a veil and went about clutching prayer beads. Amirullah built a high wall around his house so that no one from the outside world could see his pretty daughter-in-law. Then, reading out from several holy books, he informed his daughter-in-law that it would please Allah to see a woman obeying and looking after her husband and his parents for the rest of her life. *"Ji achha, Abbaji,"* said Aunt Fajli, nodding and accepting every word he said.

Amirullah was a special friend of Allah. Allah was so fond of him that He often visited him in his house to chat. But, blessed though he was by Allah's mercy, Amirullah was plagued by jinns and evil spirits that lived in some of the trees near his house. They began to attack Aunt Fajli almost as soon as she stepped into the house. Sometimes they stayed with her for a day or two, at other times for a week. Amirullah had to get rid of them personally. When they left Aunt Fajli, she fell to the ground with a thud. That was the sign that the jinn had departed.

Whenever she was possessed Aunt Fajli dropped her veil, went out of the house without a burkha, smiled at passersby, and spoke complete nonsense. Once she saw her own husband at the main crossing in Noumahal and said, "Hello Musa bhai, where are you off to? Come here, have some peanuts!"

Getting rid of a jinn was most difficult. Aunt Fajli first had to be caught firmly and dragged back to the house. Then she was locked up in the darkest room, which Amirullah entered with a stick in his hand. His first question was always, "Why are you doing all this?"

Aunt Fajli replied, "I don't like it here. I feel like roaming all over town. I feel like eating peanuts and sweets, especially chum-chum. Hee hee hee!"

Obviously, it was not Aunt Fajli who spoke these words but a jinn whose name was Sharafat. He had entered her body and made her drop her veil, slip her sari from her shoulder, dance obscenely, and speak without thinking. It was all Sharafat's doing. Naturally, Aunt Fajli herself could never be so completely shameless.

Amirullah began by speaking gently: "Look, we have not done you any harm, have we? Why are you creating such trouble for us? Go on, leave my daughter-in-law alone. She is a very good woman, totally devoted to her husband, and very virtuous. Don't trouble her any more. Go away."

At this, Aunt Fajli would jump up on the bed, begin dancing, and burst into song: "Come, my friends, let's hold hands and sing and dance together."

Amirullah could not bear to watch his daughter-in-law dancing with her arms raised. He lowered his gaze. But when he spoke, his voice was stern. "I know very well how to get rid of you." This made Aunt Fajli jump down from the bed, lift her sari to expose her feet, and twirl on her heels. "You can't do a damn thing to me!" she giggled.

Amirullah's face set in grim lines. "You are crossing all limits!"

"Yes, so I am. So what? I shall do exactly what I want. If you try to stop me, I will kill you. I'll chop you to bits with a knife. You don't know me!" Aunt Fajli began thrashing her arms about.

At this, Amirullah gripped his stick and raised it. The more his daughter-in-law thrashed her arms, the harder he brought it down on her back, neck, even her head. Never before had she been beaten like this. One evening, Grandpa had thumped her back because he had caught her sleeping instead of studying, her head resting on her book. But the next day he had made amends by taking her to a sweets shop and letting her have her fill of chum-chums.

When Amirullah began beating her, Aunt Fajli felt as if all her bones were going to be crushed. "Let me go. I promise I won't do this again!" she pleaded tearfully.

"Really? You promise to go away?" Amirullah asked, breathing heavily.

"Yes, yes, I promise!" She fell at Amirullah's feet.

"What's your name?"

"Sharafat."

"Where do you live?"

"In the neem tree."

After this, Aunt Fajli's tired body would lie limp on the floor. For a long time, she wouldn't open her eyes. Then, all of a sudden, she would wake up with a start, shake her head, and, on seeing her father-in-law, pull her veil back to cover her head. "Abbaji, why are you here? Why is the room so dark?" she would say. Then she would rise and go out, muttering to herself, "It must be time for Abbaji's namaz. I still haven't given him water to wash his hands and feet. It's so late!"

Amirullah and the rest of his family would stand in the courtyard and watch the return of the old, familiar Aunt Fajli. The jinn had clearly left her. Everyone heaved a sigh of relief.

The jinn Sharafat often took over Aunt Fajli. When she was free from jinns, she was very devoted to Allah, very devoted to her husband and father-in-law. She did not laugh; her veil did not slip. But sometimes the beatings left black bruises on her back. Black marks on fair skin, like the ugly spots on the beautiful moon.

Aunt Fajli removed her hand from Ma's back, wiped her eyes with a corner of her veil, and said, "This is the path to peace, Borobu. Come to Abbaji's meetings and hear his words about Allah and the Prophet. That will help you in your afterlife. After all, this life and everything to do with this world is only transitory, isn't it?"

This was precisely what Ma wanted — to get rid of attachment to worldly pleasures, worldly people. Baba could therefore do what he liked. It would make no difference because she would be immersed in Allah.

"You know, Borobu," said Aunt Fajli, "Abbaji only has to pray to Allah for you and your soul will be released from the prison of your grave. You will easily cross the bridge that will take you to heaven. When you stand there to be judged, your virtues should be greater in number than your sins, don't you think? If you keep getting caught up in the trivial matters of this world, what will you travel with when you cross over?"

Ma nodded in agreement. It was true; she had done little for her spiritual fulfillment. What was she going to do on the last day of judgment? She did not even do her namaz five times a day anymore. Dust had gathered on her Koran; she hadn't even brought it down from the shelf for many days. She could not find happiness in this world — what if she found none in the next one, either? Suddenly, Ma was afraid.

After offering Ma the necessary advice, Aunt Fajli ate a plate of fish curry with rice, belched a few times, draped herself in her black burkha, and returned to the house in Noumahal.

The very next day, Ma put on her burkha soon after breakfast. Where could she be off to? Noumahal. A week went by. Then a month. "Where are you going, Ma?"

"Noumahal."

That was all we were told. Silently, the four of us sat at the dinner table, or on a sofa, or on the veranda, and watched her disappear. Going to Noumahal became an addiction, and no one in the house could stop her. This addiction had to do with Allah, and its hold was stronger than opium.

A month later, who knows what got into her, but she caught me by the arm while I was playing outside, pulled me toward her sharply, and said, "Come!" I looked at her in surprise. Her sari looked rather untidy under her burkha and her hair was disheveled.

To be honest, I didn't mind. Any chance to get out of the house was exciting. It didn't matter where I went. Before we left, however, I had to be dressed properly, so Ma made me wear the long salwars that were part of my school uniform. They were the only salwars I had because I was still young enough to wear only shorts at home. I wore a long dress over the salwars, and the white veil — which was usually folded and worn tucked into a belt — was unfolded and placed over my head and chest, although such modesty was unnecessary since my chest was still quite flat.

When I was dressed to her satisfaction, Ma put me into a rickshaw. I thought I looked distinctly odd but had no wish to protest and miss going out. I spent the journey looking at film posters, reading the signs over shops, and staring at all the different people on the streets. But the journey ended too soon — I did not like that at all. If only the rickshaw could take me day and night this way, and take me much, much farther away!

I do not know when Peer Amirullah's house, once built in a clearing in a jungle, turned into something like a colony. A number of houses had been built over a large area. The one with the highest veranda and whitewashed walls belonged to Amirullah. Ever since Ma had become his follower she had stopped referring to him as a relative. Instead, she called him *Huzur*, Sir, since no kinship term was appropriate for the peer. He was above all that.

The first thing Ma did when she arrived at Amirullah's house was to touch his feet, no matter what he might be doing at the time — sleeping, eating, or preparing for his namaz. It wasn't just Ma; everyone had to do so before they did anything else: light the oven, stand for their namaz, even go to the toilet. Since Amirullah was Allah's favorite servant — no, he was more than that, he was like a buddy — Allah was said to visit frequently. No one knew when this happened. Ma thought it took place in the dead of night. It was her belief that they spoke in Arabic. In fact, she thought Arabic was Allah's mother tongue. If she could learn it, perhaps she could exchange a few words with Allah in her afterlife.

The idea of learning Arabic appealed to her greatly, so much so that she had great admiration for anyone who could speak it. She was like a dog with its tongue hanging out, and from her tongue dripped the temptation to go to *behesht,* to heaven. When she thought of Huzur conversing with Allah in the middle of the night, her eyes drooped in deep reverence. If she could please Amirullah, perhaps Allah would show her some mercy. After all, she had sinned a lot, running crazily to the cinema and thinking of worldly pleasures. Would Allah ever forgive a sinner like her?

Having touched Amirullah's feet, Ma sat on the floor and broke into loud sobs. Tears ran freely down her cheeks, falling on her chest, her sari, and her blouse. Aunt Fajli's full, pink lips were badly chapped, but she placed a hand on Ma's shoulder and said calmly, "Why shouldn't Allah forgive you? Just ask for His forgiveness. He is merciful. He is great. Of course He'll pardon you. He doesn't turn anyone down if they raise their hands and beg for His kindness."

It was not just Ma who was keen on pleasing Amirullah. A number of other young women were, too. The minute Amirullah finished his tea in the evening and stretched out on his bed to rest, Ma and the other women began fighting over who would massage Huzur's arms, his legs, and his head. If Ma got his feet, her face lit up instantly and a smile hovered on her lips. This was because a person's feet — even Amirullah's — were bound to be dirty. If she could massage his feet it was a way of proving to him that even the dirt on his feet was holy and pure for her.

This massage went on for a couple of hours. Then the young women began offering Huzur sustenance: orange juice, lemon sherbet, *kheer,* followed by food served on gleaming silver plates. There was fish dopiaza, chicken curry made with very tender pieces of chicken, basmati rice. After his meal, when Huzur belched with satisfaction, he was given paan covered with silver foil. Paan was something of an addiction with him. His daughter-in-law sat on a mat on the floor and filled the betel leaves with nuts and spices. Huzur put those in his mouth, one by one, chewed them six or seven times, then spat out the red juice into a spittoon. If some spittle hit one of the young women she would lick it happily, while most of the others quickly bent over the spittoon. Soon, a war broke out over who would be the first to eat the paan already chewed by Huzur, or drink its red juice.

When I looked at those women I was frightened. They reminded me of the times Ma went to the cinema and had similar fights over tickets. There was always a separate queue for women at the Alaka. When the victorious ones emerged from the crowd their bodies were wet with perspiration, the buttons on their blouses torn, their hair totally disheveled. But their faces were triumphant and happy and in their fists, tightly clenched, were the tickets.

Now, Ma and the others were fighting over Amirullah's paan juice as if it was some heavenly nectar. Ma, certainly, was convinced that although the paan had been chewed, it was no ordinary man who had chewed it, but one with whom Allah Himself conversed secretly, late at night, while everyone else slept. A man who could speak easily of the supreme powers of Allah, His magnanimity, what He had ever said and where, and to whom, what He had hinted at — everything. If she ate the paan from Amirullah's spittoon a place for her in heaven was guaranteed. In fact, that was what Amirullah himself had implied with an air of mystery, his eyes twinkling, as if he was playing hide-and-seek with a group of children. "You want a ticket to heaven?" his enigmatic smile seemed to say. "Then keep your eyes and ears open; try to work out what is going to please Allah. He has given you a brain and enough intelligence."

Ma picked up a half-chewed paan from the spittoon and put it in her mouth. I sat behind the battlefield — alone, scared, my face going red with embarrassment from time to time. Still, a belief began to take hold: If I clung to Ma strongly enough, I could also manage a trip to heaven. Aunt Fajli was sitting apart from the fray, looking at the women who were fighting. She made no attempt to claim a share of the chewed paan. She did not need to, since — according to Ma — she already had a ticket to heaven. All she had to do was somehow pass her time on earth. After all, *she* had not sinned by going to the cinema. She leaned toward Ma, half crouching in the middle of the battlefield, and whispered, "Why stop at just the paan, Borobu? If you touch the spit or phlegm of someone favored by Allah, you will earn a lot of virtue."

The words sank immediately into Ma's mind.

Before going to look for Huzur's spit or phlegm she gave me a chain with a hundred prayer beads and sat me down on the floor in a different room. I was also given a piece of paper with *"sallallahu Ala Muhammad"* written on it, which I was supposed to say five hundred times. This, Ma said, would earn me virtue. Her sole aim in visiting the peer's house was to add to her fund of virtue, and she wanted the same for me. I had to admit that I had enjoyed the ride in the rickshaw, but what kind of a house was this? No one was allowed to play, to speak with a raised voice; everyone was to stay fully covered at all times, from the hair on their heads to the nails on their toes, never allowing their clothes to shift and expose even an inch of skin. I thought it would be better to be in a stinking toilet than to sit clutching prayer beads in such a weird house.

Just before dusk fell, Huzur began his public meeting. Ma dragged me to witness it. If my veil slipped from my head, she nudged me sharply with her elbow. On the way to his house she had told me, firmly and repeatedly, that I should touch Huzur's feet as soon as I saw him, and make sure that my veil didn't slip from my head. When we arrived I made no attempt to touch Amirullah's feet, and my veil slipped more than once. Having found a seat among the women in the room where the meeting was being held, Ma sat down next to me. The women were sitting behind a curtain, in accordance with normal practice. The men were in the main room. Through a chink in the curtain I could see Amirullah sitting on a mattress, with two or three open books in front of him. He was leaning over them and muttering something in Arabic, which his audience was hailing with shouts of appreciation. "Aha, aha!" they exclaimed.

Then Amirullah took off his glasses, began polishing them, and said, "Those who don't believe in Allah, who have the slightest doubt about Allah and his Prophet Muhammad, who don't follow all the orders Allah has given, well, do you know how Allah is going to burn them in hell? O brothers, you will be burned in that unbelievable fire. Can you imagine the heat if the sun descended and hung just one foot above your head? Hell's fire will be that hot. Thousands of snakes and scorpions will bite you. Do you know what you'll be fed? Boiling hot water and pus! Nothing else. Allah will pull your tongue out and nail it over your head. He will then throw you into the fire. You will burn, your body will char, but even so you will not die. Allah will keep you alive so that you suffer more. Snakes will coil themselves around you; scorpions will sting. You will not be able to enjoy worldly pleasures for long, O brothers. Doomsday is nigh. Prepare yourselves. Israfil is waiting to blow his horn soon, he is holding it to his mouth; Allah is about to issue His final command."

Wailing broke out behind the curtain. Some of the men were wiping their eyes with handkerchiefs. Others cried more openly, their shoulders shaking. Who knew who had enough honor, and who didn't?

"You can gain nothing by thinking of *this* world, my brothers. Think of the next one. Try walking on the path shown by Allah. If the great Almighty forgives you, only then will you be saved from the confines of your graves and the pain of being burned in hell. Remember, the fire in hell is seventy times stronger and fiercer than any fire on earth."

I sat silently behind Ma, the prayer beads still in my hand. I was sorry to see her cry. Her whole body was racked with sobs. It surprised me greatly to see so many people crying in fear of being burned by a fire. It was exactly like frightening a child. Perhaps I ought to cry, too, just like the others. I waited for tears to gush, but my eyes remained completely dry. Having heard how Allah might roast people alive, He began to strike me as someone cruel and heartless.

After his long and terrible description of the tortures of hell, Amirullah joined his palms sideways and raised them in prayer:

"O Allah, forgive these men, forgive every sin they have committed. You are great, you are all-merciful, you are the savior. I am begging you, on behalf of the sinners sitting in this room, to pardon them, O Allah!"

Amirullah's voice began rising and, in keeping with it, the sound of wailing rose from the people. I sat like a statue, except that my eyes darted everywhere, on this side of the curtain and that. What a strange world it was!

Baba heard that Ma was going to the peer's house regularly and that she had become his devotee. One day he announced that no one should visit Amirullah, and if anyone did, he or she would not be allowed to live in his house.

Ma heard this announcement and said with undisguised contempt in her voice, "Even my left foot has no wish to live in the house of a *kafir*.* No one ever praises the name of Allah here. If I continue to live in this house, I shall be banished from heaven!"

Since she began to visit Amirullah, Ma had stopped cooking at home. Every morning, Moni brought the shopping bag and asked what should be bought, whether she should cook the fish with gourd,

---

* Infidel.

if the meat curry should have pumpkin in it, what about spinach, should the dal be thick or runny? Ma simply said, "Cook whatever you want," in answer to all her queries.

Moni was totally confused. Ma had never behaved like this before. She used to cook herself; Moni only helped with cleaning and chopped the vegetables. Now she was expected to handle everything. Ma had even handed Moni the key to the storeroom — she was free to decide how much of the stored groceries could, or should, be used. With such unexpected freedom, Moni felt as if she had turned into the lady of the house, a well-to-do lady, a memsahib.

When Ma returned from Noumahal after a complete session of paanjuice–phlegm–spittle–discourse–prayers, she spent most of her time sitting on her prayer mat. After her namaz she counted her prayer beads, then read aloud from the Koran. After that was over, it was time for another namaz. She did the recommended five — *fazar, johar, assar, magreb, esha* — and, for good measure, a sixth called *nafal namaz.* Her household duties were no longer important to her. She did not even have time to wonder whether her children had been fed. When she spoke to us, she did so more slowly and much more gravely than before.

"My children," she said, "taking lessons in worldly practices is not going to do you any good. Start thinking of your final journey to Allah. Do your namaz every day, do your *roja,* your fasting, in Ramadan. Earn for the permanent life. Don't become a kafir like your father. Think of Allah, He is merciful, He will forgive you. Read the Koran. See, I am telling you all this, which means Allah Himself is advising you through me. He is everywhere; He can see and hear everything; without His will not even a single leaf can move on a tree."

Ma's face looked like a dry, colorless leaf, one fallen from a tree in the heat of summer. She sighed, continuing, "Your father does not do his namaz. Anyone who fails to do it is a kafir. I live in the house of such a kafir only because of you. If I cook for and feed a kafir, I will be committing a sin. If you don't turn to Allah and walk on the path He has shown, I will leave you and go wherever my eyes take me. Go, dear, wash your hands and feet, it's time for namaz."

Ma made a gesture indicating that the last few words were meant for me. My heart sank. Once I had washed my hands and feet, I would have to stand with Ma, mutter my prayers, place my hands first on my chest, then get on my knees for a while and remain like that for a few moments, and then finally touch the ground with my forehead. Nothing was more uncomfortable than this procedure. But it was a command from Ma, and I had to obey.

Baba returned home and found me sitting on the prayer mat. "Nasrin, come here!" he called. I jumped up from the mat and ran to him with relief. Standing before my father, head bent low, I was sure that this time I would be spared a scolding because I had been busy doing something as important as praying, not frivolously playing or chatting idly with others. But before I could fully grasp what was happening, Baba grabbed my neck and pushed me so hard in the opposite direction that I landed right before my desk. "What nonsense have you started doing instead of your studies?" he barked, grinding his teeth. "Following your mother's example, are you? Will Allah feed you if you call him? Won't you have to find food for yourself? Go to your desk and study. If I see you leave, I will break every bone in your body!"

Ma was sitting on her prayer mat, fuming silently. How dare Baba make her daughter get up and leave her namaz! No doubt he wanted to turn me into a kafir like himself. But Huzur had said to her, "You must stay calm, Hamima." Amirullah had given her a new name — Idulwara Begum had became Hamima Rehman. Every woman who went to him, no matter how old or young, was given a new name. Renu was now called Nazia, Hasna's name was Mutashwema, Ruby was Maheda. Hamima, recalling the peer's words, tried to keep calm, but it was not easy. How long could she be patient? There was a limit to everything. After all, it wasn't as if Baba had given birth to their children — that particular task had been performed by Ma. If she could not exercise even the smallest influence over her offspring, why should she stay in this house?

Baba changed into a lungi, tied it firmly over his stomach, and stood over me as I sat at my desk. He continued shouting: "If you can't do as I tell you, get out of my house. I pay for every mouthful you eat, for your clothes, for everything — you *have* to listen to every word I utter if you wish to live here. And if you don't want to, then go. Go and beg at every house you can find. Why don't you go? You don't have to stay in a kafir's house. Go!"

I could see that these words were actually addressed to Ma. I was not doing namaz voluntarily, nor had I left it unfinished of my own free will, so my role in the conflict between Ma and Baba was minor. This thought brought me some comfort.

Ma entered the room as soon as Baba left. "Of course I'll go!" she declared. "You think you can keep me tied here? That I have nowhere to go? Better to live in a jungle with wild animals than with a kafir. When I do leave, you'll find out what I mean. I'm not going to tell anyone or do a song and dance before I leave. I'll just slip out one day. You've turned the children into little devils, just like yourself. If I stay with them I'm going to lose whatever virtue I've earned."

Ma's words were not addressed to me, either. They were meant for Baba. But both spoke in my presence. Since neither wished to see even the shadow of the other, the storm they brewed up raged in my room and over me.

Having finished her speech, Ma suddenly slapped my cheek, leaving the impression of her fingers on it.

"Why did you leave your namaz? Aren't you afraid of Allah? How did you become so reckless? The devil always tries to disturb people if he finds them praying. You allowed him to do just that, didn't you? How dare you leave your namaz half finished! When the dancing flames in hell burn you forever, who will go there to save you? Your father?"

I couldn't speak. My head was still reeling from the impact of the slap.

When the new day dawned Ma began my religious education with renewed vigor, more so because I was born on an auspicious day, on the same day that the Prophet Muhammad was born. I returned from school to find her waiting for me to sit down and read the Koran.

In the evenings a number of girls from the neighborhood came to the front yard. Just as I was about to organize a game of gollachhut, Ma called me inside. I was made to wash my hands and feet and sit with the Koran. I had to wear a salwar, cover my head with a veil, and read *"Alhamdulillah he rabbil al amin aar rahamanir rahim . . . kulhuallahu ahad allahusasamad. . . ."* My playmates waited for me outside.

One day I broke off and said irritably, "What is all this I'm reading? I don't even know what it means."

Ma replied coldly, "There's no need to worry about its meaning. Just reading the book of Allah is good enough."

Hoping that Ma would soon release me so I could rush off to join my friends, I would follow Ma's instructions and read various verses from the Koran, glancing out of the window from time to time. Suddenly I realized that the light had faded, that it was now quite dark. The girls who had been waiting for me had all gone home. A painful lump rose in my throat, but I'd finish reading, then kiss the Koran just as Ma instructed before taking it from its stand and replacing it on the top shelf of Ma's cupboard.

Every morning Sultan Ustadji came to teach me Arabic, but that wasn't enough. I was supposed to spend my evenings reading the Koran as well. As things were, my Arabic teacher was causing me a great deal of grief. The veranda we sat on was white with a thick layer of pigeon droppings. If I wrinkled my nose at the stench, he said, "Why do you pull a face like that when I ask you to read the words of Allah?" Then he'd curl a fat finger and rap me sharply on the head. One morning, instead of saying *"Alif laam zabar aal, laam khara zabar la, yaao pesh hoo,"* I happened to say, *"Laam yaao pesh lahoo."* At this, the bearded fellow rose, broke a stiff, hard branch off a colorful red, blue, and yellow *patabahaar* tree, bared his teeth at me, and said, "Put your hand out!" One was always supposed to obey a teacher. So I held out my hand, palm upward. Sultan Ustadji brought that branch down on it, again and again, until my hand turned red.

Now, it seemed, I was not going to be spared in the evenings, either. If I nodded off while reading from the Koran, or missed a word, Ma would box my ears, punch me in the back, or give me a tight slap. She was convinced my heart was not in the pursuit of religious studies. All I could think of was the mundane world — games, music, and dance. Ma said clearly I would have to spend all eternity in hell.

Having successfully ruined my evenings, one day Ma spoke to Dada, slowly and seriously. "Noman," she said, "aren't you going to start doing your namaz?"

"Yes, Ma," Dada replied with a smile, "I'll do it soon."

"If you don't do your namaz and roja, I am telling you — for the last time — that you will lose me. I shall leave you, forever."

Dada heard this threat, grinned broadly, continued to swing his legs from his chair on the veranda, and said, "Ma, I swear I'm going to start doing namaz. Please don't leave us."

I came out on the front veranda and took a deep breath. The field stood empty. A gust of wind rose from the field and went straight into my heart, whistling and moaning softly.

A week later, Ma raised the subject again. "You said you were going to start your namaz, Noman. Have you?"

"I will, next Friday, the holy day," Dada replied gravely.

Come Friday, Ma said to Dada, "Go to the mosque for the Friday namaz."

Dada scratched his neck. "I don't feel too well today, but from next Friday on I am definitely, positively going to start. I promise!"

This pleased Ma greatly. "Do you remember the *kalmas,* the prayers I taught you?" she asked.

"Of course. How could I forget? What do you take me for, Ma? A man who doesn't remember the kalmas, the four pillars of Islam, is not a Muslim at all."

That day, when we sat down to eat, Ma served Dada the largest piece of chicken. He had taken the trouble to remember the prayers and was going to start doing his namaz regularly starting next Friday.

The week passed, and it was Friday again. This time, Dada said, "Nothing can happen on this earth unless Allah wills it. Even a leaf cannot move on a tree unless Allah wants it to. No one has the power to do anything against His wishes. How can *I* start doing namaz without an order from Him? He's not doing anything to make me start my namaz, is He? What power have I got to start unless He makes me? If I tell you, yes, I have enough power, then that would be a lie. It would be sinful, wouldn't it? *La sharika lahoo.* Allah's powers cannot be shared. Allah is one and unique." Dada stopped for a minute, then burst into a song: "If it dances when Allah pulls the string, how can you blame the puppet?"

Ma gave up on Dada; but she found I was within her reach and asked, "Oy, have *you* done your namaz?"

"Baba has told me to do my lessons for school," I replied, running toward my desk.

"Look at her! Hardly out of her nappies and she's learned to answer me back. Like father, like daughter. Doesn't believe in Allah! How can Allah ever get you to do a good deed when you've been possessed by the devil?"

Ma suddenly burst into tears. "Satan has entered this house. I had such faith in my children, such hope. They've all turned into kafirs, they've been destroyed. Oh Allah, take me away from them!"

Allah did not hear Ma's appeal. He did nothing to take her away. She continued to stay with us in San Souci, within its high compound wall, among the flowering plants and fruit trees. Baba's threats had no effect on her. She still went regularly to Amirullah's house in Noumahal. On a Thursday evening, having attended the prayer meeting and heard a description of Koran, the words of Allah and hadith, the words of Prophet Muhammad, she returned home with her eyes red and swollen from crying. She was convinced that the day of judgment was just around the corner. She had to hurry and prepare for it. It was also her belief that Peer Amirullah would make a special request to Allah to get her a ticket to heaven. As for her children, she had decided to stop trying to make them turn to Allah. They were being led by Satan, too firmly rooted in this world to think of the next one. Ma was now more concerned with her own future. When everyone stood in the field of judgment waiting to be judged, they were all simply going to chant: *"Ya nabsi, ya nabsi!"* No one would have the time to look at or think of anyone else.

Ma continued to walk on the path of Allah, but discovered eventually that the path was not without a price. Amirullah had told Ma a little obliquely that whoever led others to heaven encountered quite a few obstacles on the way himself. Removing those obstacles required money. Even the Prophet needed to have money; even He couldn't do without it. There was a special name for the money paid to clear the path to heaven. It was called hadia. Collecting enough hadia was somewhat difficult for Ma. Baba no longer gave her money, not even to buy the small things — he did all the shopping himself. Baba's Taj Pharmacy, where he saw patients in the evening, was quite close to our new house, so he went to the market either in Ampatti or Durgabari before returning home. What Ma still had was the jewelry she happened to be wearing when our house was robbed: the heavy gold bracelets on her forearms and the gold chain around her neck. The local jeweler's shop, Matri Jewelers, was within walking distance. One afternoon Ma sold her chain and took the money to Amirullah's house to pay the hadia. She also removed rice, dal, and cooking oil from our storeroom and took it to the peer's house. This gave her a certain measure of reassurance. At least no one could say that she went to the prayer meetings empty-handed.

Since Baba had stopped giving her an allowance she did not even have money to pay for a rickshaw. She started walking to Amirullah's house. She did not care if I had fever, or if Dada had fractured his leg, or if Yasmin fell from a tree and cracked her skull. Nothing stopped her from paying Amirullah a visit. It was not only on Thursdays that she disappeared. I began to find her missing even on Mondays and Tuesdays when I returned home from school. Where had she gone? To the peer's house of course. She was absent almost every day now, ignorant of the everyday details of our lives. Baba was increasingly restless. He would return to the house twice during the day to see if his household still existed, to make sure it had not vanished into thin air. He placed a padlock on our storeroom and another on our black front gate every night at nine o'clock. All this infuriated Ma even more. She thought the devil was pursuing her, trying to stop her from turning to Allah, so her devotion to Him grew stronger and she began to serve Peer Amirullah with much greater fervor. If she found the front gate locked when she got home, she went straight back to Noumahal, thus absenting herself even during the night.

After putting up with her absence for seven nights, Baba finally sent Dada to bring her back. She returned feeling victorious, knowing full well that she had been missed and that the house could not run without her. She said to us, after making sure that Baba was within earshot, "I will stay with you only if you do your namaz regularly. It's that simple."

Baba heard her, leaned back in his sofa, and spoke gently: "Do your namaz, read your Koran. Has anyone ever stopped you? But why do you have go to that peer's house? Do you think those who don't go there will never get to heaven? The children need to go to school. They have their studies to think of. You do nothing to look after them, instead you spend all your time in that house. Does one have to neglect one's family to do namaz and roja? Who has told you that? You're simply being used by that cheat and hypocrite!"

"Don't ever say that!" Ma shot back. "He is very dear to Allah, a saint, and you're calling him a cheat and a hypocrite? How dare you! Your tongue will drop off, I tell you. I will have nothing to do with a kafir like you. You ruined my life. If Fajli hadn't rescued me at the right time and shown me the way to Allah, I would still be running to the cinema, wearing my right sandal on my left foot! I was blind, but thinking of Allah has opened my eyes. Now I know how dangerous it is to form strong attachments to worldly things. Who will help me cross over to the other world on the final day? My husband?

No. My children? No! No one can help me, no one except Allah."

Aunt Fajli had said to Ma: "Borobu, if you live with someone who does not do his namaz, you will be considered a sinner. Dula-bhai is a kafir; if you have anything to do with a kafir, Allah will burn you, too, in that fire in hell."

Ma had no wish to burn in hell. Her life on this earth had caused her enough pain already, and she wanted no more. Her prayer beads moved very quickly in her hand, as did her lips: *"Salliala saiadena Muhammadur Rasoolullah."* In the dark room the beads glinted like the eyes of a cat. Ma stayed awake all night, sitting on her prayer mat.

The sound of her weeping woke me in the middle of the night.

"Why are you crying, Ma?" I asked, raising my head from the pillow.

Ma did not reply. She just went on crying.

"Won't you sleep tonight? Come to bed, Ma."

Ma did not stop sobbing, nor did she come to bed.

By the time she did the first namaz of the day, the fazar, dawn had broken. It was only then that she went to bed. Later in the morning, I asked her, "Why were you crying, Ma?"

She sighed deeply and said, "I was thinking of the suffering of the grave. When the angels ask me questions about my life, what am I going to answer? The grave will be covered, closed at the top and sides, so tightly, so absolutely tightly that . . ." She choked. Words failed her.

It was now obvious that Ma could not be forced to stay at home. Baba removed the padlock from the gate. It no longer mattered *when* Ma got home, as long as she came home. It was my belief that Baba wanted Ma to come back not because he loved her but simply because he wanted her to be around to keep an eye on us, so that none of us came to harm. While all this was going on, word reached us that Sultan Ustadji, who had also taught Ma when she was a young girl, had died. "There's no need to study Arabic anymore," Baba said. "Just pay attention to your schoolwork."

Ma's jaw set at these words. She intensified her prayers to Allah: "Please make my children strong believers, Allah. Release them from the suffering in the grave. Save them from the fire in hell, take them to heaven. You are all-forgiving. You are the Lord of the Universe."

After this, Ma began hiding coconuts, guavas, mangoes, jamun, even jackfruit under her burkha, smuggling the fruit out of the house to feed the people at Amirullah's. She had stopped going into the kitchen almost entirely, but now she started cooking again. Young chickens were killed, and she cooked their fresh, tender flesh with her own hands, using all the right ingredients to make it tasty. Then she filled a bowl with chicken curry and slipped out the front gate. She was going to offer it to the peer. Ma also took a few old saris, which Aunt Fajli had asked for, to make a quilt.

Huzur had promised Ma that when the angels came to her grave to ask her questions, he himself would answer them for her. He was going to become a *gausul azam* very soon, someone in whom Allah confided, telling him many secrets. This news had been given to Huzur in a dream. It was Ma's dearest wish to see Allah at least once. But would He ever reveal Himself to a sinner like her? The thought brought tears to her eyes. With one hand she clutched the bowl of chicken curry under her burkha, with the other she wiped her tears.

One night, having returned from the peer's house, Ma muttered: "Humaira has had a gold pendant made with ALLAH written on it. She's also had half a dozen bangles made, with thirty grams of gold. Does anyone ever give me anything? No one in the world is as deprived as me!"

She cast her burkha aside and called out to Moni to give her her dinner. When Moni brought her a plate of rice, Ma shouted: "Why is this rice so cold? Isn't there any warm rice at all? What are you trying to feed me? You will all be happy when I die! You think I don't know that? Who has ever given me anything in this house? I haven't even got a good sari. Who's going to get me one?" So saying, she pushed her plate away.

Moni took the plate back to the kitchen to heat up the rice. Ma stood near my desk and began speaking loudly so that Baba could hear: "Men usually keep their wives covered with gold but what do I get? I've been appointed here just to act as a guard, a *chowkidar.* Well, even a chowkidar gets paid. But me? I'm working for free!"

"But you are our mother!" I said, my voice low. "Would you take a salary?"

Ma promptly snapped at me and made me shut up. "How on earth am I going to manage?" she demanded. "My father married me to a doctor. He had so hoped that his son-in-law would help my brothers and sisters get an education. Has he helped any of them? Has he ever asked how they're doing? Does he think of anyone at all? Look at my arms. I haven't worn a single bangle, or any other jewelry, for such a long time. And other men's wives? They are loaded with it! He keeps me like a poor beggar, and yet makes such heavy demands. Look after my children, he says. Bring them up properly!"

One day when I was six Aunt Fajli arrived from her in-laws' house with the news that a *dojjal* with a huge ax in his hand was soon going to be out in the world, testing everyone's beliefs about Allah and seeing if everyone performed his or her duties, namaz, and roja. A dojjal, I learned, was an avenging angel. Anyone found lacking in belief deep inside would be hacked into five pieces.

After that, out of sheer terror, everyone in Grandma's house began reading the kalmas twice a day. Who knew, this dojjal might turn up at any time! I began having frequent nightmares in which I was hacked to pieces, from which I woke with a start. Uncle Sharaf said, "Everyone in Peer's house is safe. Their beliefs are quite strong. The dojjal couldn't do them any harm."

Ma was of the same opinion. "Fajli need not worry at all," she said.

As one day slipped into another, I asked Uncle Sharaf, Uncle Felu, and Ma: "Why, that dojjal didn't turn up, did he?"

"No, but he can still come, any time. Fajli's father-in-law has said that doomsday will be upon us right after the dojjal's arrival," Ma said.

"And what will happen on doomsday?"

"The worst," Ma replied with a sigh. "The angel Israfil will blow his horn. The world will be destroyed. Everything Allah has created — the sky and the earth — will disappear."

I tried to imagine how the earth was going to be destroyed. Soon I could picture the scene quite clearly: The sky would cave in and squash the earth, every building would be flattened, people would be crushed like ants. Huge banyan, neem, coconut, date palm, and every other tree would be buried under the earth. Even if you passed the test the avenging angel set you, you would never be spared on doomsday. That day, death was inevitable. Shortly before we left Grandma's house, Aunt Fajli announced that it was sinful to wear gold jewelry. Every woman who heard this news took off what she was wearing and put it away. Uncle Hashem had been recently married and his bride was wearing a lot of gold.

Other women from our neighborhood were still visiting our house, lifting her veil to see her face.

"Parul, take off all those gold pieces you're wearing. The world is coming to an end. If you are caught wearing jewelry at such a time, Allah will see it as a sin," Aunt Fajli said. She began taking off Parul mami's jewelry herself, handling each piece and casting it aside as if she was holding a dead rat by its tail. "Chhotobu," said Uncle Hashem, "I thought taking the jewelry off a new bride brought bad luck."

Aunt Fajli shrieked at this, her shrill voice ringing out. "What do *you* know about good or bad luck, Hashem? The day before yesterday, Abbaji saw the Prophet in his dream. And do you know what the Prophet told him? Those portions of one's body that are covered with jewelry will burn in the fire in hell."

Grandma took Aunt Fajli aside and asked her: "Where have you kept your own jewelry?"

Aunt Fajli replied, prayer beads moving rapidly in her hand, "What would I do with jewelry? Your son-in-law took it all and sold it."

A crease appeared upon Grandma's brows.

A year had passed since that day. Apparently it was now all right to wear gold in Amirullah's house. I raised my eyes from my book and looked at Ma's sad face. "It's sinful to wear gold!" I exclaimed. "Didn't everyone in the peer's family give up wearing jewelry?"

Ma didn't reply. She simply gave me a withering look, as if I had truly been possessed by the devil, and the words that I had just uttered had been spoken by him, not me.

A few days later, Ma went to the local jeweler's shop and returned with a pair of gold bracelets. The owner of the shop was known to Baba. Ma told him that he would pay for the bracelets later, in instalments.

~ 7 ~

Religion

Every Friday Grandpa came back from the mosque after the namaz with *batashas* in his pocket, sweet, pale yellow discs, made with gur. As soon as we saw him reach the pond, Uncle Felu, Chhotku, Yasmin, and I ran to get our share. Grandpa was always kind to the young children in his house, but not to the adults. Having given us our batashas, he went home and started to drive everyone crazy. That was the term Grandma used, when Grandpa began shouting: "Get me my stick, and tell me who did not go to the mosque. I shall beat them to death today!" All the boys were supposed to go to the mosque. The girls were not allowed to, so they had to do their namaz at home. Grandpa did not mind his womenfolk stepping out of the house, but when they did, they had to be clad in a burkha.

On Fridays, he liked to take things easy. It was an old habit. Between his return from the mosque and his afternoon nap, he asked questions: Which of his sons had failed to go to the mosque? Which daughter had gone out of the house? Did she drape her burkha before she left? Grandma got fed up with his questions. After his nap, however, Grandpa went back to being his normal genial self. He tied his lungi tightly and went off, moving his hands as if he was pushing aside the air in front of him. He went to Notun Bazar, no longer concerned with who was at home and who was not. The thought of going to his restaurant and meeting people was enough to entice him out of the house. With the exception of Grandma, none of the grown-up woman in our house wore a burkha voluntarily. Aunt Runu and Aunt Jhunu left home with their burkhas stuffed into a bag. When they returned, they tried to get hold of Chhotku, or whoever happened to be standing by the pond, to ask if Grandpa was at home. If he wasn't, they quickly slipped into the house. If he was, they waited at a neighbor's until Grandpa left. Grandpa had sent only his eldest son Siddique to a *madrasa,* a religious school. Everyone else went to ordinary schools and colleges. Grandpa was a strict disciplinarian when it came to education. "Knowledge is invaluable wealth; there must be absolutely no lapses on your part when it comes to studies," he said frequently and sternly. But, of course, he only said that to his sons. To his daughters, he said, "Girls need not bother with higher studies!" Despite this, Aunt Runu went to college and received her bachelor's degree. Grandpa kept trying to get her married. Every now and then he would invite prospective grooms and their families to come and inspect Aunt Runu. She, in turn, would smear her face with mud and grime, and deliberately make her hair look disheveled, so that no one found her suitable for marriage. Sulekha's mother would turn up often, sit on Grandma's bed, help herself to paan and lime, and say, "Are you planning to keep Runu in your house forever? Why don't you get her married? Idul and Fajli were married so easily!"

Grandma would begin preparing a paan for herself and reply, "No, let her study a bit more. She ought to get a job. She can always get married later. These days, even a woman has to earn. It's not right to depend purely on the husband. Who knows what might happen in the future?"

Proposals for marriage came for Aunt Jhunu as well. In fact, because she was fair-skinned, she received more proposals than Aunt Runu. But Grandma remained firm. "My daughter is still studying, and she'll study some more. What's the big rush to get her married? Besides, how can a younger sister be married before the elder one?"

After leaving the madrasa, Uncle Siddique went to the university in Dhaka, received his master's degree in Arabic, and found a job. His light-skinned wife, Halima, lived with him in Dhaka. They did not have any children yet. People said, "So what if she's fair? She's barren, isn't she?" Now and then, the neighbors gave him amulets and lucky charms for his wife to tie around her waist, but after they left, Uncle Siddique threw them into the well. Sometimes, during holidays, he came to visit us, occasionally accompanied by his wife. When I saw him walking about in the courtyard, wooden clogs on his feet, I found it difficult to believe that he had come to stay for only a few weeks. It seemed as if he had lived here for thousands of years.

Uncle Hashem was far less interested in his studies. He often played and spent his days chatting with his mates. He failed his matriculation exam two or three times, then gave up studying altogether. It had been decided that Uncle Siddique would take Aunt Jhunu with him to Dhaka and get her admitted to Eden College. The others — Fakrul, Tutu, Sharaf, and Felu — did their studies as half-heartedly as they did their namaz and roja. But their circle of friends increased daily. By the time they finished chatting and having a good time it was always quite late at night. Influenced by his friends, Uncle Tutu started smoking.

Whenever he could, Grandpa tied his sons to pillars and thrashed them, as if he wanted to — quite literally — beat some sense into them. But it was no use. None of them improved their exam scores. Grandma consulted Uncle Siddique, and decided that her sons, too, would have to be sent to Dhaka, one by one. If they were put in a school over there, they might grow up to be proper men. Grandma was going gray worrying about her sons' future; she did not want them to turn into vagabonds like their father.

Grandpa announced that he would go on the hajj. This infuriated Grandma. "How will you find the money to do that?" she snapped.

"Allah will give me the money," Grandpa replied mysteriously.

As things turned out, it was Baba who gave him the money, not Allah, on the understanding that Grandpa would return it when he got back. He filled a trunk with his clothes and a few packets of chira and other long-lasting edibles. Then he had his name written on the trunk with white paint: MUHAMMAD MANIRUDDIN AHMED. ADDRESS: AKUA MADRASA QUARTER, MYMENSINGH. The year he sailed for his hajj was the same year that Neil Armstrong went to the moon. The hajj drew Grandpa, the moon pulled Armstrong.

Everyone in our house was passionate about the moon. When the moon came out, mothers carried their babies out in the courtyard and chanted a little rhyme: "Come, come, Uncle Moon, put a dot on my love's forehead!"

Grown-ups liked to sit out in the moonlight and hear Uncle Kana's stories. Everyone agreed that the tales he told were the best. Aunt Runu sang: "On this moonlit night, all have gone to the forest." Before Eid, everyone wanted to look at the moon. When Grandma saw it, she greeted it with *salaam aleikum*.

On this particular occasion, Uncle Siddique happened to be around. He had come to spend the holidays. When he heard Grandma greet the moon, suddenly he said, "Ma, Neil Armstrong has gone and pissed on the moon. Why are you saluting something that's got a Christian's piss on it?"

Aunt Fajli was among those who heard this remark. Sometimes — after being possessed by a jinn or if she felt feverish, had a tummy upset, or a headache — she was allowed by Amirullah to spend a few days with her parents. This time, a headache had brought her to Grandma's house. Having heard Uncle Siddique's comment, she said, "Abbaji has told us that no one has actually landed on the moon. It is Allah who has created the moon. It is He who makes both the sun and the moon rise and set. The moon is holy and pure, Muslims look at it to celebrate Eid, and observe roja during Ramadan. This business of a man landing on the moon is just a rumor spread by Christians. It is their propaganda."

Uncle Siddique burst out laughing. "Fajli," he said, "I taught you science when you were small, didn't I? Didn't I tell you how the earth was created? Have you forgotten everything?"

Aunt Fajli began drawing water from the well to wash her hands and feet prior to doing her namaz. "What are you trying to say, Miabhai?" she retorted, "Do your scientists know more than Allah? What Allah has said is the only truth; everything else is a lie." Aunt Fajli set her full bucket down in the courtyard and confidently straightened her back. Uncle Siddique looked at the sky, as if he was about to start counting all the stars, and said quickly, "You are never possessed by jinn, Fajli. What possesses you is your father-in-law!"

I didn't know who was right, Uncle Siddique or Aunt Fajli. Both were given special treatment in Grandma's house. Pulao, meat curries, and other tasty dishes were made when Uncle Siddique came. While no one fussed quite so much over Aunt Fajli, a great deal of fuss *was* made when someone from her husband's family came to visit. I was not close either to Uncle Siddique or Aunt Fajli, but her in-laws and their relations appeared even more distant. When they came, a sunburned, snotty-nosed girl like me was not allowed to go beyond the well. If I got any closer to the house, Grandma would say, "Don't hover here. Come back only when the guests have gone."

So I would stand at a distance and watched the proceedings. The mattress that was normally rolled up during the day was unrolled, and Grandma spread a new sheet over it. I could see Aunt Fajli's husband and father-in-law sitting on it and having their meal. Grandma would bring bowls of fresh, hot food from the kitchen, and Aunt Fajli, her veil pulled over her face, would serve them. After their meal, they would have a little rest, lying on the mattress, chewing paan. It was only then that the women would sit down to eat — Aunt Fajli, her mother-in-law, her sister-in-law, and her daughters, Humaira, Sufaira, and Mubashwera. Grandma was the last to eat, after everyone else in the family had been fed. After that, I was free once more to go into her house, easily crossing the no-entry line drawn near the well between her courtyard and ours.

Now, Uncle Siddique continued to speak as he walked on the paved courtyard. His wooden clogs made a clicking noise. "Very well," he said, "if what Allah has said is the only truth, then do what Allah has decreed. Your husband can sleep with your maid; there's absolutely no problem with that. Do you know why? Because Allah has said, *la ehellu lakannisau meen vayadu ola al tabadalla bihinna meena ajoajeu olao aijabka husnu hunna illama malakatu yaminuka,* which means it is perfectly legitimate to have sex with a female servant."

The water in the bucket remained untouched. Aunt Fajli couldn't wash herself. She stomped into the room and snatched her burkha from the rack, breaking into sobs. When she cried, her cheeks turned red like ripe mangoes. She looked quite pretty when that happened, like a lady in a painting. "Ma, I am leaving. I cannot possibly spend another second in this house. I cannot bear such humiliation!" she shouted.

Grandma ran back into the room, pulled the burkha out of Aunt Fajli's hand, and said, "Why are you crying? Siddique always speaks without thinking, so sometimes he speaks nonsense. That's no reason for you to leave the house at night. What will your in-laws think? They won't be pleased, will they? Go, if you must, but at least wait until Eid is over."

Aunt Fajli snatched her burkha back in one swift motion and began putting it on. "No, I won't spend another moment here. Do you think I come here because I want to? No! I come only because back at home there's always so much noise and so many people that I get headaches. But if my brothers are going to insult me here, why should I stay? I had thought of celebrating Eid with you. Even that is not to be. Miabhai made such an awful remark about Humaira's father. How many men in this world are as holy and pure as him?"

Grandma failed to make her stay — Aunt Fajli was absolutely determined to go, so Uncle Hashem escorted her back. The atmosphere in the house was quite grim that night. I sat quietly and stared at the moon, wondering with great amazement how anyone could possibly have gone there. Why, it was so small! Ma used to tell me that an old woman sat in the moon, with a spinning wheel. But according to Uncle Siddique, on the moon there were no plants; there was no water, and certainly no old woman. The shapes on the moon that made it look as if a woman was sitting there were only craters and shadows. But it really didn't matter to me what the moon was, or what it looked like. I secretly made friends with it. The moon traveled in the sky to accompany me wherever I went. If I stopped, so did the moon. If I rested for a while in Grandma's courtyard, like me, the moon took a rest in the sky. Then it followed me to my own courtyard. I went to stand by the pond and found it there as well.

On the morning of Eid, everyone had a cold shower, using a bar of red Cosco soap. I wore a new dress, new shoes were put on my feet, and my hair was tied with a red ribbon. A drop of scent was applied and another drop put on a tiny piece of cotton, which was tucked behind my ear. The men wore white pajamas and *panjabis* and donned caps. They, too, placed bits of cotton dabbed with scent behind their ears. The whole house was filled with the beautiful smell of attar.

I left for the open prayer ground with all the men. What a huge place it was! Large sheets were spread on the grass for the Eid namaz. With the sole exception of Uncle Siddique, all my uncles — Baba, Dada, and Chhotda — were there. The field was packed with people. When the namaz started, everyone bent down together. I watched the spectacle, enchanted. It was a bit like doing physical training during our school assembly. When we bent down to touch our toes, perhaps this was how we looked. After the prayers, Baba and the other men embraced one another. Only men were allowed to do that. When we got back home, I said to Ma: "Let's embrace each other for Eid!" Ma shook her head and said, "No, females aren't supposed to embrace." When I asked her why, she simply said, "That's not the custom." The words *Why not?* sprang to my lips and struggled to get out.

People started to make arrangements for the sacrifice. A black bull had been brought three days before, and was now tied to the banyan tree. Tears were streaming from its dark eyes. Suddenly I felt my heart ache. Here was a living being, chewing his cud, switching his tail; yet, in a few moments he would become buckets of meat. The imam of the mosque sat under the tree and sharpened his knife. Uncle Hashem went and brought a heavy bamboo pole. Baba spread a large mat in the courtyard where the men would sit afterward and chop the meat. Having sharpened his knife, the imam called out. At once Uncle Hashem, Baba and a few other men tied the bull with a rope and placed the bamboo pole between its legs, so that it stumbled and fell. The bull cried out in pain. Ma and my aunts were standing at the window watching the sacrifice. All eyes were dancing with joy. Only Uncle Siddique, still wearing a lungi and devoid of any scent of attar, stood in one corner of the field and said, "A poor, defenseless animal is going to be brutally killed, and people are actually *happy* to see that happen? And so is Allah? None of you have a shred of sympathy. That is the real truth."

He removed himself from the horror of the sacrifice. I remained standing. The bull thrashed its legs and bellowed again. It took as many as seven strong men to hold it down. It threw them off desperately and rose once more. Again, the bamboo pole was used to make it stumble and fall. This time, the imam acted quickly. As soon as the bull fell, he raised the knife, shouted "Allah hu Akbar! Allah is great!" and slashed its throat. A stream of blood spurted out. The bull was not yet dead; it continued to roar with its half-slit throat, its legs flailing.

An ache formed in my heart, sharp and persistent. I was not required to stand and watch anymore. Ma had told me, as she did on the morning of every Eid, that it was my duty to watch the sacrifice. When the imam began skinning the dead animal its eyes were still full of tears. Uncle Sharaf and Uncle Felu were glued to the spot, refusing to move from the scene of action. I left for Monumia's shop to buy balloons.

The meat was divided into seven portions. Three were for Grandma's family, three were for us, and the remainder distributed among our neighbors and the poor. The best thing about Eid was that Baba stayed in a good mood all day, speaking gently, not shouting at or beating any of us for not studying. We spent all our time eating pulao, korma, *shemai*, and *jarda*. If we made any mistakes, we were forgiven by the elders. The work of cutting the meat continued all day. Huge ovens were lit and the meat was cooked in very large pans. In the evening, when the cooking was finished, Ma and Grandma bathed and put on new saris. Aunt Runu and Aunt Jhunu got dressed and waited for an opportunity to slip out to visit their friends. Guests started pouring into the house. Uncle Siddique, still wearing a lungi and an ordinary shirt, returned after a walk round the neighborhood. He said, "There is so much blood everywhere . . . the entire area is drowning in it. I don't suppose anyone knows how many bulls were killed today? Those animals could have been given to farmers. Many of them can't plow the land because they don't have oxen. Why are men such monsters? I just don't understand. One single family wants to eat all the meat they can get from a bull. And yet, think how many don't even get a handful of rice!"

There was no point in asking him to have a bath and put on new clothes. Grandma gave up, and simply said, "All right, so you did not wish to take part in the celebrations. Don't you even wish to eat? Aren't you hungry?"

"Why, yes! Give me whatever you can. I'll eat anything, except that meat," Uncle Siddique replied, heaving a deep sigh.

Grandma's eyes brimmed over. How could she bear the fact that her eldest son, her firstborn, would not touch the meat from the sacrificial bull on Eid day? She wiped her eyes, vowing silently not to touch the meat, either. When did a mother ever eat anything, anyway, without first feeding her child?

Very soon, the news of Uncle Siddique's refusal to have the special meat spread through the house. The grown-ups began to feel a little uncomfortable. Ma said, as she served the meat, "Miabhai is going to return to Dhaka without eating this meat. He says he can't bear the idea of a sacrifice. What about the meat we buy in a butcher's shop? Does that come without killing an animal?"

After Eid, my life resumed its old pattern. By this time, I had lost a front tooth. Uncle Sharaf would poke me from time to time and chant:

Toothless, toothless, where do you go?
Eat some shit, and your tooth will grow.

Ma had dropped my tooth into a mouse hole and said:

Mouse, mouse, give you my rotten tooth, I do.
Give me one like yours, new and as sharp, too.

I would have to wait until the mouse obliged. Until then, Uncle Sharaf was going to flash his toothy grin every day. Aunt Runu more or less confirmed what Uncle Sharaf had said. "Your new tooth will never appear unless you eat shit," she told me.

The very mention of shit made me want to throw up. Going to the lavatory every day was a horrible experience for me. I never spent a second more than I had to. Dada, I had noticed, spent as long as two hours. I never understood how he could do it. Anyway, Aunt Runu's words annoyed me no end. "You have teeth!" I retorted, "Did you eat shit, Aunt Runu?"

"Oh yes!" she replied nonchalantly. "When I was small."

Although Uncle Sharaf chanted that rhyme, he was repulsed by this particular subject far more than me. He would refuse to eat and knock his plate over if he saw a hen leaving droppings in the courtyard, or if someone so much as mentioned the word *shit*. One day, as he sat down to eat, I happened to say, quite innocently, "Uncle Sharaf, did you know that unless one eats shit, one cannot get new teeth?" Hardly had the words left my mouth when Uncle Sharaf came flying to punch me in the back, and throw his full plate away into the courtyard, as if it were a piece of broken brick.

Mind you, *I* was not allowed to punch *him* in the back when he chanted that objectionable rhyme because he was older than me. Anyone older than me had to be treated with respect. They could do whatever they liked, but I could not hit them back, nor tell anyone if they swore me to secrecy and stripped me naked whenever they wanted to. If I opened my mouth, I would be the one to get thrashed. I was simply supposed to accept — without asking questions — whatever the grown-ups decided to bestow on me, be it punishment or reward. Whatever they did was for my own good. They themselves had taught me to believe this.

When Tutu and Sharaf had their circumcisions, to turn them into proper Muslims, they were dressed in new lungis. When they walked, they kept their legs wide apart, so that the newly cut tips of their penises did not hurt. If they caught me laughing, both showered blows on my back. I was not allowed to laugh. In fact, I was not even allowed to look at their lungis, or the way they were walking. Anyone older than me was free, at any time, to set boundaries that I could not overstep.

After Eid, Uncle Siddique stayed with us for a long time. He spent the days reading, reclining in a chair. In the evenings he would walk in the courtyard, wooden clogs on his feet. Sometimes he came over to chat with Baba at night. Uncle Siddique never raised his voice. If he heard anyone else do so, he clicked his tongue regretfully. Uncle Hashem had a habit of shouting every now and then: "I've fallen! Oh God, I've fallen in!" This brought everyone running to the well, and they found Uncle Hashem clutching the edge, his body swinging inside.

"Stop this dangerous game, Hashem!" Grandma scolded him. "One day you really will fall right into it."

Uncle Hashem clambered out, grinning. Uncle Siddique stared foolishly, his mouth hanging open. "That was a *game?*" he asked. "And it was supposed to be funny? I found nothing funny in it. Has Hashem gone mad?"

But Uncle Hashem did not stop there. Sometimes he caught either Uncle Felu or me, held us upside down over the well, and said, "Drop you! I'm going to drop you!" When he did that to me, I screamed with all the power in my lungs, and everyone rushed out once more to see what Uncle Hashem was doing. Again, Uncle Siddique just stared blankly.

One day, Aunt Fajli turned up, fully aware that Uncle Siddique was at home. "I have something to tell you," she declared as soon as she saw him, without wasting any time on greeting him, or any other preliminaries. Uncle Siddique smiled and laid a hand on Aunt Fajli's back. "Why are you so cross? You were not like this before. At least take off your burkha and sit down. Then we'll talk."

She brushed his hand off and replied, "No, I have not come to this house to sit and chat. I have only one thing to say, and I will leave as soon as I've said it."

She took only the veil from her face, sat down on a bed, and went on, "You said the other day that Allah has said a man can sleep with his maidservant. Where did you find such a thing? In which verse of the Koran? It's wrong, totally wrong! Allah did not mean a maidservant. The Koran is quite clear about this. It mentions female slaves. A sexual relationship with a female slave is considered legitimate. But there are no slaves anymore. After all, we pay our maids salaries, don't we? We don't actually *buy* them!" Aunt Fajli smiled. It was a smile of triumph.

Uncle Siddique sat cross-legged on the bed, hugged a pillow, and said, "Ah, is that all? And this was so important that you would not take your burkha off, relax for a minute? Just say your piece and walk off? All right, tell me this: Why do you think the system of slavery disappeared? Why do we not have it anymore? *Can* you tell me? Who stopped the system? Your Allah? Or was it your Prophet? It was simply the people, do you understand? If the people had not put a stop to it, can you imagine how terrible life would be, even today? Besides, just think for a moment. Whether it's a female slave or a maid, how could Allah decree . . ."

Aunt Fajli interrupted him, raising her voice: "What Allah said was valid in those days. Women had no one to take care of them, offer them security. A female slave had nowhere to go. That is why Allah —"

Uncle Siddique cut her short. "If you think the Koran was written for a specific period of time, that's fine. Remember that, and kindly let it remain in the past, in that particular period. What's the point of making a song and dance about it today? And there's something else. Why did Allah say things that related only to those times? He knew the past, He knows the future, He is omnipresent. Then why didn't he write in his Koran that in the future slavery was going to be abolished? He could even have written that one day the world would have electric lights, motorcars, airplanes, rockets . . . why, He could have mentioned something about man going to the moon in a rocket! I totally fail to see why you are so concerned with things that do not apply to this age, the times that we *are* living in. You worry too much; you're afraid of every little thing."

Aunt Fajli got up with a long face. She lifted her veil with one hand and said, "I had no idea you had sunk so low, Miabhai. Shame on you! Even to look at you would be a sin for me." She shot out of Grandma's house, came over to our house, and promptly lay down, saying, "Borobu, please let me sleep here for a while, I've got such a raging headache!"

Ma went to the kitchen to prepare a meal for her: fine white rice and roasted pigeon.

When Uncle Siddique talked to Baba, it was usually to discuss purchasing land. "Buy some land in Dhaka, Rajab Ali. You can get it cheap right now. Later, you'll never get it at the same price."

Baba nodded and said, "Yes, let me think about it."

I longed to talk to Uncle Siddique and hear stories of Dhaka. What was Dhaka like, what did it have? But I noticed that he never even looked at me, possibly because his "princess" was now an ordinary creature, raised in the dirt and dust. However, on one particular occasion, on the day before he left for Dhaka, I did get to talk to him directly. I was on my way to the lavatory, when I found a torn piece of paper lying on the ground. It had a few words in Arabic written on it, so I gave it to Ma. Ever since I had learned to recognize Arabic letters Ma had taught me to collect anything I found written in the holy language, to make sure it did not get mixed up with other rubbish or stepped on. I had to pick it up and throw it into water. Normally, that was exactly what I did. I kissed it quickly, then floated it on water, like a boat. Today, I took that piece of paper to show Ma, simply to prove that I was a good girl; I had not stepped on it. Ma was shaking some clothes out to dry and hang on a line. "I can't take it right now. Give it to your uncle," she said to me.

Uncle Siddique took it from me and read the words aloud fluently. This made Ma cast him an admiring glance. Anyone who knew Arabic was immensely honorable, and ought to be revered, although Uncle Siddique did not go to the mosque on Fridays, or do his namaz for Eid. No one seemed to mind.

"What will you do with this piece of paper?" he asked me.

I clutched Ma's sari, leaned against her — more mentally than physically — and replied, "I shall give it a little kiss, then throw it into the pond."

Uncle Siddique threw it down on the ground at once. "You want to kiss that? Do you know what's written in it? It says, 'You son of a bitch, I'll fuck your mother.'"

Ma flushed with embarrassment. The wet clothes remained in her hands, still twisted. Phulbahari, who was walking from the well toward the house with a full pitcher under her arm, stopped in her tracks. Grandma was watering a chile plant. The jug slipped from her hand and all the water ran out, making a wet patch on the ground. I took a couple of steps toward Uncle Siddique, my eyes nearly popping out with amazement, and said, "Uncle Siddique, isn't Arabic Allah's language? You mean it can be used to write dirty words, too?"

Uncle Siddique walked about, his clogs clicking on the floor, and replied, "Why not? Arabic is spoken by the Arabs. They drink, they do other things that are wrong, they murder. They use foul and abusive words. They take as many as fourteen wives, or even a hundred."

"Stop it, Siddique!" said Grandma.

Grandma's firstborn, brought up with a great deal of care and affection, sent to a madrasa, where he learnt Arabic so well, stopped at his mother's command.

Ma stared suspiciously at Uncle Siddique. She found it very hard to believe that she had grown up with this man in this very house, in this courtyard, under that banyan tree. They used to return from school at the same time, have a quick meal, then rush to the lake attached to the Naseerabad Madrasa. They swam all afternoon. When they finally emerged from the water their eyes were always red. They knew that if they went home with red eyes, Grandma would beat them both. So they sat on the steps of the lake, picked a couple of yam leaves, chanted a rhyme to put a spell on them, and rubbed their eyes with the leaves to remove the redness. Both children waited until the magic spell took effect, and returned home as if nothing had happened.

At the time, the streets were empty; only one or two horse-drawn carriages could be seen. Ma liked to stop for a moment at a street corner to look at an English lady who lived in a two-story house. She sat on the balcony in the evenings, drinking tea, and when she laughed, her long, white legs seemed to laugh, too. Uncle Siddique grabbed a corner of Ma's dress and dragged her away, into their own alley, saying, "They are Christians. If you look at them, Allah will punish you!"

A table and a chair arrived for Uncle Siddique to use for his studies, but none for Ma. Grandpa secretly brought grapes and oranges for him, and Siddique hid them in his drawer and ate them all himself. He never shared a single grape with his sister. But Ma had the responsibility of looking after that mean and selfish boy's books and clothes. If he found ink marks on his table, or if anything was out of place, he did not hesitate to punch Ma in the back.

When did that boy grow up? Today he had grown to such heights that he appeared to touch the sky. And Ma? She was still rooted to the ground, where she had always been. Ma had felt envious then, and she felt envious now. But to whom was her envy directed? This man who was standing here, the one she called Miabhai? It occurred to Ma then that he was a man she did not know at all.

After the war of 1971, Ma turned to the peer once again. Amirullah had not run anywhere to hide; he had remained perfectly safe in the city. He even befriended a few Biharis. He had left India to come here only because it was a Muslim country. If Pakistan itself broke in two, what was the point in staying on? It was with the peer's blessings that some of his followers attacked ten Hindu houses in Noumahal and set them on fire, shouting, "Allah hu Akbar!" When they did that, the peer patted their backs reassuringly and said, "There is nothing wrong with doing this. This is simply an effort to save Islam from its enemies."

Ma was not entirely clear about what this "effort" involved. However, since she was the peer's disciple, and no disciple should ever doubt what the leader said or did, Ma did not ask any questions that could potentially hurt or upset him. She just waited for the next directive and accepted it without protest. This involved buying plain white cloth and making herself a few long salwars and kamiz. She would give up wearing saris and wear these new clothes from now on, she declared. Peer Amirullah had told them quite clearly, "All women must dress the way the Prophet's wives did." No one was allowed to grow their hair. Everyone — male and female — was to keep their hair at shoulder length. Ma's hair was not thick, although she braided a tassel onto it to make it appear so, but it was long enough for her to sit on. She took a pair of scissors and snipped it off. With her hair now reaching only her shoulders, she donned a loose-fitting salwar and kamiz, and draped an urna over her chest. She no longer looked like the old, familiar Ma. "Why are you wearing these?" I asked, feeling upset.

"I will never wear saris now," Ma informed me. "That is what Hindus wear. It is a garment worn by kafir. If I wear one now, it would be a sin!"

Since she had decided to obey every command issued by Peer Amirullah, Ma forgot many things. Her childhood friend, Amala, for instance, who was a Hindu. She forgot the days when she had attended Hindu festivals with her friends and bought toys and dolls at their fairs. She had been offered sweets after Lakshmi puja at a friend's house, and, before that, stood with all the others, hand in hand, to watch Durga puja. She even forgot that when I had cut my own long, rippling hair so that it went only a little way below my neck she had thrashed me black and blue. "What have you done to your beautiful hair? I have taken such good care of it, I massaged it with oil and washed it regularly — what a waste!" she had ranted.

I saw that same woman change before my eyes. She stopped

joining us at the dinner table. We would all sit down to eat together, but Ma would serve herself and eat separately, sitting either on the floor or on her bed, plate in hand. What was the matter? Ma said, "It's sinful to eat at a table. Jews and Christians do that."

In our area, there were only two or three Muslim families. Everyone else was Hindu. They had several festivals throughout the year. The leaves of woodapple trees were often required for Hindu ceremonies, and since we had one our Hindu neighbors would come in through the front gate and asked if they might take some. I always said yes. They climbed the tree and took as many leaves as they wanted. They also took the blossom from a creeper over our gate. Some even plucked a few woodapples, hidden under the leaves. I had no objection to that. I never liked woodapples anyway. Sometimes, Ma made a drink from their juice and held it to my lips. I always wrinkled my nose when she did that, and pushed her hand away.

Ma had made friends with some of the girls who came to our house to collect the leaves. "Hello, what's your name?" she would ask them. "Where do you live? What does your father do? How many brothers and sisters do you have?" But now that she was visiting the peer, Ma had to put a stop to this practice. She chased out every Hindu boy or girl who came to ask for leaves, and told us: "Don't give them any more leaves for their puja. They are kafirs. It would be a sin to help them." These words made me feel terrible. "Why do you call them kafirs? I know them all, they are very good people," I protested.

Ma started counting her prayer beads. "Anyone who isn't a Muslim is a kafir — Hindus, Christians, Buddhists, all of them."

I wanted to argue. So I continued to speak, taking the precaution of moving out of her reach. "Suppose," I said, "a child was born today. The parents are Hindus or they might be Christians. The child had no say in the matter. Obviously, he or she did not *choose* to be born to those particular parents. He or she might have been born to the imam of our mosque. When he or she grows up, that innocent child will naturally learn to do what the parents teach him or her. So the child celebrates puja or Christmas. What will happen to this child in the end? Will he or she go to heaven or to hell?"

Ma's lips moved as she counted her beads. She did not answer my question. I took a couple of steps forward. "Tell me, Ma, where will he go?" I insisted.

This time, Ma replied, "If the child converts, if this child believes that Allah is one and Muhammad is His prophet, he or she will go to heaven. If not, he or she will be sent to hell."

"To hell? Why? What did the poor child do? How can he be blamed for anything?" I asked, narrowing my eyes.

"He was born in a non-Muslim household," Ma said, uttering each word succinctly, "*That's* his fault, *that's* what he must be blamed for."

I saw my chance, seized it, and shot the final arrow from my quiver: "You have often said yourself that nothing can possibly happen on this earth unless Allah wills it. So it was Allah who wanted that child to be born in a non-Muslim family. If anyone must be blamed, it should be Allah. Surely it should all be *His* fault? It's not right to put the blame on a perfectly innocent child!"

Ma reached out instantly and caught me by my hair with the same hand in which she was holding her prayer beads. "How dare you!" she fumed, pulling my hair sharply, "How *dare* you talk about Allah like that? Who has taught you all this? If I hear you talk rubbish about Allah or the Prophet just once more, I will strangle you myself. *I* brought you into this world, didn't I? So I have every right to destroy you. You have become a sinner. In fact, if I kill such a sinner, Allah will be happy with me."

I failed to see what it was that I had said that was so objectionable. I just wanted to get Ma to see that a child had no power to decide where it was born, which faith it adopted. Since that decision was made by Allah, the final responsibility regarding the child's future must also rest with Him. But Ma's list of dislikes and things she disapproved of grew so long that no matter what I did, I always appeared to be committing a sin.

One day, Ma saw me standing by the hand-pump, drinking water out of a glass. "Why are you drinking water standing up? If you do that, it means you're drinking the devil's urine," she told me. When I returned after a trip to the toilet, she examined my hands to see if they were damp or dry. If they were dry, she said, "Did you wash your hands? Hindus don't. The right place for those kafirs is hell."

There was a fragrant *hasnuhana* plant outside an east-facing window in my room. All night it spread its sweet scent, but if I tried sleeping with my head under that window, Ma would shout at me: "Why are you lying here with your feet pointing west? Don't you know that's where Kaba lies? It's a sin to point your feet at it. Go on, turn around, sleep with your head to the west."

By this time I had learned to recognize the four directions. When Ma pointed west, it suddenly occurred to me that a Hindu temple lay there. But I knew that if I mentioned it, Ma would call me the devil's advocate and, quite possibly, punch me in the back. So, rather meekly, I moved my feet away from Kaba in Mecca, although thousands of miles separated my poor feet from the holy place and, in that intervening space, lay mountains, lakes, rivers, lavatories, latrines, temples, churches — everything.

I could find no logic in Ma's religious beliefs. When I asked questions, I received some very simple answers, the gist of which was this: Allah had made humans with clay and jinns with fire. Every spirit, be it that of a human or a jinn, was one day going to be judged in the field of judgment. Where did jinns live? They remained invisible, but they were there, hiding in the air. Where did Allah live? Allah was light, the source of creation. He, too, was invisible, He lived somewhere up in the sky. But no matter where He was, He could see and hear everything.

Ma said all that but on the night of shab-e-baraat, having made bread and sweet dishes and arranging for prayers to continue all night, Ma also said, "Today, Allah is going to come down from the seventh heaven. He is going to watch closely what's going on in the world."

Before I could stop myself, I blurted out, "Ma, can't Allah see that clearly from the top of the seventh heaven? Does He have to climb down to see better?"

"Don't ask so many questions." Ma spoke through clenched teeth. "You must believe in Allah totally and without question. Allah is all-powerful. There is no one to show us the way except Him. There is no one to help us except Him. Allah is one and unique."

I had heard Peer Amirullah utter exactly the same words. Ma sounded like a parrot. There was a parrot in a cage in Grandma's house. If it saw anyone coming into the house it said, "A guest, a guest! Bring food, bring food!" Aunt Runu had taught it to utter those words. Once it had learned them, it stopped speaking on its own. All it ever said were the words it had been taught.

Ma did not stop simply at repeating what she had heard from the peer. She tried constantly to impose her beliefs on her children, particularly on me. She was desperate to indoctrinate me, although she did say, every now and then, "You must choose your own path. My job is to guide you, give you advice, and that's what I am doing.

When Allah asks you on Judgment Day, 'Did anyone ever tell you about me?' you'll have to admit that someone did, won't you? The truth is that what I tell you about Allah and the Prophet is something Allah wants to tell you, He just uses me as his medium."

Sometimes Ma tested my memory by asking me to repeat *naseehat,* the words of Allah, that she and Sultan Ustadji had taught me. "Can you recite the *kalma-e-taiyab*?" she would ask, her tone quite gentle. My reply always came at once: *"La ilaha illalahu Muhammadur Rasoolullah."*

As soon as I finished speaking, Ma would throw her second question at me, *"Kalma shahadat?"*

"Ash-hadu aan lailaha illalahu wahadahu la sharikalahu wa ash-hadu anna Muhammadan abduhu wa Rasooluhu."

The words simply rolled off my tongue, although they hardly made any sense. It was as if I was merely reciting a well-known nursery rhyme.

Ma's lips spread in a smile at my quick response. However, those same lips did not take long to shrink and set in a thin line when I asked her, "You keep saying Allah made us humans with clay. But where's the clay in our body? All we have is skin, and flesh under our skin, and bones under the flesh!"

Ma pursed her dark lips, making them look even darker. The gentleness in her voice disappeared. She spoke harshly. "You think the clay Allah has used is the same that you get to see on this earth?"

That reminded me of what Uncle Sharaf did on occasion. He would scratch my arm, then point at the white mark his nails left on my skin and say, "Look, that's the clay. There's your proof that Allah has made us with clay."

The thought made me fall silent, sudden doubts surfacing in my mind. Perhaps it was true that, on the top layer of seven heavens, there was a different kind of soil, different kind of clay. How could anyone know for sure? Ma found me lost in thought, and said, "There is no end to Allah's divine powers. It is all around you, but you must watch and learn patiently. For instance, just think of . . . a green coconut!" Ma stopped for a moment to cast an awed glance at the coconut trees in our courtyard. Then she started again. "Allah has filled it with such tasty milk! Would a single human have the power to fill a coconut with milk? Then think of sugarcane. It's only a stick, but a stick with a sweet drink in it!"

Ma's admiring glance swept over all the other trees in our court-yard. "Then there's jackfruit," she went on. "How beautifully the little segments have been made! Could a human create a jackfruit? Never. Allah has given so many different fruits to His servants." Her eyes rested on pomegranates. "Look at those! Allah packed every little piece with sweetness. How did He do it? Who but Allah has the power to create anything?"

Ma's description of Allah's powers stumped me completely. Ma calmed down when I stopped asking questions but her eyes brimmed with pity for me.

One day, just as Ma was about to leave for Amirullah's house, her whole body hidden under a burkha, I asked her, "Ma, why do women have to wear a burkha?"

At that moment, one of Ma's feet was on the bottom front step, the other on the ground. She dragged the latter back onto the step and answered my question. I noticed that her eyes were lined with kohl. "It is to protect our chastity," she told me. "Allah has said that any man from the outside world who is not a close relative of a woman must not see any portion of her body. It's a sin to do so."

I climbed down a couple of steps. "Why has Allah not asked men to wear burkhas? What if their bodies are seen by the outside world?" I inquired.

Ma's gray eyes began glowing ominously, like two balls of fire. "You *must* learn to obey what Allah has said. He has ordered women to wear burkhas. He said nothing about men. You must accept that without question. It is a sin to question and to doubt."

Sin, sin, sin! I took three steps backward. No matter what I did, or where I went, I appeared to be in some danger of sinning. It was a sin to turn left. And if I turned right, I sinned again. I couldn't ask questions. But then, there was my math teacher in school to consider. What *he* said was quite different. Every time he wrote out a sum on the blackboard, he said, "If you have a question, ask it. One who doesn't ask questions cannot grasp mathematics." What on earth was I to do?

Grandpa's threats were different. Sinners were to be given the fruit of the *yakkum* tree. It tasted so awful that one would throw up instantly, bringing up the entire contents of one's stomach. Grandpa was the first person in my life to mention the yakkum tree.

"What does the tree look like, Grandpa?"

"It's full of thorns, just thorns!" Grandpa shuddered. Could it be like prickly cactus? Perhaps. It was my belief that Grandpa had tasted the fruit of this yakkum tree at least once in his life and had found it so terrible that he had no wish to taste it ever again.

Since his return from the hajj, Grandpa had started to describe the food in heaven. He spoke with his eyes closed, as if he could picture all that heavenly food spread before him. A smile of supreme contentment hovered on his lips. "Aha!" he said. "The food in heaven is so superb that if you eat it once, even your belch will carry a wonderful smell!" It seemed to me that it was the lure of eating the delicious food in heaven — and belching afterward — that prompted Grandpa to do his namaz five times a day. The day he returned from the hajj, everyone in the house surrounded him, as if he had returned from a meeting with Allah Himself. As Grandpa described his visit, sometimes he spoke with a smile; at other times strong emotions moved him to tears. He told us how he had gone around Kaba and kissed the black stone called Hajr e Aswad. It had turned black from having absorbing all of mankind's sins. Then Grandpa had thrown his shoes at a mountain, shaved his head, and worn loose robes instead of sewn clothes.

A large number of our neighbors had turned up to see Grandpa. Sulekha's mother remarked, "Oh, if a man can do hajj, all his sins are forgiven. You are such a lucky man!"

I was only a small girl, sitting on the floor with my legs outstretched. I should not have poked my nose into what the grown-ups were saying, but I did. "Those who do wrong things, those who kill, say those policemen who shot Mintu . . . would Allah forgive their sins as well?"

"Yes. He forgives every sinner," Grandpa deigned to answer the little girl.

I remembered something I had heard Ma say: "There are various types of sins. The worst of them is called *kabira*. *That* sin is never forgiven." Now, I found myself asking, "Even kabira?"

This time, Grandpa made no reply. Thoroughly displeased, Ma rose from the circle that had formed around Grandpa and dragged me out by my arm, taking me to the hand-pump. "Phulbahari filled that bucket a long time ago. Go on, have your bath," she ordered.

I picked up a metal pot and began taking the cold water out of the bucket to pour over my head. Many of us had to bathe by the hand-pump. Grandma and her grown-up daughters had their shower in the bathroom, which doubled up as a urinal. The structure had no roof, and proper walls on only three sides. The fourth wall was half built. A curtain hung over the empty portion. In one corner of our own courtyard stood a similar structure, which was roofless and without a door. Its purpose was the same. Its floor was stained yellow with urine.

Since the hand-pump was in Grandma's courtyard, most of the children went there to bathe. Only Baba had his bath in the bathroom with the stained floor. Phulbahari left a bucket of water there very early in the morning. The hand-pump in Grandma's house was a recent acquisition. Before it was installed, we used the well water to bathe and wash our clothes. Even our drinking water came from the well. When the government provided a tap on the main road, we sent our maid out to bring drinking water in a pitcher. When Ma was a small girl, they drank the water from the pond. At that time, no one was allowed to bathe or wash their clothes in it.

Things had changed. There were a lot of differences between Ma's times and my own, I thought. While I was having my bath, rubbing a bar of scented soap all over my body, the smell of jackfruit suddenly reached me, rising over the scent of the soap. The fruit on Grandma's tree had ripened in the heat. Its smell triggered a funny sensation. I could feel something slimy slide down my throat. The first time I had tried to eat jackfruit, a juicy segment had stuck in my throat; I had to retch several times to bring it out. After that, Ma would squeeze its juice and gave it to me, mixing it with milk and chira. That removed any risk of it sticking in my throat, but I could not stand the smell. Ma told me to hold my nose with one hand, drink with the other. I had to laugh at her suggestion. It was like being asked to sit in our lavatory, where I had to hold my nose to block the stench.

While I was soaping I looked at the stray dog sitting in the court-yard breathing with its mouth open, red tongue hanging out.

Having finished soaping, I poured more water over myself and said to the dog, "You want to go to Mecca to do hajj? All your sins will be wiped off. Even kabira." Some of my bathwater fell on the dog, but it did not bark. It rose quietly instead, shook off the water, and left. In Grandpa's room, those still sitting around him were being offered holy water from Mecca. Grandma had rushed back to the kitchen to make *chitoi pitha,* her husband's favorite cake.

Uncle Siddique went to Karachi in an airplane the same month that Grandpa returned from the hajj. He sent us a photo: He was riding a horse; a hat was on his head, and he was wearing a suit. Grandma had the photo framed and hung it beside the bamboo pole that acted as her bank.

Some of our neighbors turned up to look at that photo, among them Sulekha's mother. She took a paan from Grandma's box, stuffed her mouth with it, then used a finger to take extra lime and put it on her tongue. She then went out, spat some of the paan juice out in the courtyard, and returned to the room. Finally, she pulled one end of her sari over her head, using her right hand to bring it farther forward, remembering not to use the lime-stained finger, and looked around to make sure that there was no one else in the room. She whispered into Grandma's ear: "I hear Siddique has become a Communist! This job that he has got abroad . . . well, that's a Communist's job, too!"

Before she started visiting Amirullah, Ma hardly ever spoke of hell, the snakes, or the scorpions; nor did she take a long time to finish her namaz. If she heard Baba or any of my brothers return, or the sound of a plate or a glass being dropped and broken in the kitchen, she did only the first part of her namaz, and then rose from her prayer mat, rolling it up, without bothering to read the final prayers. Now if Ma happened to be praying, she would not rise, even if a hurricane swept through the house. She offered every prayer, even though it was not necessary to do so. Then she did *monajat,* praying with her palms joined and raised, never bringing them down until she was satisfied that she had poured her heart and soul into praying and felt confident that Allah would hear everything and save her from being bitten by snakes and scorpions.

I could not get the story of snakes and scorpions out of my mind. The scene that rose before my eyes was this: Hell was a huge pit. A fire burned in it, snakes and scorpions were biting and stinging people, and Allah, white-faced, white-bearded, wearing white pajamas, a panjabi, and a white cap, was looking down on them, a stick in his hand, laughing uproariously. By this time, I had seen a few films. Ma had taken me, and we were taken to two by our school. One was called *Darshan,* the other was *Kabuliwala.* I saw that, in films, the villains enjoyed causing others pain. I thought Allah was a villain, because there was always so much talk about the pain He was going to inflict, but I did not dare tell Ma that. I did, however, snap my fingers dismissively and say, "If snake charmers went to hell, they'd be able to control all the snakes, wouldn't they? Haven't you seen how they handle them? They can get their snakes to obey every command." At the time, I was doing very well in school, studying not just literature but also science and other subjects, getting good marks, and moving ahead in class. I also devoured books that were not part of the school curriculum, books that my two brothers hid under their pillows.

When Ma ordered me to do my namaz, I washed my hands and feet at the hand-pump, covered my head, bowed, bent my knees, knelt down as required, and muttered the Arabic words I had been taught without understanding their meaning at all. I asked Ma, "My teachers in school tell me not to memorize anything without learning what it means. It is only the stupid students who learn their lessons by heart, and write them out word for word. Intelligent students grasp the meaning of a lesson, then write what they've learned in their *own* words. In this case, Ma, if we prayed in Bengali instead of Arabic, why would that matter? Why do we pray namaz in Arabic, the language we don't know? Doesn't Allah understand Bengali?"

"Shut up, you talk too much!" Ma hissed in fury. "Don't give me more grief, please. How I'd hoped that my girl, born on a holy day, would turn out to be virtuous, would do her namaz and roja. But . . ." her voice trailed away. She avoided my question altogether.

Of late, she started to *zikir*, meditate, alone in her dark room, saying Allah hu, Allah hu in a deep voice and shaking her head from side to side. The sound had to come from somewhere deep inside her body; it was not sufficient to speak in a normal voice. For hours on end, Ma continued to do this. Allah hu! Allah hu! The whole house reverberated with the sound. Frightened by it, our cat ran out and sat on the high compound wall. The dog started barking. Still, Ma would not stop. She was convinced that those who used this form of prayer grew wings and could fly from this world into another where, beyond the seventh heaven, there was no one but Allah and His favorite followers, those who prayed in a similar fashion. Allah would place a finger under the chin of this follower, tilt her head upward, and plant a long kiss on her mouth. His action would so move His follower that she would faint instantly.

At times, to Ma, Allah's appearance seemed very similar to that of Amirullah. At other times, He looked like one of the teachers, one who had lived in her house for free when she was a girl. Or He looked like Sultan Ustadji, dressed in a long robe. Ma shook her head firmly. No, Allah could not possibly look like her Huzur in Noumahal, or any of her teachers. Allah was without a definite form. The more He appeared in her mind looking like someone she knew, the more fiercely she shook her head, trying to banish the thought. The poor cat continued to sit on the wall.

One evening Baba returned unexpectedly and heard the noise. He had to look around a bit before he found its source. Then he came to my room and, for once, said something that did not start with his favorite Sanskrit saying, *"Chhatranam adhyanang tapah"* (The pursuit of knowledge is the only meditation for a student). Instead, he said, with one hand resting on his waist, and the other thrust into his pocket, "Has your mother gone mad? What the hell is she doing?"

I was, at that moment, reading Rabindranath's play, *The Post Office*. It had to be hidden quickly under my geography book. With my eyes fixed on a picture of the Bay of Bengal, I replied, "Ma is doing zikir, the special prayer."

"That woman is simply obsessed with the thought of going to heaven! Who has ever said that if you ignore your family and your duties in the house, Allah is going to be pleased with you? You remember the poet who said that heaven and hell exist right here on this earth, one doesn't have to travel anywhere after death to find either?"

Baba moved closer to my desk. I held the geography book tightly, so that Baba couldn't see, through even the smallest gap, the one I had hidden under it.

"Pay attention to your studies," Baba began his speech once more. "The only thing worth having in life is knowledge. What you learn today will always remain with you; it's not something anyone can take away. I had to work very hard to get an education. After school, I had to take the cows out to graze, then at night, I did my studies by the light of an oil lamp. I stood first in my class. I have made sure that each of you can devote yourselves to your studies. Pay attention to your lessons, so that you, too, may stand first. Read everything thoroughly, from the first page of every book to the last."

I could offer Baba nothing but silence after his speech.

Ma finally finished her prayer and emerged from her dark room into light. Her swollen eyes, blunt nose, dark lips, and sunken cheeks glowed with satisfaction.

When I heard Baba go out of the room, I brought the hidden book out once more. There was a time when Ma, too, would have scolded me for reading what was not a part of the school text. Today she did not even glance at my books. In her eyes, anything written about the temporary life on this earth — be it in a schoolbook, or somewhere else — was not worth reading.

Smiling to herself, Ma walked a little unsteadily toward the rose-bush in our courtyard. She began stroking the flowers. Thorns pricked her hand, but she did not seem to mind. Her smile broadened; little balls of flesh gathered over her cheekbones. If I raised my eyes from my book, I could look straight out the open door and see the court-yard. Ma among the roses. The cat had climbed down from the wall, and Ma was still smiling. Her smile made me think of the sudden bright streak a running deer must create in a dark forest. I could no longer stay indoors. Ma's smile dragged me out to the rosebush.

"What is it, Ma? Why are you stroking these roses?"

Ma replied at once: "Look, what a rich, red shade Allah has given these flowers! Their petals are so soft, arranged in layers, each of the same size, not a single one is smaller or larger. What a beautiful scent they have, too. Could a human being ever create such a flower? Allah has given us so much!"

Ma seemed totally overwhelmed, as if this was the first time she had seen or smelled a flower, as if she had realized only today that it was Allah who had created every object on this earth. "Each flower is different from the other," she went on, "and so is their scent. The same goes for the leaves on different trees, and all the fruit. Not one is identical to the other. What mighty powers Allah has!"

Ma raised her eyes from the flowers and looked at me, but it was not really my face that she saw. What she saw was the power of the Creator, who had given my face its specific shape and features. Then her eyes moved from my face to the sky, and she found further evidence of the might of the Almighty. Ma's smile turned positively beatific; she was now far above this ordinary, mundane world.

By this time it was quite dark. Ma returned inside the house, said another prayer, then stood at the door to each room, and blew. This was supposed to drive away all trouble. But today that would not happen, for dark clouds had started to gather in the sky, forming ominous black masses that crashed against each other amid the noise of thunder. A storm was beginning without warning. Coconut fronds flew in the air as freely as the hair of a young girl running through an open field. Branches from the jamun tree broke and fell on top of the guava, branches of the guava tree tangled with the mango. Fresh mango blossom rained down on the courtyard. Tin roofs of smaller houses blew off and landed on our jackfruit tree. Our woodapple and *champa* trees were uprooted.

When this happened Ma wailed and appealed to her lord: "Stop this storm, O Allah!" But her plea did not reach Allah at the top of the seventh heaven, even though Ma was a woman who did her namaz five times a day, read the Koran, wore her hair at the appropriate length, dressed like the wives of the Prophet, and was about to be given a ticket to heaven. The sound of her wail rose up to the second, or at most the third or the fourth layer, then it dropped, with a thud, on top of the raging storm. Yasmin, Moni, and I shut all our doors and windows and, frightened by the noise and fury of the storm, clung to Ma in the hope that she would contact Allah and put a stop to it. Ma began praying again and then suddenly, to my complete amazement, stopped abruptly and said, "Who knows where your father is? Noman, Kamal! Where are they?"

Ma sounded like the old Ma we all knew, worried and anxious about her husband and children. It seemed as if the storm had destroyed the woman who had ceased to care about her family. Putting her forehead on the floor Ma said, 'Wherever they are, please save them, I am begging you Allah.'"

The storm stopped much later, and my heart told me that neither Ma nor Allah had anything to do with it. At first I failed to understand why my heart should tell me such a thing. I would search in its depths for a reason, but would find nothing.

Almost a year later, the following April, long after this *kaal-boishakhi* storm in May, I would find an answer. It would take me that long to find a Bengali translation of the Koran in Ma's cupboard and read it, since I had always wanted to learn the meaning of the prayers one offered: *sura fateha, soora neesa, lahab, ekhlas.* I would see the lines in Bengali, printed under the Arabic, like a face under a mask.

Outside, the sun was scorching. The whole neighborhood was sleeping that hot afternoon. Rocket, our dog, was sleeping on the veranda, his legs outstretched. Even the trees and the plants seemed to sleep, their branches hanging lazily. Moni was sleeping in the shade of the woodapple tree, on the bottom step of the stairs going up to the roof. A bucketful of wet clothes still stood by her side; they had not been spread out to dry. I was holding the Bengali translation of the Koran in one hand and a little ball of tamarind in the other, which I was licking from time to time. The words I read froze my blood. "The moon has its own light," it said. "The earth always stands still. If it does not lean on one side, it is because all the mountains, acting like nails, are holding it in place."

I read these words over and over, first tilting my neck to the left, then tilting it to the right. How was this possible? How could anyone say such things? As far as I knew, the earth did *not* stand still. It moved around the sun.

What the Koran said was wrong. Or was what I had been taught in school wrong?

I felt very confused.

Was there no such thing as gravity? Was the earth really held in place by mountains? But my science books had told me that the earth rotated once every twenty-four hours. That meant it was moving all the time!

Which was true? Science, or the Koran?

The tamarind remained in my hand — I forgot to eat it. Completely taken aback, I sat on the floor with outstretched legs, the book open on my knees. Strong gusts of hot wind came in through the open windows, making the blue curtains flutter, lifting my hair and the pages of the book. My mind also took flight. It rose higher and higher in the sky, getting larger and larger, while my body seemed to shrink to the point of completely ceasing to exist. I remained where I was, like a dot, helpless and immobile. The sound of a dove calling in the distance brought me back to my senses. My eyes began to move once more, and I read on: Man's female companion has been created out of one of his ribs. One of the bones in a woman's neck is crooked. That is the reason why no woman thinks straight, or walks on a straight path. Women are like a field for growing crops; the men are totally free to cultivate whenever they like. If a woman is disobedient, her husband has the right to drive her away from his bed, then he may try to talk some sense into her, but if she remains disobedient, he can beat her. Women can claim only one-third of any property owned by their fathers. Men can claim two-thirds. Men can take one, two, three, even four wives. Women may have only one husband. Men can divorce their wives simply by uttering the word *talaq* three times. Women are not allowed to seek a divorce at all. When acting as witnesses to an event, two women are counted as one witness, whereas every single man is seen as a complete witness.

In all of this, I was prepared to make allowances for what was said about the earth and the moon. All right, *I* was in no position to say for sure whether the moon had its own source of light, or whether the earth moved or remained still. I had seen nothing for myself. But how could there be such differences between men and women? Once, Chhotda and I had peered into the room of a medical student in our neighborhood and seen a human skeleton. Chhotda had told me that it could have been either a man or a woman's; it was impossible to tell. There were 206 bones in the human body. My teachers in school said the same thing. I could spot no difference between Dada's neck and mine. His was as straight as mine. He jerked his head from side to side sometimes, making cracking noises. Then he would stretch his whole body, and some of the bones in his back would creak. And he did not stop there, either. There were times when he pushed me against a wall and pressed my neck. The bones in *my* neck made the same noise. As for ribs, I had as many as he. Ma had as many as Baba. Strictly speaking, Baba ought to have one less, since Ma was supposed to have been made from it. What if a man had four wives? Would he lose four ribs? I could not believe it. Grandpa had married a second woman and lived with her for a couple of weeks. Was she, too, made from one of Grandpa's ribs?

Why should anyone need two women to act as *one* witness, when the word of a single man was considered sufficient? Didn't women speak the truth? Only men were honest and truthful? Was Uncle Sharaf honest? When Aunt Jhunu's earrings went missing, Uncle Sharaf had denied stealing them. In the end, they were found tied in the knot in his lungi. The knot became loose in his sleep, and the earrings slipped out. Grandma found them and kept them safe. When he woke up and realized what had happened, he promptly ran out of the house. He was persuaded to return only when promises were made that no one would beat him.

Why could men claim more than women in the matter of parental property? Why this injustice? What gave Dada an extra share in

Baba's property? I was Baba's child as much as Dada. The only difference was in the genital region: Dada's organ was long, mine was flat. Ma often bemoaned the fact that Dada had no brains at all. Yet he was entitled to an extra share only because he had a penis and I didn't.

How could the Koran — a book so holy that it had to be kissed before it could be lifted or replaced on the shelf — speak of such discrimination? I could scarcely believe it. To tell the truth, I did not want to believe it. It was true that I was not particularly enthusiastic about reading from the Koran, but it had never occurred to me that what it said could be wrong or unfair. So, even Allah was not prepared to treat women equally? Was Allah no different from Getu's father? He used to beat Getu's mother because she did not obey his every command. The day the whole of Akua had trembled at the sound of Getu's mother's screams; I had run behind Uncle Felu, passed through a bamboo grove, and finally reached her courtyard. Plenty of others were already there. Getu's father was portly, had small eyes sunk behind fat cheeks, and a crew cut. He made a living selling yogurt and buttermilk across from the local sweets shop. When we found him, he was standing in the middle of the courtyard, his lungi raised up to his knees, his torso bare, sweating profusely, his sweat dripping onto the ground.

"You stupid bitch, who do you think you are, eh?" he was ranting. "First you forget to put any salt in my food, and then you have the cheek to argue!" As he spoke those words, he kicked his wife in her stomach, her back, her face; then, still not satisfied, he brought out a burning log from the kitchen and struck her with it. Her skin crackled as the log left burn marks all over her body, and Getu's mother writhed like a headless chicken. The onlookers were standing idly by, some with their arms resting on their stomachs, others with their arms entwined behind their backs. Some had interlocked their fingers and were resting the back of their heads on their palms. There were women, too. Some had covered their mouth with their right hand, their left hand clutching their right elbow. Others were standing with one arm on their waist, the other hanging loosely. Their eyes, however, were not idle. Every eye took in every detail of Getu's father's strength, and watched the blood gushing out of his wife's nose, mouth, and head.

What Getu's father did next was more impressive. It made everyone supporting his head or clutching her waist drop their arms.

Now those arms simply hung uselessly, the fingers looking like tiny, young bananas, not yet wholly formed. Surrounded by his audience, Getu's father spoke triumphantly, as if he had just won a war: "I want a divorce. I give you talaq, you bitch, and talaq, and talaq again!"

The headless chicken was not moving anymore, nor crying out in pain. But the eyes in the courtyard were still curious, hungry for more. Getu's mother's clothes were tattered, her dry, sun-bleached reddish hair disheveled and smeared with mud.

The show was over. One by one, the eyes, the legs, and the arms began moving away, as they always did when the curtain came down after the final climax in a film. What was left behind was the little hut, a creeper going up to its roof that would later bear gourds, a small courtyard, wiped clean with a mixture of water and cow dung, and in a corner, Getu's mother, just divorced. Like the others, Uncle Felu began moving away and so did I.

Once the drama was over, everyone found their tongue and began talking as they left: Well, she didn't put any salt in his food, so naturally he lost his temper. What else could he do? That woman was always lazy, she shirked her work. Now she'll pay for it.

She was proud, too. She did not serve her husband properly. Very snooty, didn't do as she was told. She asked for it.

Getu's mother eventually rose, left the empty stage, and spent the rest of the day sitting by the pond, crying. No crowd gathered around to watch her. Only I stared at the pond through the window, resting my chin on the windowsill. The recent rains had made the pond overflow. Getu's mother used to sit on its steps, wash her clothes, then wash herself with the same soap and bathe in the pond. After her bath, she used to return home in her wet clothes, clutching in her hand the others she had washed, the water wrung from them.

The same steps were now empty. Getu's mother was no longer washing her husband's lungis, or Getu's dirty quilts. The pond was the same as before, as were the fish in it, but Getu's mother was not the same. She sat looking like a termite mound.

Ma snapped at me and got me to move from the window. "This girl has to stare at all the low-class people, all the time!" Ma said. In Grandma's house, everyone referred to the people who lived in the slum as "low class." Those who lived in big houses were "upper class." If any of them visited Grandma they were offered the best upholstered chairs. Kheer was made with vermicelli in it, and served hot on nice plates. They ate with spoons. When they finished, glasses were filled with water from the hand-pump and placed at their disposal. After that, they had tea and, with it, glucose biscuits. If members from the lower classes turned up, they sat on the floor. No one offered them kheer on a plates, or tea and biscuits.

Only a week after divorcing his wife, Getu's father remarried. His new wife was little more than a child. When Ma heard the news, she remarked, "Getu's father is a horrible man. He divorced his first wife for no reason at all."

Phulbahari's husband lived with his four wives. Ma said the same thing about him: "That husband of Phulbahari's is as bad as the devil. He's married so *many* times!"

What she had to say about Baba was no different. He, too, was bad and wicked. He might marry Razia Begum one day. But wasn't it wrong of Ma to say this? Wasn't it Allah who had given a man complete freedom to divorce his wife whenever he liked, marry another when it took his fancy — one, two, three, four times? And wasn't one supposed to accept blindly everything Allah had ever said? These men whom Ma abused so harshly had simply done what they were allowed to do; they had not broken a single rule set by Allah. Didn't Ma realize she was actually questioning Allah, thereby committing a foul sin herself?

The Koran lay open on my knee. The hot breeze kept fluttering its pages and the curtains. My soft, thin hair blew in that breeze. I felt as if I had chanced upon a hidden treasure. I had seen, secretly, a pitcher full of gold coins, and a snake was coiled around it to guard its contents. At least, I thought that the pitcher was full of gold. But was it? What if it was empty? An empty pitcher made more noise than a full one, didn't it?

~ 8 ~

The Culture

Ma seldom took her meals with us. She would eat what was left over after she had fed everyone else. If we had chicken curry, all the best pieces were gone by the time she sat down. She got only the bones. After she finished, what little remained went to our servants. It didn't matter if nothing was left, because a separate meal was cooked for them anyway. We had fish and meat and other tasty stuff. Our maids had thin, runny dal and dried fish. This was the normal practice; I had seen it in Grandma's house as well. Grandma ate only after Grandpa had had his lunch and all the children had eaten. The maids got to eat afterward. Usually, they simply had rice soaked overnight in water, eating it with a little salt and green chilies, or they mixed it with dal that had gone off, which none of us would touch.

While we were eating, Ma didn't allow any of our maids to stand nearby, because they could cast an evil eye. One night when I was seven years old, my stomach really started hurting. Ma said, "I have noticed Phulbahari gawking at you when you eat. You've caught her evil eye." She ran to Grandma's house, got three paan leaves, and smeared them with mustard oil. Then she stroked my stomach with each of them, one by one, muttering, something like, "Out you get, evil eye, blow with the wind all the while!" Then she pierced each leaf with a pin and burned it over the oil lamp. "There, all the evil has been burned now!" she declared.

"What's an evil eye, Ma? What does it mean?" I asked.

Ma replied, "Some people have evil in their eyes, in their glance. Once a woman came to our house begging. She stood in the court-yard, looked at our papaya tree, and said, 'Look, you've got so many fresh papayas!' Would you believe it, that tree fell down the minute she stepped out of the door! No one shook it, there was no storm, not even a strong breeze — it simply keeled over, just like that. I'm sure when Phulbahari saw you eating, she thought, 'Oh, how lucky Nasrin is, she gets so much to eat!' There must have been envy in her eyes. That's evil."

The ache ebbed soon after the paan leaves were burned, although it must be admitted that Baba had given me some medicine in the meantime. Ma remained convinced that, if I felt better, it was only because she had the evil eye fobbed off.

There were three women in Akua who, according to Ma, were notorious for their evil eyes. If they looked at a tree, it died. And if they looked at a man, he became so violently ill that death seemed imminent. People shut their doors and hid behind them if they saw any of those women approaching. However, when two of Grandma's trees began to look as if they were dying, it was one of them who had to be approached to cast a spell on a bucket of water, and it was that special water that helped the trees survive.

Grandma's mother — my great-grandmother — was known for her bananas. If a woman was bitten by a dog, she would place a pill inside the banana and get the stricken woman to eat it. No one knew what went into that pill. It looked like a peppercorn, but it ensured that when the woman had a baby she produced a human child, not a puppy. After taking that pill, the woman was told not to eat bananas for the next three months. That was the only restriction placed on her, and it was a small price to pay to ensure that no puppies popped out of her belly.

Some others believed in water-from-seven-ponds. They collected a handful of water from seven different ponds and gave it to whoever was bitten by a dog. It cured people of hydrophobia, and women, in particular, continued to produce human babies.

When a dog bit me my great-grandmother was long dead, so no one gave me either a banana with a magic pill in it or water from seven different ponds. What Baba gave me were injections, but that did not stop Uncle Sharaf from clapping his hands and shouting, "There's a puppy in your belly. Ha ha ha!"

This worried me no end. I used to press my stomach from time to time to see if a puppy was growing inside me. Uncle Sharaf did not leave it at that. If I happened to swallow the seed inside a plum, he would say, "Well now, a plum tree is going to grow inside you. Its branches will burst through your head one day!" This made me check my head every day to see if I could feel a branch or a twig cracking open my skull.

There was more. If my head accidentally knocked against someone else's, I was supposed to knock it again — deliberately this time — or else a pair of horns would shoot out of my head. I knew this, but once when my head knocked against Uncle Fakrul's while we were at the hand-pump, I made no attempt to knock it a second time. Uncle Fakrul had probably not even realized that it was my head that his own had struck, not the handle of the hand-pump. He happened to be squatting by it at the time, rubbing soap into his hair. The lather was all over his face and his eyes were closed. I arrived at this moment to fill a jug of water, and the collision took place.

I spent the whole evening looking into a mirror to see if horns were going to make an appearance, but nothing happened. I told Uncle Sharaf about my fears, which gave him the chance to tease me every day after that. "Those horns will come, sooner or later; oh yes, they will!" he kept saying. Much to my relief, they didn't.

After his bath one evening, Uncle Fakrul wore a freshly washed lungi and shirt and was standing by the well, staring hard at a pile of jute stalks. Ma asked him what so attracted him in that pile, to which he replied, "Oh, nothing. It's just that I was wondering, if that whole pile was set on fire, how would it burn? I'd like to see it."

Ma raised her voice and called out to Grandma. "Listen to this, Ma! Do you know what Fakrul wants to do? He'd like to set fire to that pile of jute!" Grandma was in the kitchen, making tea and toast for all the grown-ups. That day, just as it started to get dark, those jute stalks did catch fire. Everyone started looking for Uncle Fakrul. It turned out that he was not home, having gone for a walk soon after tea. Grandma decided not to waste any more time investigating the crime. It was far more important to put the fire out, so she drew bucket after bucket of water from the well and threw it on the fire. It didn't work. The fire crackled and the flames rose as high as the top branches of a coconut tree. The plants near the well were all burned. By the time Uncle Fakrul returned, the worst was over. He looked openly dismayed. "Oh no!" he cried. "I had so wanted to see it burn, and I had to be out when it happened!"

The blame fell on Phulbahari. Uncle Tutu swore he had seen her smoking by the well. She must have thrown her bidi stub into the pile of jute stalks. Ma threatened to beat her to a pulp, and she was forbidden to smoke in the house. Phulbahari stopped smoking for a while, but later she started again, sitting on the veranda attached to the kitchen.

One morning, in San Souci, I suddenly thought of Phulbahari as I was brushing my teeth with powdered coal. By this time I was a little older and had graduated from shorts to long salwars. The thought of Phulbahari brought back many other memories. She was dark and her face pockmarked. Whenever something went wrong, she was invariably held responsible. I began to feel sorry for her. She used to make a special sweet in winter — *bhaapa pithey* — stuffing it with gur made from dates, wrapping it in a piece of fine cotton, and steaming it. When it was ready, I could see the steam rise through the cotton. After we left Grandma's house, winter came and went every year, but no one made bhaapa pithey. Today, on this misty morning, all of a sudden, my heart longed for that sweet. Then it occurred to me that it was not just Phulbahari's pithey that was missing in our new house. Rather, it was virtually everything else that had made the cold winter mornings so enjoyable at Grandma's. None of us drank date juice anymore, or gathered white flowers from under *shiuli* trees. Ma used to place cotton shawls around us, tying a knot behind our necks. Each of us had suddenly become modern. We now spent winter mornings inside, wearing thick woolen sweaters and having bread and eggs for breakfast.

Moni brought a jug of water for me to use after I finished cleaning my teeth. I hadn't asked her to do this for me, but she did it. Phulbahari was just the same. If I started hiccuping, she would quietly hand me a glass of water. If I stumbled and fell, she used to come running to pick me up and stroke my knees and toes. Moni did not look like Phulbahari, but worked just as silently, providing what I needed even before I could ask for it.

How did they do it? Women like Moni and Phulbahari were always up early to sweep the courtyard. Then they made breakfast and served it at the table. When breakfast was over, they washed the dirty dishes. While I was getting dressed for school, they brought me my shoes and helped me put them on. If I left my clothes strewn all over my room, they picked them up and folded them neatly. If my clothes were dirty, they washed them. At night, they made the bed and tied the mosquito net, tucking it in securely.

Live-in servants went to sleep long after their employers did, having eaten the leftovers and washed all the dishes. They slept on the floor and didn't have mosquito nets. In the morning the mosquito bites on their faces made them look as if they had measles. On cold winter nights they had to make do with torn old quilts — no one gave them blankets. This was the accepted practice. I, too, got used to it and started slapping or punching them when it suited me. If I went anywhere in a rickshaw with them, they sat at my feet. Even if there was room to sit next to me, they were not allowed to do so.

They were given a new set of clothes and shoes only once a year. Baba bought them the cheapest clothes he could find. The soaps they used were also the cheapest, and they had to massage their hair with soybean oil. Coconut oil was bought only for us.

When I sat down at night to study they fanned me throughout to keep the mosquitoes away. If I wanted a glass of water, they ran and got it for me. None of us ever had to pour a glass of water out of a jug — we were used to being handed one. It seemed that they were born only to serve their masters. They would die serving them. If they fell ill, they were treated as if it was their fault. If they died, it was simply their bad luck. They were dirty, we were clean. They were low class, we were upper class.

In school, I had learned grammar, history, geography, mathematics, and science, but the real world had taught me something entirely different. It had given me lessons in class distinction. What I had learned in books — do not be proud, do not look down upon the poor, all men are equal — came crashing down in real life. This tradition of exploiting the poor and the deprived was too old, too deep-rooted. I, too, became part of it, bound to it by an invisible chain.

Every day, as soon as I got up in the morning and washed my face, Moni brought a cup of tea to my room. I began to drink tea in the morning even before we left Grandma's house. There we used to have two breakfasts. The first, smaller one was at around seven o'clock, consisting of chira and tea. I would drop grains of chira into my tea and scoop them up with a spoon before putting them in my mouth. The bigger breakfast, served at ten o'clock, included thin chapatis with meat curry from the previous night, or fried eggs.

One day in San Souci, just as I had started sipping my tea, a commotion broke out in the kitchen. Ma was thrashing Moni, slapping and kicking her. Moni was dressed in one of my old dresses. Ma pulled it so hard that it tore. Apparently, Moni had eaten some of the meat curry from a pan and, even after being caught by Ma, had said that the cat was the culprit.

"It wasn't a cat, it was you!" Ma snarled. "You are a big thief! I give you so much to eat, but still you want more. Didn't I give you enough of that meat curry? How dare you touch it again!"

But Moni refused to admit her guilt. Ma picked up a broom and brought it down on her back with as much force as she could. "Go on, admit it now. You ate the meat, didn't you?" Ma's sari slipped from her bosom, but she paid no attention. Modesty had ceased to matter. All she wanted was to hear Moni's confession.

Moni stood absolutely still, silently accepting every blow. Tears were streaming down her cheeks and onto her chest. I could not help poking my nose into this affair. "Say it, Moni!" I urged her. "Just say you won't do it again."

This time, Moni responded. "I won't do it again!" she repeated pathetically.

Ma stopped. Then she shouted at me and told me to stay out of it. This was, in fact, a common occurrence. Moni was used to being thrashed every now and then.

The very next day, she began to tell Ma the story of her life. "I was very small then. My mother was still breast-feeding me. My sisters, Nuni and Chini, were not that much older. My father left us all one day, just like that. He went to Jamalpur to work as a mason and didn't come back. Then Ma heard that he had got married again and was living there with this other wife. He wanted a son very badly, you see. He got married a second time to get a son."

Ma dozed as Moni continued her story, deftly running her fingers through Ma's hair to look for lice, crushing any she found between her nails. "After he had three daughters, my Baba got so cross that he couldn't live with us," Moni went on. "If my Ma had had a son, Baba would not have left us. But how could she? Allah didn't give her one. Even He did not think of her. But how can I blame Allah? It was all my Baba's fault. He was a heartless wretch. How could he simply walk out on us? If I had him to look after me today, would I be working as a servant? Never. He was perfectly able to give us enough to eat."

Moni sighed, wiped her eyes on her right arm, and started again: "My Ma went to Baba's brothers for help and then to her own brothers, but everyone just shooed her out. I remember when we went to my uncle's house someone was making rice in their kitchen. It was bubbling away, and its smell . . . oh, how lovely it was! I can still smell it sometimes. No one offered us even a single plate of rice. We were so hungry that all of us started crying — Nuni, Chini, and me. Ma picked wild rice growing from the ponds and boiled that for us. Sometimes she went from door to door and begged for rice water. Each of us turned into a bag of bones. Nuni fell ill. She kept crying and asking for fish curry and rice. Who was going to give it to her? Ma prayed so hard she cried her eyes out, but Allah took no notice. Nuni died. You should have seen Ma crying when Nuni was being buried! Anyway, in the end, she started looking for work in people's houses but most women didn't want a woman with two girls. So Ma got Chini and me to start working as well. We were to end up as servants. Chini found a job in a house where the master was, well, a bad man. He used to touch her breasts. One day his wife caught him and what did she do? She got rid of Chini! It wasn't Chini's fault, was it? Ma had to start all over again to find her a job. But no lady would keep Chini in her house. They were scared. Said they didn't want a young girl. Now, finally, Chini is with a lady who lives only with her children. Her husband lives abroad."

Ma said, "It's itching on the right; you might find lice there. Look carefully." Moni began lifting Ma's hair, as instructed. "You need a fine-tooth comb," Moni said. "My Ma used to get rid of lice in our hair by using a fine-tooth comb."

Moni wore a faded old dress under which she wore torn pajamas. On only two days out of the whole year did she get to wear a pair of sandals: when we celebrated Eid. But she had to take her sandals off the next day and keep them safe to be worn the next Eid. On the morning of Eid, Moni would have a bath, put on a new dress and her sandals, and then come to us for some talcum powder. Someone would kindly put some powder on her palm, and she would go running happily to look at herself in the cracked mirror in the kitchen. She would dab all the powder on her face and reemerge, a shy smile on her heavily powdered white face. As a mark of respect, she would then touch the feet of all the adults. Immediately afterward, she would return to the kitchen and work all day helping prepare special dishes for Eid. Huge pots and pans were used to cook pulao, meat, and other delicacies. Moni spent a lot of time blowing hard into the oven to light it and keep it going. She then washed the dirty plates and utensils. Her new dress became dirty and stained, looking old even before the day ended.

Her story still not finished, she continued to look for lice and kill them. "Some people told Ma to marry again," she went on, "but Ma thought, What if the second man does the same thing, what if he leaves me, too? So she didn't try to find another husband. When I save up enough money I will go back to my village with Ma and Chini. I'll build a hut somewhere and keep hens. Those hens will lay eggs, and we can sell them in the market. We'll manage very well."

Moni's dreams floated before her eyes like a swan on a lake. Her salary was five takas a month. She had never been paid, never held the money she had earned in her hands. Ma kept every penny. When the time came for her marriage, Ma would buy a pair of gold earrings with Moni's own savings, and a nose stud, too.

This idea did not appeal to Moni. "What will I do with gold earrings?" she asked. "I might get married, but what if I cannot produce a boy? Suppose my husband throws me out of his house? No, when I leave, just give me all my money, please."

The swan in Moni's eyes flexed its neck proudly. In her dream house, her mother lived with Moni and Chini, had plates of rice with meat curry, and slept under a blue mosquito net, wrapped in quilts embroidered with fine designs. Moni hadn't learned to dream of anything bigger or better than this.

A couple of weeks later, I returned home from school and found that Ma and Baba were not home and that the girls from the neighborhood had not yet come to play. Moni, alone in the courtyard, was washing dirty pots and pans with coconut fiber and ash. Watching her, I had a sudden urge to wash some of those aluminium pans myself. It might be fun to turn the burned and blackened ones into bright and gleaming objects. I snatched the pot Moni was working on and began scrubbing it. Moni instantly turned pale. "Please," she pleaded, swallowing hard, "please don't do this. If your father found out, he'd kill me. Please go inside. Let me do my work."

"No one will know. Don't tell anyone. Come on, let's wash these quickly. Then we can play hopscotch." One of Moni's eyes began dancing with joy. The other still looked doubtful. She might have played hopscotch before, but not in this house. Servants were not allowed to play here.

"Will you really play with me? But if your mother finds out she'll beat me." Moni looked around although she knew very well there was no one at home.

"No, no one will know. When someone opens the front gate it'll make a noise, won't it? We'll stop playing at once, that's all!" I said reassuringly, looking at Moni's apprehensive eyes.

We drew squares on the ground and played hopscotch, Moni and I. A low-class girl with an upper-class one. I had never seen Moni look so happy. She seemed to have forgotten that I was her master's daughter. It was as if we were close friends, both from the same class. We were soon covered with dust. When the game was in full swing, each of us winning a few squares, the black front gate suddenly opened with its usual creak. Moni and I leaped in different directions — she toward the kitchen, I to my room. I quickly wiped out the squares on my way, then sat at my desk. Moni gathered all the plates and glasses she was supposed to have washed and ran to the hand-pump. As she hurriedly bent over the well, she dropped everything she was carrying. Glasses, plates, bowls, and cups slipped from her hands and crashed to the ground, breaking into a thousand pieces.

Ma, who had just come through the gate, witnessed this scene, the destruction of her favorite dinner set. She caught Moni by her hair and banged her head against the hand-pump. Moni's forehead was cut open and blood began streaming forth. The handle of the pump was smeared with blood. Moni stared at me, her eyes wide with fear. She got the sack immediately.

Tying her two torn dresses and the sandals she wore on Eid into a bundle, she wiped her eyes and said to Ma, "Give me my salary, all the money I've been saving."

"How dare you ask for your salary?" Ma shot back. "Will you buy me another set of plates and everything else you've broken? No. *I* am going to replace that whole set with the money I'd kept aside for you, understand? Go on now, get out of my sight!"

Moni left, the little bundle tucked under her arm. What had she earned after working in our house for two years? Two torn dresses and a pair of sandals with black straps. Moni would now go back to her mother, who would get her another job at five takas a month.

And she would start dreaming again. I leaned against a pillar on the veranda and watched her go. She melted into the darkness without looking back. Phulbahari had left like this, limping, not once glancing back. Crickets were chirping somewhere. The grass and ground turned damp in the evening mist. So did I. I could feel the dew on my eyelashes. The scent of shiuli flowers wafted in from the house next door and filled our courtyard.

Ma was trying to give up thoughts of the mundane world, but it held her in its grip, refusing to let go. The loss of a few plates and glasses had upset her so much that she couldn't concentrate on her evening namaz.

Having got rid of Moni, Ma had to spend the next few days cooking and working alone in the kitchen. This made her very irritable. When Baba came home, she shouted again, "Why won't you let the girls come into the kitchen? Don't they have to get married some day and cook for their husbands? Every girl has to learn to cook before she gets married. Look at these girls. They behave like boys!"

Baba coughed, cleared his throat, and replied, "These girls are getting an education. Why should they work in the kitchen? Haven't we got others to help with the cooking? I don't want either of my girls to go anywhere near the kitchen. They must spend their time on their studies."

"Studies?" Ma retorted. "When you aren't at home, all those girls ever do is play. Get me someone else to help with the housework. I can't manage alone. Whoever comes to this house has to be taught all the work, and once they've learned everything they leave."

Ma went on strike. Or so she told Baba. No one saw her light the stove. No one knew who would chop the firewood, grind the spices, wash all our dirty dishes. Who, for that matter, was going to cook? Wash our clothes? Sweep and mop the floor? Baba would have to realize that the entire household had come to a standstill. If he asked for food, he was told, "Food? There isn't any. There's no one to cook, is there?"

What Ma did without Baba's knowledge was feed us secretly. If a beggar turned up at our door, she got *her* to work in the kitchen, grind the spices, wash the dishes, chop the vegetables, even cook food. In return, Ma fed her.

In the end Baba found a homeless girl sleeping on the pavement in

Notun Bazar. He woke her up, asked her name and address, and brought her home.

"Keep her," he told Ma, "at least for the time being."

It was to be a temporary measure, but Ma found it necessary to interview the new arrival. The girl stood, holding on to one of the veranda's wooden pillars. Ma sat on a chair. The girl, perhaps eight years old, had snot hanging from her nose, her body was unwashed, her hair was dry and sun-bleached. She was wearing just a pair of shorts, which might have been white at one time but had now turned a shade of brown. There were thick streaks of dried mud on her legs. Her skin was cracked like the earth during a drought.

"What's your name?" Ma asked, irritated.

"Renu," the girl replied, sniffing.

"What kind of work can you do?"

Renu did not reply. She simply gazed at the plants in our courtyard and at the hens and ducks. Ma cast a sharp eye all over Renu, from head to toe, asking again, "Have you ever worked in anyone's house?"

"No." Renu shook her head.

"Don't you have parents?" Ma's tone was stern.

"A mother. No father," Renu replied indifferently, as if it didn't matter in the least whether one had parents or not.

Now Ma's tone became gentler. "Brothers or sisters?"

"Nah!" Renu still sounded as if she couldn't care less.

"Can you grind spices? If I asked you to wash clothes, could you do that?"

Renu nodded. Yes, she could. Ma wrinkled her nose, possibly because Renu smelled pretty foul, and asked, "Can you make rice?" Renu nodded again, thereby passing her test. She was employed at once.

Ma sent her to the hand-pump to have a bath and told her to use soap to wash herself. After that, she poured a little oil on Renu's palm so that she could massage it into her hair. Then Renu was given one of my old dresses to wear and a plate of leftover rice and dal to eat. When she had eaten, Ma told her to sweep the house, then grind some spices and cook the rice. Ma kept an eye on Renu from a distance while she went about doing these tasks.

Moni left, Renu came. One lower-class girl left, another lower-class girl came. The town was filled with lower-class girls and our comfortable lifestyle continued undisturbed.

Soon Ma began leaving all the household chores to Renu and resumed her visits to Amirullah's house. After each discourse she returned home with her eyes red and swollen from crying. Then she spoke angrily about the ways of the world. Only a moment later, however, if she found that Renu had not boiled the rice properly she did not hesitate to slap her.

Ma might be in a good mood, but this could change in a second. Our domestic staff lived in a state of perpetual fear, but there were times when Ma's heart brimmed over with affection. At night, she started teaching Renu to read. Renu placed a finger under each Arabic letter she was shown and repeated after Ma: *alif, bay, tay, say.* Still in an affectionate mood, Ma gave Renu two of my old dresses.

Before Renu could settle down properly in our house, our dog, Rocket, was found lying dead on the veranda. Ma sent word to Baba so that a cleaner could come and take the corpse away. Baba sent one of the men from his pharmacy. He tied a rope round Rocket's neck and dragged him out, leaving a mark on the ground as he went. I ran to the bathroom to have a good cry. That was the only place in the whole house where I could hide and be alone. Rocket would never again come speeding to greet me. If I stood with a biscuit in my hand, he would no longer jump up to get it. When I left the house, Rocket often followed me. Our neighbors were surprised to see that we had an Alsatian. As I reached the main crossing, I would say to Rocket, "Go on, Rocket. Go back home," and he would run back like an obedient child. He had been beaten by other dogs, then neglected, and so became sick. For days on end he just gazed at us with tears in his eyes before he finally died quietly. No one took him to the veterinary hospital, and had I said anything I would have been angrily shouted at.

After Rocket died, Ma brought a small pup from Grandma's house. It was a local dog, not an Alsatian. I wanted to call it Rocket, but Ma decided on Poppy. There was no disputing Ma's decision so everyone started calling it Poppy. (When we were in Pabna, the jailer there had a dog called Poppy — that was why Ma had chosen the name.) She already had other animals to look after — a goat, hens, and pigeons. She took good care of the dog and no longer said, as she used to, "A dog is an unholy animal. No angel visits a house if there is a dog in it."

Poppy was very attached to her. Ma was his owner. She would pick up pieces of meat from her own plate and put them on Poppy's. I tried to teach the dog little games but he never learned — I would throw a ball in the air but Poppy couldn't catch it. He was just an ordinary dog, good for nothing but barking at strangers. Nevertheless, Ma continued to shower affection on him, as she did on Renu. Renu massaged Ma's hands and feet at night, and ran her fingers through her hair. Having finished with Arabic, Ma had begun to teach her Bengali. Even so, Renu couldn't forget her own mother. She was found crying for her whenever she was alone. "I do so much for you, and still you can't stop crying!" Ma scolded her. "You will always remain a servant, understand? You'll spend your life slaving away in one house or another!"

Baba heard about Renu's longing to see her mother. He went looking for her and, eventually, found her. He said to Ma, "Keep them both. Renu can do all the light work and her mother can handle the heavy stuff."

The next day, he bought a printed cotton sari for Renu's mother. Ma examined its quality and said, "The weaving's very well done and it's expensive. Why, even *I* am hardly ever given such a good sari! If I get just one like this every year, I'll consider myself lucky."

Renu's mother began her new job, but Ma found fault with almost everything she did. When Baba returned home, Ma complained to him, "This woman's character seems, well, doubtful."

"Why? What's she done?" Baba's eyes were curious.

"A man came from the pharmacy this afternoon. I found her talking with him, whispering something. I gave her a blouse to wear with her sari, but she didn't. She likes to show her breasts, especially when there's a man around."

Baba remained silent.

His silence infuriated Ma.

The month limped to a close with Renu and her mother doing most of the housework. Ma started to go out again, returning home quite late, then spending a long time for zikir. One moment she was there, the next moment she vanished from sight. Almost automatically, Renu's mother took over running the entire household. When Baba went shopping, he asked Renu's mother — not Ma — what was needed in the kitchen, what spices we had run out of. When she had a free moment, Renu's mother braided her hair, humming under her breath. This irritated Ma so much that she said, "Stop singing, Renu's Ma. You were hired to work. Do your work, and keep your mouth shut." Renu's mother stopped humming.

Renu and her mother were still with us when the most terrible thing happened. Everyone else had gone to sleep. I had just secretly finished reading Sarat Chandra's *Devdas,* hiding the book safely under my mattress and closing my eyes, when an awful commotion made me spring up. At first, it was difficult to grasp where it came from, or what had caused it. Then, having strained my ears for a few moments, I realized Ma was screaming and someone was banging a door very loudly. Perhaps they wanted to break it down. Had robbers and bandits attacked our house? My limbs went numb and I began to sweat. I shut my eyes tight, held my breath, and lay down, pretending to be fast asleep. If they found me like that, perhaps they would take pity on me and spare my life. Would they hesitate to chop my head off? Someone was running along the corridor outside my room. Then more footsteps. Someone screamed shrilly, someone else was speaking in a low tone. There was no way of telling what was being said.

Yasmin was also awake. "Bubu, what's happened?" she whispered.

"I don't know," I whispered back.

I could hear my chest hammer away. Then, gradually, the commotion in the corridor subsided. It was only then that Ma woke Dada and Chhotda and told them what had happened. Bandits did not feature in her story — Baba did. At two-thirty in the morning, Baba had been discovered lying in Renu's mother's bed in the kitchen.

Ma was a light sleeper. She had awakened in the middle of the night and decided to check if all the doors and windows were bolted and locked. She did this from time to time, because our house had once been robbed. When she reached Baba's room, she realized that the door that opened onto the corridor was unbolted. So she went into the room, lifted the mosquito net, and found Baba missing. She checked the bathroom. He was not there. She checked the veranda. He was not there, either. Then she heard strange noises coming from the kitchen. She listened carefully and realized that she heard Baba's voice and the sound of a creaking bed. The sound came from the wooden cot on which Renu's mother had been sleeping for the past week.

Baba had gone to sleep with Renu's mother so late at night! I simply stared lifelessly at the inside of my mosquito net. Yasmin lay next to me, her eyes wide with silent amazement.

Ma, who was seeking to detach herself from this mundane, humdrum world, spent the rest of the night sobbing and moaning. Dada, Chhotda, Yasmin, and I also stayed awake, our silent sighs keeping her tears company.

⸺ 9 ⸺

The Peer's House II

Inside the house, about half a dozen women were seated in the peer's room, all clad in long, thin robes that reached to their feet. Their heads were covered with veils. The dresses clung to their bodies so closely that, from a distance, it seemed as if they were wearing nothing at all. Only one of them was in a sari. Four medallions hung from her neck, and one end of the sari was pulled over her head. Appearing to be greatly distressed, she placed both hands on the peer's feet and said, "If I do not get a son, Huzur, my husband will divorce me."

When Amirullah replied, he spoke very slowly, running his fingers through his beard. His eyes, filled with boundless compassion, remained fixed on the beams of the ceiling. "Think of Allah," he said. "Only He can give you what you want; I am only His servant. Take His name — and you must do meditation — in the middle of the night. He is all merciful, pray to Him. Pray with tears in your eyes, Aleya. How else will you be able to move Him, tell me? If one of His servants stretches out a hand, begging for His kindness, Allah does not let that person go empty-handed. There is no end to His mercy."

Aleya threw herself at Amirullah's feet, bursting into loud sobs. If a son was guaranteed, she was prepared to take Allah's name all night, not just in the middle of the night. Amirullah removed his hand from his beard and placed it on Aleya's back. Then he brought his gaze down from the ceiling and rested it on Aleya's hair, which had escaped from her veil. "Allah is one, unique, without a form, all-powerful," he went on. "He has no beginning nor an end. He has no ties — no father, no mother, sons or daughters. He sees all, yet He has no eyes.

171

He hears all, yet He has no ears. He has no hands, yet there is nothing that He cannot do. He is present everywhere. He does not eat or sleep. Nothing and no one on earth can be compared to Him. He has always been present, and He always will be present. He provides what others lack, but He lacks nothing Himself. He is immortal and indestructible. He is the ultimate preserver of honor. It is He who gives us honor. Appeal to Him, Aleya. Raise your hands in prayer. You will certainly be blessed with a son, and then society will treat you with due respect."

Standing hesitantly behind Ma, I heard these words and began thinking about the shapeless form of Allah. It reminded me of the magician who came to our school one day. He had been draped in a black cloth. When the cloth was removed, there was no sign of him. He seemed to have quite literally vanished into thin air. If I could acquire an invisible, shapeless form I would roam all over town, walk on the banks of the Brahmaputra for as long as I liked, and no one would be able to find me to drag me back to the house.

Amirullah pulled his feet from under Aleya's body. Humaira, Aunt Fajli's daughter, came running from a group of young women and took Aleya out to the courtyard. Aleya stood under a hibiscus bush and untied a knot in her anchal. Then she passed neatly folded money that she had brought as the peer's fee to Humaira. Humaira curled her fingers around it, came back to the room, and handed it to Amirullah. His was an experienced hand. The money passed quickly from one hand to another, as if it were a relay race. Amirullah thrust his hand deep into the pocket of his robe, for the moment a mobile cash box. My eyes remained glued to that hand in his pocket. The peer's sharp glance now turned to me. "Who's that with you, Hamima?" he asked. "Your daughter?"

Ma brought me forward, pulling me by the arm. "Ji, Huzur. This girl was born on the twelfth of Rabi-ul-awal. She does namaz with me and has started to read the Koran. Please give her your blessings, Huzur, and pray that she grows up to be virtuous." She gave me a little push and added, "Go, touch his feet."

My whole body stiffened. I couldn't move an inch. Touch that man's feet? I had absolutely no wish to do so. Ma pushed me again. I began stepping back, inch by inch. To no avail. The peer — his long, white beard flowing down from his face, his body covered in a long robe, a round cap on his head with the word ALLAH written on it —

reached out and grabbed me with his paw, as if I was a ripe fruit falling off the tree. Then he held me so tightly against his chest that I was quite lost within the folds of his robe and began to choke. The peer closed his eyes, muttered a few words, and blew all over my face. As he blew, my face was sprayed with spittle.

I struggled out of his robe and ran to hide behind my enchanted mother. As I wiped my face on my sleeve I heard the peer ask, "Is your daughter taking lessons only in worldly matters?"

Ma sighed. "Yes. I have no say in this, Huzur. My children's father believes in worldly matters, so that is what they are being taught. But this girl is very interested in learning about Allah and the Prophet, so I thought that she would like it here and would think more about Allah."

Amirullah clicked his tongue in regret. Then he leaned back in his bed and said, "Do you know what the problem is? Once you start to think only of this world the devil enters your soul. It is very difficult then to free yourself from his clutches and turn to Allah. Look at these women here: Nazia, Nafisa, Munajjeba, Motia. They used to go to college at one time, all of them. Now their minds only dwell on lessons taught by Allah. They are preparing for their final journey, acquiring the virtue that will see them through. They now accept that what they were being offered in the name of education was a pack of lies. True knowledge was hidden from them they were kept behind a curtain of terrible darkness."

At this point Ma made a gesture, one that meant that she wanted me to go out to the courtyard. Then she picked up a palm-leaf fan and began fanning Amirullah. I had hardly taken a step toward the courtyard when Humaira swooped down on me like a bird of prey and took me to a room in the northern corner of their house. There were several beds in this room but during the day each mattress was rolled up. Mats were spread out on wooden cots. Aunt Fajli's daughters sat here to count their prayer beads or to do their namaz. None of them went to school. They were being taught lessons at home that would lead them onto Allah's path.

Humaira was older than me by about five years. She had a perfectly round face. "You are my aunt's daughter. We are cousins. Do you know that?" she asked, tapping my shoulder. "Why do you go to school and learn useless stuff? Allah will be cross with you, don't you see that? He will be very angry with you!"

So saying, Humaira made me sit down on a mat and sat beside me.

"Your father is a kafir. If you listen to him, Allah will send you to hell." Humaira closed her eyes to imagine the horrors of hell, and shuddered. Then, for some reason I couldn't quite understand, she clutched my hands tightly. I started to go cold. I could picture the scene myself: A fire was burning in a huge pit over which there was a massive cauldron of boiling water. Innumerable people were floating in it, shrieking with pain. I was among them. Suddenly, Humaira and I were joined by seven girls who came and stood before us, their sharp glances piercing my body. I was a totally strange creature, one who went to school. Waves of compassion rose in their eyes, as if they were all sitting in the garden in heaven and watching me from there. I was, of course, burning in hell. Some of them cried out in sympathy. A tall woman said, "Humaira, does she want to turn to Allah?"

"Yes, but her father won't let her." Humaira sighed as she replied. Was her sigh so deep because she was my own cousin and concerned about me?

The tall woman clicked her tongue in sympathy. *Tch tch.* So did the others. *Tch tch. Tch tch. Tch tch,* like a lot of cats drinking milk, making slurping noises. I counted them silently. Seven, six, five, four, three, two, one. Tall, short, medium, short, short, short, medium. In my mind, I arranged them according to their height, as if they were standing in my school assembly: short, short, short, short, medium, medium, tall.

A sharp nudge from Humaira brought me out of my reverie. "Look!" she said, raising her chin and pointing to the others, "See these girls? Their fathers have left them here to walk on Allah's path. They live here. They are learning the Koran and the hadith." Humaira sighed again, very deeply. "If your father was given proper advice and guidance, I am sure he would have turned to Allah, too, and sent his children to walk on the same path."

It is difficult to tell whether or not the correct advice and guidance would have worked on my own father. It had, however, worked very effectively on a judge. He had left his sixteen-year-old daughter, Munajjeba, to dedicate her life to the service of Allah. She was the tall girl, Humaira told me. A judge's daughter. Where did her father work? Dhaka. Humaira uttered the word *Dhaka* in such a way that clearly implied that the judge was a man of importance.

What had happened was this: Munajjeba was good in her studies but fell in love with a thoroughly unsuitable boy. Some people claimed to have seen her lying with this boy in a field after dark. Every tongue in the neighborhood began wagging. The judge took his daughter out of school and kept her at home. It was at this time that someone told him about the peer, who had a number of young girls in his care. He taught them the Koran and the hadith and the girls learned to be virtuous and do their namaz regularly. None of them was allowed to step out of the house. Each was kept in strict purdah. Hearing this, the judge came to attend one of Amirullah's discourses. The way he spoke and the way he treated him melted the judge's heart. A few days later he brought his sinful daughter — who was clearly walking down the wrong path — and left her in Amirullah's care. Her name, Rubina, was changed to Munajjeba. Now Munajjeba spent her days wearing long dresses that kept her chastely covered, her head always veiled. She never left the house, and when she heard Amirullah's description of hell during his meetings, she cried her eyes out.

That was the beginning. After Munajjeba, other girls arrived, each the daughter of someone important: a police officer, a lawyer, a senior government official. Hazrat Ibrahim had acted upon Allah's instruction and sacrificed his own son. If he could do it, why couldn't a modern father bring his daughter to serve Allah? This was Humaira's view. In this house, girls were advised to fall madly in love with Allah. And they did, too, within just a few days of their arrival. They were totally infatuated with the shapeless, formless Allah. This made Amirullah sigh in relief. To him, the girls were not Nazia, Nafisa, Motia, or Munajjeba — they were fresh blossoms in the garden of heaven.

Extra rooms had to be built for the girls. Amirullah cleared his forest of all the wild plants and made lots of small rooms. None of them had windows. The girls gasped for air in the sweltering heat, but the peer said, "Our Prophet lived his life in this type of room; living in such a room will bring virtue. If you can put up with discomfort, as did our Prophet, he will stand by you himself to prove your virtue when the time comes for you to be judged."

The girls almost swooned, stirred by deep emotions. No, they did not need windows. If the Prophet's house had been without a door, they would have been prepared to do without a door as well.

After two or three years the fathers of these virtuous and religious women came to take them back. The girls refused, very firmly, to return home. Munajjeba's mother came to fetch her, because her father was seriously ill and confined to bed. Munajjeba did not go — she had no wish to return to a tainted world. It was her belief that the instant she stepped out of the courtyard of Amirullah's house, the sin that existed in the world outside would cause blisters to appear on her body.

She was not the only one. When the other girls were old enough to be married, their fathers found suitable men and came to collect them. The girls were adamant. They expressed their views quite clearly. The world was about to come to an end. This was no time to think of marriage. That was what their peer had told them. Therefore, they were not willing to do anything considered incorrect or unsuitable. Their fathers returned without them, defeated by the girls' determination to cling to the holy soil of Amirullah's house.

Why was it not the right time for marriage? They had their answers ready. Huzur, when he was in his deep meditation, had spoken directly with Allah. They talked often as they walked together in the garden of heaven. Munajjeba only had to close her eyes to become a bird and fly around in the same garden. Allah Himself had said to Amirullah, "The end of the world is nigh. It is time for Israfil to blow his horn. The day of judgment is approaching fast. It is not advisable to think of marriage and raising families in the few days left before the end. Forget all that. Just think of acquiring virtue."

The girls believed that their Huzur would personally help them cross the bridge that led to heaven. He had told them that he would hold the hands of his favorite followers and take them with him when he passed through to heaven's gate; without them, the peer himself would not step in heaven. This was why none of the girls wanted to be out of his sight. He had offered to depart for Mecca soon with his followers, to remain in the land of the Prophet until Judgment Day.

"Allah will send a vehicle for us to go to Mecca," declared Munajjeba.

None of them had any idea what kind of vehicle it might be, but they were absolutely sure that it would come to this house one day. Humaira believed it would be a *burrakh*, the same winged chariot in which the Prophet had once visited heaven. Lists had been prepared for who would go in which group. Munajjeba heard that her name was on the first list. The list was kept under the peer's pillow. Every single girl looked terrified, as if the day of judgment would be upon them the very next morning.

Slowly, that fear began to take its root in my mind, too. Baba wanted me to get an education and grow up to be a worthy human being but if the day of judgment was so close, wouldn't it arrive long before I grew up? The earth would be destroyed. Everyone would be judged in the field of judgment where Allah Himself would sit with a pair of weighing scales to see how much good there was in every person.

My heart trembled at the thought. When I stood face to face with Him, Allah was bound to ask me whether I had done my namaz regularly, kept a fast to observe roja, counted my prayer beads, read the Koran, and generally followed His advice. What was I going to say? If I said yes to all His questions He would no doubt catch me out since He had already written down everyone's future. What mystified me was why, if the future of all creatures was known to Allah, did everyone have to gather in a huge field and account for themselves? Why did Allah need to ask questions about who did what on the earth? It struck me as perfectly unnecessary.

Each time I tried to imagine this field of judgment I thought of a field near Uncle Siddique's house, in Dhaka. This was where the bridge stood that had to be crossed to gain entry to heaven. The magician in our school who had vanished under a black cloth could easily cross that bridge, I was sure of it. The scene rose clearly in my mind, although all I could see was a rope. No, it was so thin it had to be called a thread. I was walking on it, my legs shaky and unsteady. The magician, however, was walking confidently, his body firm and straight. He was a Hindu; his name was Sameer Chandra. If he managed to cross the bridge, where would Allah send him? To hell, because he was a Hindu? Or to heaven because he had crossed the bridge successfully?

If I was the judge, I would send him to heaven. But I had been told that a Hindu simply had to go to hell, no matter how good and kind and virtuous he was, because that was the fate Allah Himself had decided for him. It was already written. I did not like this business of everything being written in advance. If that was the case, why go through the drama of judging everybody, for surely what would take place in the field of judgment could be no more than a simple drama? And to think that people were getting so excited about taking part in it!

I was so engrossed in my thoughts that I did not notice the girls leaving the room and making their way toward Amirullah's. Even Humaira left me. I sat there alone, waiting for Ma. It was impossible for me to guess when she might be free to go home. Each time I had come to this house she had told me we would leave in the afternoon, and then we left only when it started getting dark. If she promised to leave as dusk fell, she would actually leave late at night. But there were times when, for some mysterious reason, she put on her burkha much sooner than expected and told me to hurry.

Today she didn't seem to care at all that I was waiting for her in this room. I could see her running about, whispering with the other women. When she finished talking, I guessed she would turn to her Huzur and fan him, press his legs, make him lemonade, give him a paan, then hold the spittoon for him. Her work here would be done, at least for the moment, after he spat into the spittoon, thus giving her the chance to eat his spit or phlegm and rub it on her face or head. I tried to see the woman Ma was talking to. I could see no more than her bottom, which was looked like the bottom of a pitcher. Suddenly, two girls swept into the room like a hurricane and ran toward the window, quite oblivious to my presence. They were not from the previous group, but totally new, at least in my eyes, although they were similarly dressed, covered from head to foot. One of them was saying to the other, "Look, look, that's Muhammad over there, Fatema apa's son."

Another voice. "See the one rubbing his neck? That's Muhammad, Aunt Hajera's son."

I could see nothing except those girls' behinds. More girls entered the room, skipped over me, and threw themselves at the window. A portion of the main courtyard was visible from it. A few young men who had come to attend Amirullah's meeting were standing there. Only a handful of men — most of them related to Amirullah — were allowed to come inside the house where the women lived, but the men now standing in the courtyard did not fall into that category.

"Look, over there! That's Muhammad, Nurun-nabi's son," said a third voice.

The girls started laughing. Some tried to slip in between the others; others stuffed a corner of their veils into their mouths and tried to look over the heads of those who were closer to the window. But those in the front refused to make way for those behind. "Go on, you've had your fill! Let's have a look. Get back!" exclaimed the ones who were pushing. I stood right behind everyone else and, through a gap in the crowd, caught a brief glimpse of the men. They were all wearing white pajamas, panjabis, and caps. Some stood with their arms akimbo; others were rubbing their necks or scratching their bottoms. Some were yawning, some washing their hands, some slapping their arms to get rid of mosquitoes. I failed to see why these girls were so keen to look at these very ordinary men.

Some more girls from the first group that I had met rushed in to look out of the window. All of them wanted to see the Muhammads. Why were they all called Muhammad? The question crossed my mind, but I couldn't utter it. It stuck in my throat like a black tamarind seed. There was only one window in this room and that was only because it was an old room. The girls couldn't look at the various Muhammads from the new rooms built without windows.

One of Aunt Fajli's sons was also called Muhammad. He was her first son — before him had come his three older sisters, Humaira, Sufaira, Mubashwera. After producing three girls in a row, Aunt Fajli was frequently possessed by jinns, but after Muhammad was born the jinns began to leave her alone. However, Muhammad was then followed by three more girls. The jinns renewed their attack with greater force. Even Humaira, I heard, had been possessed a few days ago. In fact, possession was quite a common occurrence in this house. Some young girl would be possessed almost every day. Amirullah had to be called in to get rid of the evil spirit, in a dark room, with all the doors and windows, if there were any, closed.

This reminded me of the first time I had witnessed the procedure. The girl was called Juthi. She was in the same school as me, but one year my senior. She was very pretty. One afternoon, she happened to be sitting under a banyan tree singing quietly to herself. When the bell rang, all the other girls left, but Juthi continued to sit there, singing. The bell rang again for the next class, but Juthi just went on singing, her hair blowing in the wind.

Our Urdu teacher — we called him Urdu Sir — was a *maulvi*, a holy man. Informed about Juthi, he dragged her away from under the tree and told the other teachers that she had been possessed by a jinn. By this time Juthi was already shouting, "Let me go, let me go!" But, keeping a firm hold on her, Urdu Sir began preparing for an exorcism. The first thing he did was take some holy water, mutter a few lines of prayer specific to the task, and then sprinkle the water on Juthi's face. But this was not all. Urdu Sir then set fire to one end of a branch from a neem tree, held it before Juthi, and beat her with a thicker branch. He didn't stop until she fell over. I stood with all the other girls in the school and watched this spectacle, my eyes filled with horror. I felt very sorry for Juthi. Sitting in this room in Amirullah's house now, I felt extremely uneasy. What if I was also possessed by a jinn? What if Amirullah had to take me to a dark room, stick in hand, as he had done with all the others?

I shriveled up with fear, so much so that I didn't even notice the other girls moving away from the window. Ma came in briefly to tell me that we would return home as soon as the meeting was over. This brought no comfort, for I had already experienced the length of Amirullah's meetings. I knew it would take place in a large hall. The girls would go straight from the inner part of the house to the portion of the hall that was curtained off. Everyone would have to sit on a mattress on the floor. Only Amirullah sat on a divan, on a thick mattress. When he entered the hall, which was filled with the scent of incense, his right hand would be raised, his face grave. Everyone would rise to their feet and say, *"Salaam aleikum ya Rahamtullah."* The hall would echo with the sound of so many voices. Amirullah would reply in his deep voice, *"Waleikum assalaam!"* and invite his audience to sit. The women — some smelling of talcum powder, some wearing kohl — would peer through a chink in the curtain to look at Amirullah and to cast sidelong glances at the other men.

The routine was the same today. Amirullah ran his fingers through his beard and began speaking: "Look, Abu Bakar, this world that we live in is an unreal world, so what's the point of making a lot of money here? Will anyone ever be able to take it with him in the end? Tell me, will you take your possessions with you to your grave?"

Abu Bakar — short, with a dark beard, seated in the front row — replied, "No, Huzur."

"So what will you give your heart to, eh? To Allah, or to the pursuit of wealth?" The peer addressed the question to Abu Bakar, but his glance swept over all the heads in the room, each covered with a white cap.

"To Allah, Huzur," said Abu Bakar, sounding as if he had been hypnotized.

The women stared hard at Abu Bakar through the curtain. Today his name would be on every one's lips. Huzur had spoken to him voluntarily. This was a rare honor. Some were of the view that Huzur would now make a special recommendation to Allah to send Abu Bakar straight to heaven.

The meeting always lasted exactly an hour. This time, Amirullah spent the time describing the poverty the Prophet had to suffer. His only possession was a torn blanket. The congregation wept noisily upon hearing how he had suffered. The more you cried in this house, the more you were praised. There was something else that earned one a good name: having a dream. Aunt Fajli had dreamed she was sitting by the side of a fountain with the Prophet. Flocks of white birds were flying around and a soft breeze was blowing. Although she couldn't recall what they talked about, Huzur had told her that her place in heaven was now assured. After that, Aunt Fajli had risen in everyone's estimation. Some had asked her what the Prophet looked like, and her face lit up as she described her dream: "His face is so bright; he is so handsome. How wonderfully soft his hands felt!" Her eyes closed slowly as she spoke, as if she could still feel the softness of his touch. They had moved to the fountain to wash themselves and had only just started when she woke up.

After hearing of her dream, various other members of the congregation began dreaming of the Prophet and were similarly hailed with words of praise. Ma felt profoundly unhappy that the Prophet had never appeared in her dreams. Before going to sleep she thought very hard about him, so that she might see him, but that didn't happen. Ma considered herself a sinner.

As soon as the meeting was over, the men formed a queue to touch Amirullah's feet and thrust money into his hands. This was the hadia. The amount was unspecified. One was supposed to pay whatever one could. Those were Amirullah's instructions.

Abu Bakar bent with deep reverence over Amirullah's feet and said, "Huzur, I am very worried. The world is soon going to come to an end and we'll all have to face the day of judgment. I no longer pay any attention to running my business. After all, when I go, I'll go empty-handed, won't I? Who knows what's in store? All my life, I never really thought about this. Please pray for me, Huzur. Without your prayers and your blessings, I will be lost."

Huzur promised to pray and to bless.

Having collected the hadia from the men, Amirullah entered the section where the women were sitting. Every woman not from his own family would now touch his feet and offer him money. After this was done Huzur would retire, recline on his bed, and various young women would throw themselves at him and massage his body.

I pulled at Ma's veil and said plaintively, "Come on, Ma, we must go home. If Baba gets back and finds me gone, he's going to beat me!"

Ma snatched her veil out of my grasp. "Stop pestering me!" was all she said.

I stood alone in the dark courtyard, under the hibiscus bush. Somewhere, I had heard that a jinn was more likely to attack if you left your hair loose, so I quickly covered my hair with my urna. I was not used to wearing long salwars and an urna, the garments older girls wore. At home, I still wore shorts, but here, in Amirullah's house, your age didn't matter. Unless your clothing was approved by him, you were not allowed to pass through his front gate. It was an extraordinary new world functioning within the familiar old one.

On our way back, as we began our ride in another rickshaw I asked Ma, "Why has Israfil been sitting for millions of years, holding a horn to his mouth? Why does Allah make him do that? I mean, *He* jolly well knows when the day of judgment is going to arrive, doesn't He? Surely He could ask Israfil to pick up his horn and sound it when the time comes? Poor Israfil having to stay put, not moving an inch."

Ma replied from under her burkha: "Allah is the Creator. Israfil is only an angel, so he has to obey the Creator's command. Every angel must do that. Never question Allah's will. Learn to be afraid of Him."

"Your Huzur said we must give our hearts to Allah, learn to fall in love with Him. How can we love someone if we are afraid of him?"

I had always found it difficult to utter the words *fall in love*. There was an unwritten law that that particular phrase must never be used. But then, that law applied only to love between a man and a woman, because it was somehow wrong. People who fell in love were bad people. Aunt Jhunu, I knew, secretly loved someone. Dada wrote poetry with a girl called Anita in mind but that, too, was done secretly. "There was something between Aunt Jhunu and Uncle Rashu," Dada had once said. Even in my school, girls did not use the word *love*. They said "That girl over there has 'something' going on with a boy!" At first, I found it quite difficult to understand what "something" meant, but eventually I got into the habit of using it myself.

But *love*, or even the phrase *falling in love*, could be used freely when referring to Allah. I had never heard anyone say, "Huzur has 'something' going on with Allah!" Humaira, it was rumored, had a love affair going on with her cousin, Atiq, but it was always referred to as "something," and the word was whispered. Yet no one had any hesitation in saying that Humaira was deeply in love with Allah. In fact, it was always said very loudly so that everyone could hear.

In answer to my question, Ma said briefly, "You can love Allah *and* be afraid of Him."

"But you always say Allah keeps a record of every human being — when he's to be born, when he's to die, even who he'll marry. Allah also knows who'll go to heaven and who'll be sent to hell. It's all written down, all decided. Well then, this man Abu Bakar . . . if Allah has decided already to send him to heaven, surely he's not going to go to hell even if he's a sinner? And if you take me . . . if going to hell is what's already written for me, what's the point of my praying to Allah? Is He going to change what He wrote down Himself?" I said all this in one breath.

"How come you behave as if you haven't got a tongue in front of others? When you're with me, you can't stop chattering." Ma said in a very cross tone.

"But, tell me, Allah is capable of doing anything, isn't He?" I insisted, my voice trembling with curiosity.

"Yes. Allah can make anything happen. But if He does *not* want something to take place, then no power can work against His will. Not a single leaf on a tree would move unless Allah willed it."

Ma's body was covered from head to toe with a black burkha. Her face was hidden behind a thin veil that hung down from her forehead, so that her eyes could spot potholes before she stepped into them. Right now, the fury of her glance pierced the veil. I looked at her fiery eyes and said, "Suppose Allah was sitting with empty hands. Could he create a flower out of nothing?"

"Yes."

"Suppose He had a hankie in His hand. Could He turn it into a pigeon?" I asked again.

"Certainly," Ma said firmly.

"That man who came to do tricks in our school — that magician — he can do all those things too. He can even vanish into thin air and remain invisible, just like Allah!" I declared, triumphantly.

"*What did you say?* You've lost all your virtue. You dare to compare a magician with Allah? You stupid girl! Is this why I take you with me to hear Huzur speak? You're much worse than you used to be! I bet you've learned to talk like that from your father. I will sew up your lips, I swear, if you say such things just once more."

In the face of such rage, I felt like a pricked balloon. Ma had once told me that the saint Abdul Kader Jeelani had emerged from his grave after Allah ordered him to do so. I felt quite sure that if that magician was buried in a grave, he could come out, too. But I did not mention this to Ma, for I had no wish to take more abuse. However, another question that was struggling to escape from my mind slipped out before I could stop it. "Why do people in your Huzur's house keep getting possessed? Jinns don't attack us, do they? You keep telling us Allah Himself comes down to visit that house. If that's true, how come jinns dare to appear in Allah's space?"

Ma dug her elbow into my stomach and gave me a sharp, painful nudge. "Shut up! Not another word, do you hear? When we get home, you must do your namaz and beg Allah's forgiveness. You're not afraid of Allah, are you? No, of course not. How else would such devilish thoughts get into your head?"

I received no answer to my questions.

One day, I showed Ma my science book and asked, "Allah created Adam, didn't He?"

"Yes."

"But look at this!" I pointed to an early *Homo sapiens* in my science book. "Here's the first sign of life on earth, one cell grew into multiple cells. Ancient man evolved from a species of apes. Those men lived in caves, fought among themselves, ate raw meat, and so forth. Then, much later, they learned to light a fire. Then they made more progress, and gradually became civilized. The first man that Allah made — the prophet Hazrat Adam Allah-e-sallam — did he look like this hairy, naked ape, who walked in the garden of heaven?"

Ma wrinkled her nose, as if a bad stench was coming from the book, and said, "Get out of here, go! Every word written in that book is a lie. What Allah has said is the only truth. Nothing else matters."

I had to go away. It was impossible to raise the matter with Baba, for I invariably lost my voice if I went anywhere near him. Who was right? Which was true — Allah or science? Who was going to tell me? There did not seem to be a great deal of reason in what Allah had said. *Reason* was a word I had recently learned. Baba had lately started saying, "Never act without reason. Ask your conscience before doing anything whether you should — or should not — do it. If the answer is yes, only then may you perform that task. Every human being has a conscience. Man is an animal, but a rational one. If man did not have the power to think rationally, there would be no difference between him and an animal."

This particular speech was delivered — and repeated subsequently — when, during a game, I lit a match and accidentally dropped it in a heap of firewood. Luckily, there was no major disaster. Had the wood caught fire and spread, the whole house would have been gutted.

There didn't seem to be a great deal of reason in what Allah had said. What science said appeared far more reasonable. The first man was supposed to have been created by Allah and then simply dropped from heaven to land on earth with a loud thud. That sounded like a fairy tale. If I mentioned this to Ma, she came back with, "If you say such bad things about Allah, your tongue will drop off." To test this, I sat in my room one day with the door closed, and said "Allah you are bad, you are ugly, you are rotten, you are a crook, you son of a bitch, you son of a pig." My tongue remained in place; it did not drop off. Now there was no doubt in my mind. Nothing happened if you abused Allah. Ma was quite wrong. I had learned something else. It was just not true that Allah would give you whatever you wanted. So many times after my namaz I had asked for chum-chums, or the snacks that I had seen Uncle Sharaf and the others eat. I was never given anything. In my old school, Rajbari — the one that used to be a palace — I had seen a lovely, painted, wooden horse and was tempted enough to ask for one like it. No one gave me a wooden horse. There were various other things I had wanted. After what Uncle Sharaf and Uncle Aman did to me, I wanted them to get leprosy and die quickly. They neither got leprosy nor died. I had heard Ma say a similar prayer with regard to Baba. But he remained in perfect health and in fact seemed to be getting even fitter. He never had a fever, not even for a single day.

I, on the other hand, got frequent attacks of fever. It made me very happy because I could stay away from school and studies. When I was ill, Baba spoke to me gently and stroked my head. It was only during these rare moments that it became easy to receive his affection. He bought bunches of grapes and oranges and placed them on my bed. I ate them all by myself while my sister and brothers looked on. If they insisted that I share my fruit with them, I gave them just a little. Ma brought me pieces of salted ginger. But when it was time to take my medicine the joy of being ill vanished quickly. Baba wanted me to swallow various pills and tablets every hour. Usually I said, "Yes, I'll take them," and then threw each one out of the window when no one was looking.

Once, when my temperature did not come down even after a week Baba got suspicious. He began bringing me my medicines himself. "Open your mouth," he would say, pouring water into it and thrusting a capsule or tablet in. It invariably got stuck in my throat, which made me retch. Undaunted, Baba said "Open your mouth" as soon as I stopped vomiting. He didn't give up until the capsule or tablet made a successful entry into my stomach. When Baba was not in the room Ma came in, muttered *suras,* and blew on my chest. That felt quite nice. After all, someone's soft breath on my chest was much better than foul-tasting medicine. Then she made me drink several glasses of pretty dirty water that had been blessed by the peer. When I recovered, Ma claimed that it was her prayers and the holy water that had done it. Baba maintained it was his capsules.

I didn't feel close to Baba at all. If he came anywhere near me, I felt I was being approached by a monster and my life was in danger. Yet when he told me that high fever was a symptom of disease, that diseases were caused by germs, and that the medicines he gave me could kill those germs, I found his words perfectly reasonable.

In the slum behind Grandma's house this business of uttering *suras,* blowing on the chest, and drinking holy water was quite common. I remember that when Getu fell ill a clergyman used to come to their house every other day and blow on a glass of water. That water was supposed to cure him. In the end, Getu's body just kept swelling more and more and more, and then he simply died. He was only six years old. On one occasion, back in Grandma's house, Aunt Jhunu appeared to have gone mad. A clergyman came, chanted some *suras,* and blew on a glass of water. Aunt Jhunu drank that holy water, but it didn't work. When Ma learned about Baba's affair with Razia Begum, she secretly got hold of a clergyman to free her husband from the clutches of another woman. Since it was not possible to blow on Baba's chest or make him drink holy water, the holy man was invited into Baba's bedroom — in his absence naturally — to blow in there. Knots were then tied in four pieces of thread, which were placed in four corners of the room and buried under the ground. "Now your husband's mind will turn homeward. His eyes will stop roving," he assured Ma. I had overheard Grandma and Ma discussing this matter in whispers. No one knew better than Ma that Baba's eyes continued to roam. Even so, her faith in things like charms, prayers, exorcism, and black magic was totally unshakable.

When Ma said everything written in my schoolbooks was a pack of lies, I couldn't believe her. Before she began visiting Amirullah's house, she had seen nothing wrong with school. If anything, her main regret in life was that she hadn't had the chance to acquire an education herself. There were times even now when she wished she had finished school, not because she had failed to acquire knowledge, but because without an education she couldn't get a job and escape Baba's control. She couldn't stand on her own two feet.

How quickly she had changed before our very eyes! Was she on the wrong track, or really on the path of truth? I simply couldn't tell. Perhaps Ma could be forgiven for speaking without reason, but what about people with college degrees? I didn't hear many of them debating where the earth or the human race had come from. Like Ma, they seemed perfectly willing to accept what Allah said. Otherwise why would they do namaz or roja? The slum was behind Grandma's house, but in front of it were educated people's homes. If they, too, were prepared to accept Allah's dictates without question, this Allah had to be quite something. To be honest, even Baba kept roja during Ramadan.

When I was younger, I was quite keen on fasting the whole day. I used to get up with all the others before dawn, have a meal that started with meat and fish curry and finished with rice mixed with milk and bananas. In the afternoon, Baba would say to me, "Now you must eat something." I always shook my head and said, "No, I am observing roja."

"Roja for children is different, don't you know? You must eat something now, and then again after sunset. You have to do two rojas," Baba would say.

What this really meant was that he didn't want me to starve all day and suffer hunger pangs. When the siren blared just before dawn, on most days no one bothered to wake me up. But inevitably, the noise in the kitchen woke me, and I would jump up to join everyone else for the early meal. The reason I was so eager to keep the fast was not because I believed that was what Allah would like me to do; it was simply that I had noticed children got a lot of attention if they fasted. Maybe that's what I wanted: the attention and affection of grown-ups. Besides, it was like a game at that age. Fasting game. At the end of the game, I sat with the rest of my family before platefuls of chira, fried eggplant, warm *jalebis,* savories and sweets, waiting for the second siren of the day.

After a month of fasting, when it was time to celebrate Eid, Baba spared no expense. He bought new clothes for his children, new saris for Ma, and either a bull or a goat for the sacrifice. But that was all Baba did in the name of religion the whole year. Once he hired a clergyman to teach him Arabic every morning. He didn't tell anyone why he was suddenly so interested, but I remember that he had told Ma over dinner about a strange case a few days before his first lesson. Apparently Baba had seen a peculiar man in the house of a patient. He had long hair and a long beard; his clothes and shoes were torn, but when he wrote the word "Allah" a voice spoke up quite spontaneously from the paper, chanting "Allah hu, Allah hu!" Baba took the piece of paper away and examined it thoroughly. There was no contraption attached to it. Then he searched the man to see if he had a gadget hidden among his clothes. No such thing. Was he making the noise himself? No. So how could an ordinary piece of paper sing the praises of Allah? Baba certainly couldn't work that out. Ma was most impressed by this story. Once he told it, Baba simply sat in silence, toying with the food on his plate. Then he said, "I'm not hungry," and pushed it away. Sometimes, when his blood pressure rose, Baba would go to bed early. He did that night. Normally, he never told any of us — not even Ma — what he did outside the home, which patients he saw, where he went, or what he said. That night, his behavior was different.

About a week later, a *moulaui* — who was generally known as the blind-at-night moulaui because he couldn't see very well after dark — suddenly turned up at our door, clutching a book of the Arabic alphabet. Baba had asked to see him, he said. Sadly, Baba's enthusiasm did not last very long. He struggled with *alif zabar aa, be zabar baa* for a couple of days, then on the third day told his teacher, "Maulvi saab, have a cup of tea. I don't much feel like doing a lesson today. I'll go back to it tomorrow, okay?"

Tea and biscuits were served to the maulvi in the living room. When he returned the following day, and the day after that, no one could find his pupil. Five days later, the maulvi was given a month's wages and his services dispensed with. That was the only time religion reached out and grasped Baba, keeping him within its clutches for a few days. After that, he went back to being his former self — arrogant, hardworking, dutiful, hair brushed back, shirt tucked in, a tie over his shirt, jacket over his tie, an overcoat on top of his jacket in winter. And his shoes? They squeaked throughout the year, in every season.

Uncle Siddique used to send a magazine from Dhaka every month called *Udayan*. When it arrived, we spent a few minutes looking at the pictures, then promptly used its pages to cover our books. I had learned to put covers on my books almost as soon as I learned to read.

I saw Ma use the paper bags in which Baba brought biscuits. When I became older and my sense of aesthetics developed a little, I took on this job myself, using colorful pages from calendars (usually from the Glaxo company). Then *Udayan* came into our lives. It was published by the Russian embassy. Uncle Siddique worked at the embassy's cultural center as co-editor of the magazine. When he visited us in Mymensingh, he always brought a number of books with him and left some of them in our house. Perhaps he hoped that my brothers would read them. Neither of them ever bothered. However, I occasionally spent the lazy evenings leafing through their pages — *Lenin for the Young, The History of the Second World War, What Is Socialism: The Reason Behind It, Maxim Gorky's Mother, My Childhood,* among others.

When Uncle Siddique came to visit Ma cooked special dishes for him. When he left, she said, "What has he turned into? A man who went to a madrasa, now a Communist. *Chhee chhee!* What a shame!"

Her *chhee, chhee,* an expression of horror and disgust, made me look up. "What is a Communist, Ma?" I asked her.

"Someone who does not believe in Allah," Ma replied morosely.

That was my first encounter with nonbelief, my first wonder. So there were people on this earth who did not believe in Allah! I knew Uncle Siddique had said that Neil Armstrong had pissed on the moon. I had heard him say that Arabic was no different from any other language, that obscene words could be written in Arabic just as easily as in any other. But no one had told me that he did not believe in the existence of Allah! I longed to find out why he didn't believe, but there was no way of asking him. He lived far away. When he came to see us, he seemed to think his princess was still a little girl. He had no idea that she was growing up quickly, or that dozens of questions were bristling in her mind. She appeared timid and shy, so he thought it enough to give her several candies to keep her happy.

I began to answer my own questions by leafing through the books he left behind. When I had read them thoroughly it dawned on me, even at that young age, that the world did not begin and end with chants and prayers and magic spells. There was another world outside all this, the world of reason. Not everyone read the Koran and hadith, or did namaz and roja; nor did they build idols and bow before them. And not all Christians wore long black robes like nuns and priests. These were only symbols of something different, something bigger, something beyond the belief.

While these thoughts were churning in my mind, causing a great deal of confusion, Uncle Siddique sent word one day that he was going to bring a foreigner home with him. At once, the whole house became active. Everything was swept, brushed, dusted, mopped, and polished. Fresh, clean sheets were laid on our beds, and a tablecloth was placed on the dinner table. New curtains hung from the doors and windows. We were all told to have a bath before lunch, wear our best clothes, and wait quietly in the living room. When Victor E. Piroiko arrived and offered us his hand, we would have to offer him ours, shake it, and say, "How do you do?" We were made to memorize the words, but that was all we were required to do. As soon as the official greeting was over, we were to disappear inside the house. Since Dada could speak English, it was decided (by him) that only he would join Victor and Uncle Siddique for lunch. Everything went according to plan. Well, almost. Victor came, shook hands with us, but the words *How do you do?* got stuck in my throat. They refused to come out. Those words reminded me far too much of a game we played, *ha-do-do.*

This was another change that had come over me lately. I was finding it increasingly difficult to blindly repeat anything I was told to say.

Ma had cooked lots of things that day. After lunch, Victor was taken on a tour of the house. Then he disappeared into the bushes behind a building in our courtyard and peed there.

It was the first time I had seen a white man.

Even Ma was impressed, although she had grown up looking at

Englishmen and -women. "How terribly white his skin was!" she exclaimed, her eyes filled with wonder.

After Victor's departure, Dada continued to sit on the front veranda, swinging his legs, looking at the house, a smile of gratification on his face, as if the house had been honored by Victor's visit. Dada was still wearing smartly ironed trousers and a shirt, and on his feet were a pair of gleaming shoes.

The next day Ma went on her usual visit to Amirullah's house. After her return, she said, "So what if he was white? I saw the fellow standing while he pissed. He didn't even wash his hands afterward. Only the devil — and of course his followers — would do that. And why shouldn't he? He's a Communist, isn't he? He doesn't believe in either Allah or the Prophet. If I'd known before I would never have bothered to cook so much!"

Ma was convinced that the world was now full of the devil's followers.

10

Favorite

The Vidyamoyee School for girls was well known, built by the sister of Maharaja Shashikanto (or was it Surjakanto?). Anyway, it stood in a huge compound surrounded by a wall and a wide green lawn. Painted red, it was two stories tall with porches running all along its sides. Large trees, banyan and *peepal,* cast deep, dark shadows. On one side of the yard was a pond filled with blooming lotuses.

Aunt Jhunu had attended this school. When I passed the admission test, she took me on a guided tour and showed me where classes were held, where the staff room was, and where I had to go for the assembly. Then she took me to a room, Class IV, and found a seat for me in the front row. Before she left, she smiled and whispered in my ear, "Girls from senior classes might come and tell you something."

"What? What will they say?"

Aunt Jhunu looked at my apprehensive face, smiled mysteriously once more, but did not divulge the secret.

The first day passed without event, but on the second day, it happened. During the hour-long lunch break I was standing near the stairs, having finished eating, watching a group of girls playing in the field. Suddenly, I became aware of someone, clearly from a senior class, leaning over the railing and looking at me, a smile on her face. I didn't know who she was. I looked away and began walking toward my own classroom. Hardly had I taken a couple of steps when I heard her say, "Stop! Listen to me for a second." I stopped automatically.

The girl came closer, "What's your name?"

"Why? What do you want my name for?"

She was tall and dark and her long hair was braided. She laughed.

"Because you're very pretty, that's why." She took my hand in hers, pressing my fingers gently. I stiffened and pulled it away. The girl, whose name I still didn't know, said, "Don't be afraid. I'm not going to hurt you."

I looked down at the floor and my heart beat faster. The girl moved even closer, lowered her voice so that no one else could hear, and said, "Will you be my favorite?"

It made no sense to me. I had no idea what being a "favorite" meant. Tears welled up in my eyes and began flowing down my cheeks. The girl wiped them away with her hand and said, "What a silly girl you are! Why are you crying?"

At that moment, some other girls appeared, climbing up the stairs. The one who was talking to me moved away quickly.

In each classroom a fan made of colorful cloth hung from the ceiling. A rope was attached to it, pulled by ayahs who sat outside the classroom. After lunch that day I sat under the moving, swaying fan, but couldn't help breaking into a sweat, convinced that the older girl was trying to talk me into going somewhere with her. Who knows where she would have taken me!

The next day, I was again standing alone near the stairs. The same girl turned up and thrust a ripe guava into my hand. "I say, Miss Shy, won't you be my favorite? Say you will. I'll love you lots."

"No," I replied, my voice barely audible.

The girl smiled sweetly and tried to hold my hand again. I curled it into a fist.

A few girls from my own class — I hadn't yet learned their names — came up to me after school, and said, "Who's your favorite? That tall girl?"

I still didn't know what being a favorite entailed. All I had gathered so far was that a lot of whispering went on, speculating over who might be someone else's favorite. No one was prepared to reveal the name of her favorite because, it seemed, it was all a big secret.

Later, Aunt Jhunu told me about the whole thing. Apparently, it was an old tradition in Vidyamoyee School — older girls chose pretty young girls from junior classes as their favorites. It meant forming a special friendship, but it had to be kept secret. No one must know. No one must see them talking after school, or during the lunch break, or gym class, behind the compound wall, by the pond, or under a tree. The two girls would hold hands as they talked, and the older one would bring little gifts for the younger one. The girl Aunt Jhunu had chosen to be her favorite was called Beauty. She was really beautiful. Aunt Jhunu smiled in a certain way when she spoke of her. That tall girl had given me a similar smile.

As the days went by, I kept thinking this whole favorite issue was quite exciting. Now I longed for someone to come up again and ask me to be her favorite. They would need to ask me just once and I would agree happily, cross the line that separated me from the others, and join them. Who knows where all the pretty girls in my class flew off to when the lunch bell rang! Sometimes, snatches of conversation reached my ears: the new chain Mamata was wearing around her neck was a gift from her favorite. Shahana's friend was called Bonna. Some denied this, but others swore that Shahana and Bonna had been seen standing very close to each other behind a banyan tree.

All this happened only to others, and I remained as shy and stupid as ever. I had no favorite, no friend. If I was asked a question in class, I just stared foolishly. During our music and dance clases, and even during gym, I fared the worst. Once, during a Bengali class, I was asked to name a flower. I began thinking that there are so many flowers to choose from, so which one has the sweetest scent? A rose? A tuberose? A champa? Shiuli? Something else?

The teacher, irritated by my silence, said, "Can't this girl speak? Is she dumb?"

Yes, that's what she was. Dumb. A perfect idiot, which was why she could never bring herself to say to her teacher, "May I please go to the bathroom?" Not even when the need was urgent, because the teacher could well say yes — or no. If she said no, I knew I would have to sit very still, holding my breath, and everyone looking at me would know why I was sitting like that. If the teacher said yes, I would have to get up and leave the classroom, either running quickly or walking with my legs held as close together as possible, while the whole class looked on, wondering which kind of business I had to attend to — the small one, or the big one. It was profoundly embarrassing to ask in public and imagine the consequences, and so one fateful day I became mute and failed to utter those crucial words.

I just kept sitting, trying to control myself. Even when the teacher left after class and I managed to reach the toilet at the far end of the playing field, I could not bring myself to go in and finish my business. There were too many other girls about. I stood in that crowd waiting for the others to leave. Many more turned up after me, happily jumped the queue and went in, but I still remained where I was. The urge became stronger, great forces struggling to get out began a major fight with my gradually weakening body. *Wait,* I told this force silently. *Just wait a little while longer!* It didn't work. In an instant, my white salwar became colored. I continued to press myself against the wall, too embarrassed to look up, standing totally alone.

Who was going to rescue me from this disaster? I had no idea, but someone eventually did. It was the same tall girl who had once wiped my tears and given me a ripe guava. She approached me, smiled, and said, "Why are you standing here all by yourself?" I couldn't speak. Silently, I beseeched the earth to split open and swallow me up, but it did not oblige. My head hung low, as if it was about to dislodge itself from my neck.

The girl seemed to understand my predicament. She marched off, discussed the matter with the headmistress, and returned, having collected my books from the classroom. Then she arranged for the cleaning woman, Ramratia, to take me home straightaway. Had I been discovered by someone else and this kindness shown to me by some other girl, I wouldn't have minded so much.

I tried very hard to keep the whole thing a secret from people at home. It proved impossible. No one failed to notice my unexpected return from school, wearing white salwars with yellow patches on them, accompanied by the cleaning woman. The grown-ups smiled; the younger people laughed uproariously. Dada was no longer the only one among us to be called "shit-pants." He danced with joy, and erupted into poetry:

> Shit-pants comes back from school
> What a brilliant story!
> Ramratia comes with her,
> To add pride to glory!

For a whole month I was teased mercilessly, primarily by Dada. Occasionally, Ma took my side. "Stop it!" she said to him. "Her stomach was upset that day; it's not her fault." I seized this chance to pull a face at Dada. "Didn't *you* do the same in your school?"

"Never! Not when I was as old as you, if at all. It was only when I was little," he replied spiritedly.

At home, I could somehow comfort myself with the thought that Dada had done the same terrible thing before, but in school there was no one to offer me any comfort. I knew now that no one would ever again ask me to be her favorite. Whenever I saw the tall girl from a distance, I turned around and walked off in the opposite direction. If I caught any other girl looking at me, I began to shrink within myself. Did she know? Perhaps the whole school knew! My ears would go red with embarrassment.

After the war was over and we finally returned to school, everyone was promoted to the next class without being asked to sit for an exam. Now, during our school assembly, we stood under a new flag and sang *"Aamar shonar Bangla"* instead of *"Pak sar zameen."* Everyone had changed. People held themselves with far more pride than before; they spoke a language that was more lively, more assured. It seemed as if in the last nine months people had added nine years to their lives. Little girls were no longer little girls — they had seen their houses being burned, some had lost their brothers, some their fathers; some watched their elder sisters — victims of rape — grow bigger every day, carrying unwanted fetuses in their wombs. Each of us had been through a similar experience: We had walked for miles, had been forced to make our way through corpses, our ears ringing with the sound of screams.

Memories of that embarrassing and humiliating day faded into oblivion. No one remembered. No one cared.

I was different, too. I no longer hesitated to take part in games, even the one that involved chanting a rhyme and putting a garland around another girl's neck. The rhyme in question went like this:

> In the sahib's drawing room,
> We saw such lovely girls;
> Their skin was white,
> Their eyes were bright,
> They had such golden curls!

As soon as it was over, a garland would be placed on one of the other players. She was then asked to choose which of the two teams she wanted to join, Rose or Lotus.

My ears no longer went hot with embarrassment. Mind you, I was still quite an idiot when it came to sports. On our annual sports day Shahana and her four sisters — Heera, Panna, Mukta, and Jharna — won every race they took part in, although none were good students. I watched Shahana with a mixture of admiration and enchantment. Eventually, I became great friends with her, in spite of the differences in our nature.

However, I have to admit there was one occasion when once again my eyes lowered themselves, my heart trembled, the tip of my nose went red, and my whole body tingled, just because someone touched my hand. I dreamed of her frequently, and every time I thought of her during the day I smiled shyly. Just before falling asleep, I would see her again — her face, her smile, the way she talked, the way she walked, the way her hair, caught in a braid, rested on her back. I was convinced I would never see anyone so beautiful in the whole world. No one else could have such attractive eyes. I would forget every-thing, everyone, if I could just look into those eyes. I trembled with this strange, strange thrill.

This is how it began: One day, on my way to school, Chhotda and Milu, a friend of his, stopped me and handed me a letter. It was addressed to a girl called Runi who lived in the school hostel. She was about to take her matriculation exams. Milu had written the letter. My job was to find her and secretly pass it to her. No one must know, either at home or at school.

It seemed to me a very simple task. I found Runi and gave her the letter. She didn't open it immediately, but instead tucked it into her bosom. I looked at her eyes, those amazingly beautiful eyes. I wanted her to remain standing before me so that I could spend longer, much longer, gazing into her eyes. But Runi left. From that moment on, my own parched eyes began looking for her everywhere. If I saw a cluster of girls, I stopped and searched among them. Was she there? Every now and then I glanced out of the classroom window in case I spotted her walking across the field outside or ran into her unexpectedly.

Two days later, after school, Runi came running from the pond and gave me another letter. This time, it was for Milu. I took it but did not move. Runi smiled very sweetly. "What is it? Do you want to say something?" she asked. I shook my head. What could I say?

"You are very shy, aren't you? You hardly ever speak. Why don't you come to my room at the hostel one day? We could talk for as long as you like!" said Runi, taking my arm and pulling me closer. Her body smelled of fresh flowers. It was like a fairy tale. Runi was a flower — a jasmine perhaps — turned into a princess by some magic spell. I began trembling. My heart thumped. Somewhere deep within my being I could feel a hundred lotuses unfurl. I prayed for Milu to write to Runi every day, so that she would send her replies back through me, and I would get to see her more, much more closely. Runi would place her finger on my chin, speak in her slightly husky voice, and the few loose strands of hair around her forehead would blow gently in the breeze. I would lay my head on her breast and inhale the scent of jasmine.

I couldn't concentrate on my studies. I scribbled Runi's name over and over in my exercise books. While doing my math homework, almost involuntarily, I drew Runi's deep, dark eyes in the margin. I came back with zero on my homework nearly every day. My whole world, small though it was, was in Runi's grasp. The playing field lost its attraction; I began to spend far more time by the pond, dreaming of Runi. In its dark waters, I could see her dark eyes. Again and again I rubbed the spot on my arm where her hand had rested, feeling her touch once more. My dolls were forgotten, as were all other games. All that I craved now was Runi's touch, to be sought out and experienced in absolute secrecy.

I never spent a long time talking to Runi. In the few minutes that she could spare — never enough for me — it was she who talked. I simply listened, enchanted, sitting either on the stairs in her hostel or on her bed, my legs dangling. Runi always looked like a jasmine princess who had sprung out of the pages of a book, where she had been sitting alone in a forest, singing softly to herself. I wanted to give her all the love in my heart without telling a soul about it. I just longed to show her how strong this love was. I didn't have to talk, for one look at her eyes was enough. If I could touch her just once, every happiness in the world would be within my grasp.

Runi gave me bangles to wear, and a necklace. She moved closer as she slipped them on me, her body touched mine and I smelled jasmine again. My eyes dropped shyly.

When I returned home, the bangles and necklace had to be taken off and hidden. Baba did not like me to wear jewelry. Ma had had my ears pierced in the hope that Baba might be encouraged to buy me earrings, but he abused her instead. One day, on my way home from school, I met a street vendor selling bangles. I bought several glass ones and returned home, my arms loaded. Baba took one look at me and snatched them away. He smashed each one to pieces, saying, "If I see you wearing such stupid stuff again, I will break every bone in your body."

On another occasion, he caught me walking about with *alta,* a decorative coloring, on my feet. He demanded an explanation at once. "What's that red stuff on your feet? Is it blood? Did you cut yourself?" Ma smiled indulgently and said, "Don't be silly. That's alta, it's just a red liquid women like to paint their feet with. Your daughter wanted to try it, that's all."

I had to hide the jewelry Runi gave me but I didn't mind not being able to wear it. I knew in my heart that she loved me — it made no difference whether I wore the bangles and the necklace.

It was at about this time that I found myself sitting up in bed one night. No one had awakened me. An unseen force made me leave my bed and walk under the cover of darkness until I came to a bed on the floor where another body lay, the body of someone from a lower class. Moni had returned to our house, now older. Renu's mother was sacked as soon as Baba was found in her bed, and after that Ma hired a series of women to work in our house, ending with Moni. Ma found her sitting by a pond; she hadn't eaten for days.

I slipped into Moni's bed, my hands roaming all over her body. I removed her clothes and felt her breasts, which had suddenly grown as large as ripe guavas. No one had touched her beautiful breasts before. Now I did, fondling them, kissing them, smelling them as if I had been reunited after a long absence with my dearest friend. Moni was like a doll I had bought at a fair, a living, breathing doll. My own breasts had only just begun to appear;. a pair of buds on my chest waiting shyly to blossom into full-blown roses.

Who would have though that a foolish, unsmart girl like me could do something like this?

Back in school, I stopped passing Milu's letters to Runi. Instead, I stole writing paper from Dada's drawer, paper bordered with flowers and vines and birds, and wrote letters to Runi myself, pouring my heart out. She sent me her replies. Her letters carried her jasmine scent. My dull, uneventful life had suddenly become heady with excitement, as if someone had put me on a beautiful swing decorated with flowers and pushed me high up in the sky. No one knew. I led two lives quite happily. There was the same old me that everyone shouted at frequently and often thrashed, but inside there now lived someone else, someone who had learned to swim under water, like a diver, in the sea of love.

Chhatranam adhyanang tapah is a Sanskrit saying, something well-known sages had said, meaning that a student's only mission is the pursuit of knowledge. What else had they said? I did not have to respond, because Baba would rattle off the answer himself. "You cannot achieve anything in life without hard work. So stop wasting time on games and idle chatter or lounging around uselessly. Try to gain as much knowledge as you can. If you are seen as an educated person, the whole world will respect you. Do this not just to impress me, but for yourself, for your own benefit. If you neglect your studies now and think, 'My father will feed me anyway, so why should I bother?' do you know what will happen to you? You will have to beg in the streets to feed yourself. Work hard now, and only then will you reap the fruit of your labor. Have you seen how hard a farmer works? If he didn't, he would never be able to grow any food. Only diligence and hard work can help people become doctors or engineers or judges. You must never go to sleep before ten o'clock at night.

"Does your tutor come regularly?"

This time the answer had to come from me. "Yes, he does," I muttered.

"If you don't do well in your next exams," Baba spoke slowly and clearly, "I will skin you alive. I swear."

His squeaking shoes told me that he had moved away from the door and had left my room. Every day, he stood there and showered advice on me. He was determined to have us all educated so we would make "something of ourselves." Once, Dada failed to do well in his exams. He was so terrified he stayed away from home for three days. Baba sat with a thin cane in his hand waiting for Dada to turn up, pouring jug after jug of cold water over his own head to keep cool. Oddly, the parents of Dada's friends who had scored more or less the same marks were so happy their sons had passed that they distributed sweets all around.

Three days later, Baba left the house and went looking for Dada. When he found him, he dragged him home by the ear. If his exam results did not improve, he was told clearly, he would be thrown out of our house. Sadly, Dada only made second division. He sat for the entrance exam for medical college twice, but failed each time. Baba's blood pressure continued to rise. He threw pills into his mouth as if they were grains of chira. Dada realized that he no longer got privileged attention at home. Now, when he sat down to eat Baba picked out the best pieces of meat and gave them to Chhotda. Dada mixed his rice with gravy and toyed with it. On his plate lay a bone, sucked dry.

As many as four tutors were hired for Chhotda, one each for math, physics, chemistry, and English. He went to each tutor's house in the evenings. My own tutor came to our house to teach me, as did Yasmin's. We barely had time to rest, for the tutors arrived almost as soon as we returned from school. I had now moved from sixth to seventh grade; tuition costs had increased. Dada and Chhotda were supposed to study from dusk until midnight. I was allowed to stop at ten o'clock, Yasmin at eight. Baba laid down the law. My brothers were not required to read aloud, but Yasmin and I were, so that Baba could hear us in his room and be able to tell whether we were studying or sleeping.

Every evening, my eyes grew heavy with sleep as soon as the clock struck eight, and I would begin to nod off. Invariably, Baba would steal into my room and catch me in the act. "Go and rub some mustard oil into your eyes," he would command. "You will stop feeling sleepy." But I could not simply rub my eyes with oil. I had to tilt my head back and pour two drops of mustard oil into my eyes. Both eyes burned like hell, but Baba was satisfied that no matter what happened, I was not likely to fall asleep again.

Chhotda had a similar problem. He would put his head on his desk almost as soon as he sat down, then go to sleep. When I heard the front gate creak open, I would shake him saying, "Get up, quick, Baba's home!" Chhotda would rouse himself, having drooled all over his open book in the meantime. His eyes would be bloodshot. But he would then start reading aloud from his book, shaking his legs. To tell the truth, he didn't really read the words, he just made a funny noise. Baba heard this from a distance and thought his son was studying diligently. Chhotda would perform well enough in his exams for Baba to feel proud of him.

Whenever Baba was at home, everyone spoke in whispers. The house was as silent as a graveyard, as if all four children were trying to be great philosophers or scientists. Baba's was the only voice that could be heard from time to time. When he spoke to Dada, he had this to say: "You ass, you will never get anywhere. I tried to get you into a medical school, but you couldn't even pass the entrance exam. What will you do now? Work as a clerk somewhere? All you can hope for is a master's degree at a university. Your friend Jehangir is studying medicine and so is Faisal. How did they manage it? Surely their brains are no sharper than yours. They didn't eat anything different. I paid for so much extra coaching, but you still couldn't get a first division. Aren't you ashamed of yourself? If I were you I would have hanged myself!"

To Chhotda, he said, "You must think of nothing but your studies, Kamal. Forget everything else, because this is the most important stage of your life. You did very well in your matric. The rest of your life depends on how well you do your higher secondary. If you don't, you'll never be able to face the competition or get into medical school. And you *must* do that. A doctor's son must be a doctor. I had hoped, of course, that my eldest son would fulfill that dream, but that was not to be. You are my hope. Stop wasting your time, visiting with friends and going out with them. You must spend a minimum of eighteen hours on your studies. I want to feel proud of you. I was only a farmer's child and I became a doctor. You can be a bigger, better doctor than me. Show me that you can!"

Every morning, before leaving the house, Baba showered his advice on everyone, in every room. As soon as he was safely out, four chairs were immediately pushed back from desks. Some of us ran to the field outside, some switched on the radio or burst into song, some simply jumped back into bed. The black front gate acted as our lookout. Baba had a particular way of opening that gate — it creaked like that only under his touch. None of us needed to peer out to see if it was him. But Baba was cleverer than all of us put together. Like the monster in the fairy tale I had once read, he played tricks. When he said he would be late, he would return in the middle of the afternoon. Or he would tell us he would be back early, but there would be no sign of him until quite late at night. No one believed what he told us about his movements. We were alert and watchful all the time.

Once Baba caught me sorting a pile of long green gourds in the kitchen. He picked one up, brought it down on my back like a cane, and made me return to my desk. If he found me playing outside in the field with some other girls, he would slap me and drag me back inside, after shouting so loud at my playmates that they were frightened, too.

I have now lost count of the number of times Baba hit me, the number of times I prayed for his death. I wanted him to get very, very sick and die the same day. But his health was too robust for anything like that to happen. Far worse, however, was the threat of being vaccinated against smallpox. Whenever the men turned up in my school to vaccinate all the children, I ran and hid in the toilet. Sometimes they turned up at home. I would disappear from the house and spend the whole day outside, starving, staying out until I was sure the men had gone. One day Baba learned about my disappearing act. I was summoned and Baba himself punctured my flesh for the vaccination. I will never forget the pain for as long as I live. I could escape from every one else in the world, but escaping from Baba's clutches was impossible.

Every year I had to pass three major examinations in school, two in the first six months and a final at the end of the year. The final was referred to as the "annual" exam. I had to pass it in order to go on to the next class. Once I got thirty-three out of one hundred, the lowest grade allowed, in the first English exam, held after three months in a new class.

I felt miserable the whole day. Anxiety dried my throat so much that I drank gallons of water and sat close to Ma, hoping she would protect me from Baba's wrath. I would have to show him my report card. It wasn't difficult to imagine how hard his cane would come down on my back when he saw the thirty-three. "Wear something thick," Ma advised me, "and it will hurt less." I took her advice and spent the time waiting for Baba to get home feeling hot and uncomfortable. As things turned out, I needn't have bothered. Instead of hitting me, Baba said calmly, "From today on, I am going to teach you English." I hardly knew what to say. It would have been far better if he had skinned me alive. It was almost as if a horrible monster was stroking my back and saying, "From today on, I am going to gobble you up, bit by bit."

My whole life changed after that. Every evening, Baba would return from his pharmacy at eight o'clock, change into a lungi, tie its knot securely, slip his glasses on, pick up his cane, and sit by my desk. I kept one eye fixed on the book and the other on the cane. Baba began teaching me the rules of English grammar. As the evening progressed, I would start yawning. Each time I opened my mouth to yawn, Baba's cane fell on me with a swish, making me shudder. Baba explained the intricacies of past, present, and future tenses and their usage, cracking my skull open, pouring these in, then closing the crack with one swift blow. Those rules should have remained in my head, etched on my brain, for the rest of my life.

However, the very next day I made a mistake. I was sitting as I sat every day, one eye on the shiny cane, and the other on my book. My back was held very straight, for according to Baba, only those who were lazy and idle sat slouched over their books. The instant the wrong answer slipped out the cane rose and fell: swish! The more it swished, the more confused I got, and the number of mistakes increased. My eyes filled with tears. Swish, swish! Baba went on; the tears gathered force. With brimming eyes, I said, "I want to go and drink some water!"

"There is no need for that," Baba replied coolly. As long as he was teaching me, I was not supposed to feel thirsty or hungry or even ask to answer the call of nature. "Those are just excuses to escape your study," Baba declared. "You think you can play tricks on me?"

When the lesson finally came to an end, Ma would rub a soothing balm on my wounded back, muttering all the while: "What's the point in thrashing her like an animal? You can't *force* anyone to learn anything! But then, my girl, you do nothing to help yourself, either, do you? How will you ever do well in your exams if you keep reading novels all day? You — and the others — sit down at your desks only when your father is at home. Otherwise the whole house is like a fish market. If you paid more attention to your work Baba wouldn't have to beat you. Now go and lie on your stomach, huh!"

The caning I got every evening made me stop doing my homework and ignore all my other subjects; I spent all my time trying to master the rules of English grammar. Soon I was known as the stupidest girl in school. In my math class, the cantankerous teacher made me kneel down on the hard floor. In the science class, I was made to stand on a bench, holding my ears with both hands. Other teachers told me to stand on one leg in front of the blackboard, so that the whole class could see me, still holding my ears with my hands. That was the price I paid for not doing my homework, or preparing lessons in any other subject.

After all this, did my knowledge of English improve? No. I tried so hard to learn the rules of grammar, but as soon as Baba began roaring at me and the caning began, I forgot everything I had learned. Three months later, after the second set of exams, I managed to get twelve out of one hundred in English. When Ma saw my report card, she gave me a somewhat twisted smile and said, "When I was in the seventh grade, our English teacher asked, 'Does anyone know the English word for *gobar*?' No one knew except me. I stood up and said loudly and clearly, "Cow dung." The whole class heard me. If I had continued with my studies, I might have become an English teacher myself!"

One look at my marks made Baba's blood pressure shoot up so high he had to be hospitalized.

In his absence, our house became a fish market once more. We talked, we sang, we played the radio all day. Our desks and our books began gathering dust. Who could be bothered with them now? I spent my evenings on the roof — supposedly off-limits for me — and my nights on various novels. I could now read them openly, sitting wherever I wanted — there was no need for secrecy.

The novels were supplied by a girl called Mamata who was known to be a bookworm. She and I were in the same class and, purely by chance, became good friends. She would sit in the last row and read novels and other fiction secretly, without getting caught. One day, after school was over, she continued to sit in the classroom alone, reading her book. When the caretaker came a little later and locked the door from outside, he didn't realize she was inside. Mamata became a prisoner for the night.

I was the first to learn what had happened because the following morning I entered the classroom before anyone else. I found Mamata fast asleep on a bench. What was wrong with her? I shook her awake. Mamata told me she had been locked in. By the time she realized it, it was too late. Everyone had gone; no amount of shouting or banging on the door could help her get out. I gasped. What did she do then? "What *could* I do?" Mamata smiled. "I finished my book. It was quite late by the time I went to sleep." What was the book? Mamata showed it to me — a collection of detective novels called *Kiriti Omnibus*.

Mamata did not seem at all concerned about what her mother must have felt when her daughter failed to return home from school. "I'm quite hungry" was all she said coolly, and left the classroom. Her book stayed with me. Her mother didn't let her come to school for a couple of days. On the third day, I returned her book, having read it in the meantime. This pleased her no end, for she had started to think that the book was lost forever. From that day on she began to pass on to me every book that she read. She shared her books with no one else.

Baba was still in the hospital. Ma went to visit him every evening, clutching a tiffin* carrier filled with home-cooked food. One evening, Baba told her he wished to see both his daughters. When Ma relayed this message to me, I tried to make a number of excuses to get out of it. "I don't feel very well," I said. "I think I've got a fever. Besides, my tutor will turn up this evening. Why don't you take Yasmin?"

None of my excuses worked. Ma was determined to take me with her and I soon found myself in the hospital where Baba lay on his bed, enveloped in the smell of Dettol. There was dark stubble on his face. I had never seen him unshaven before. He seemed to have aged considerably. He called me to his side, and said sadly, "You are happy and relieved now, aren't you? Now that Monster is out of the way you are free to do what you want, aren't you?"

This meant that Baba knew I called him "Monster" behind his back. I had stopped addressing him directly as "Baba" years ago. Ever since he had started teaching me English, I had even stopped referring him to as my father. He was just Monster. The day Baba refused to give him money to buy a new pair of shoes Chhotda agreed that the name I had chosen was excellent.

I was afraid that Baba would jump up from his clean, white hospital bed and break all my bones to punish me for his new name. Instead he startled me a good deal by asking gently, "What did you have for lunch today, dear?"

Reassured I replied, "Rice and egg curry."

"As soon as I go home, I'm going to get nice, big fish for you, and chicken. I believe new mangoes have arrived in the shops. I'll get some for you."

I nodded. If I nodded, said Yes or Hmm, and indicated that I agreed with everything he said, I might be able to get out of the hospital quickly. The sooner I did so the better. But Baba surprised me even further by reaching out and pulling my head close to his chest. "Why didn't you oil your hair?" he asked, running his fingers through it. "You should oil it, comb it, and keep it tied with a ribbon. Then it will look very nice."

I held my breath. Baba rubbed his rough, bristly cheek against

---

*A lunch box consisting of several cylindrical containers bound by a band, which doubles as the handle.

mine and went on, "I know you have what it takes. I know you have brains. I realized it when I started teaching you. Tell me, if I said, 'My father has been crying for more than two hours,' what tense would that be?"

"Present perfect continuous," I muttered softly.

"Right. Correct! See, I told you you could do it, didn't I?"

Baba stroked my back, inadvertently touching the spots that were still sore from being caned. I flinched with pain, my back arching involuntarily, like a bow. But I said nothing, nor did I move away. Suddenly I felt very sorry for my father.

Baba returned home in due course, and our home was immediately covered by the cold, dark silence that descends at midnight. The same coldness engulfed my life as well. It was decided that I should go to a different school. Baba agreed that Vidyamoyee was good, but a new one, the Residential Model School, had recently started and was supposed to be better. I would go there. By this time, I had acquired friends in Vidyamoyee and developed a secret intimacy with Runi. Now, out of nowhere, a hawk was going to swoop down and snatch me from my familiar surroundings. Sounding as desperate as someone who has to flee his home to save his life but wants to hang on until the last possible minute, I said: "I don't want to study anywhere except Vidyamoyee!"

"Who are *you* to want anything? *I* want you to go to Model," Baba snapped.

"Vidyamoyee is a good school," I insisted.

Baba coughed. "The Model is even better," he replied. I mustered all my courage, closed my eyes tight, clenched my teeth, and said, "I will not go to any other school!"

"Yes, you will. You jolly well will!" said Baba, knotting his tie, looking at himself in the mirror.

I had passed an entrance exam before getting into the new school and among other things was told to write an essay on "My Aim in Life." I focused my attention on this one question, ignoring everything else. As I began writing I realized that it was easier to use English wherever strong language was required. It was ideal for hurling abuses, for instance. If I tried writing in Bengali, I was rocked by strong emotions, and powerful sentiment crashed through the barriers of reason. On this particular day, therefore, I avoided Bengali, and wrote the whole essay in English.

I said very clearly that it was not my aim to study in the new school. The building, to me, seemed haunted. I was perfectly happy in my old school and had no wish to leave. I couldn't bear being forced to do something against my will. My father was trying to impose his will on me. If he wanted to throw me into the Brahmaputra River and drown me in it, he would, just because that was what he wanted. What *I* wanted was of no consequence to him. Whose life was at stake here, mine or his? If the former — and surely the ownership of my own life could not be questioned — then I would request the authorities not to admit me to their school. I believed that they would not wish to do anything that would damage my life.

I didn't glance at any other question on the paper. This would serve Baba right, I thought, and felt quite pleased. I waited until the allotted time was up and handed in my answer sheet. Baba was waiting in the corridor outside. He pounced on me eagerly and said, "How did it go?"

"All right," I replied, my face pale.

"You answered all the questions, I hope?" he asked, smiling.

"Yes," I answered, like a good little girl.

"It's going to be tough. Two hundred girls took this test and they only have thirty seats." Baba looked worried, and beads of perspiration stood out on his forehead.

I was not in the habit of telling lies, but this one I had practiced and rehearsed so that I could make myself utter it with a straight face, without giving anything away.

Baba took me to his pharmacy after the entrance exam. He had his own pharmacy now. After the war, he had bought a shop in Notun Bazar, only a few feet away from Grandpa's restaurant, and turned it into a pharmacy-cum-doctor's-chamber. He took me to his consulting room and placed me in the upholstered chair that he normally used himself. Then he began feeding me chum-chums. "You must work very hard," he told me as I ate, "and stand first in class, every time. Pay attention to your studies right from the start."

I listened to him in silence, knowing very well that this particular dream would soon be blown away like a dry, dead leaf. Naturally, Baba had no idea, but I did. It was my special secret, like the fact that I played with Moni's naked body in the dead of night. No one knew about that, except me.

Only a few days later, Baba returned with the "good" news. I had passed the entrance exam and been admitted to the new school. My head was reeling. How could this be possible? But I should have known better — if Baba wanted something, he got it. He made it possible. He always got his own way, at least, as far as I was concerned, even if he failed with other people.

The new school stood in the middle of what looked like a desert. The building appeared empty and silent. Baba pushed me inside, saying, "I have no wish to throw you into the Brahmaputra. You are my daughter — my own flesh and blood. No one is as concerned about your welfare as your father, believe me. If you do fall into the river and start drowning, do you know who will be the first to jump in to save you? Me."

The number of students was very small indeed, and there were only five or six teachers. I went and sat in a classroom, frequently wiping my wet cheeks with my palms.

I couldn't settle down in my new school. Nor could Yasmin — she had had to change too. Before the war, she used to go to Mariam School, run by Christian missionaries. It closed after the war, and she was put in to Rajbari. Instead of "Twinkle, twinkle little star" or "Humpty Dumpty sat on a wall," she was now told to learn rhymes and poems in Bengali. The Mariam School was only five minutes from our house, and almost every evening, whenever she got the chance, Yasmin slipped out and stood in front of its locked gate. Little banyan seedlings had started to sprout from cracks in its front veranda. She heaved deep sighs. She was attached to the building, dirty and derelict though it was, to the tree that stood beside it, to the field that stretched behind the tree, to the pond beside the field. She missed the swing in her school so much that Baba had one installed in the field beside our house. Yasmin sat on it, gently moving to and fro, her eyes closed, imagining herself back in her old schoolgrounds.

". . . how I wonder what you are! . . ." she sang.

What had *I* left behind? Did I miss a veranda, or a swing? No. I did miss Runi, though, that much I knew. But was it only Runi? No. Runi was like the North Star. She shone brightly, but she was far away, too far for me. That was where she belonged, at a distance. I did not wish to drag her down to this earth, where I played in its dust and dirt. Runi was too beautiful for that.

But I missed my old routine, a life spent in the company of lesser mortals, whose noses were snotty, teeth unclean, and hair filled with lice. Such is the nature of old, established habits. People — particularly if they are introverts — are scared to step out of what is familiar and start life afresh.

In my new school, everyone was expected to bring her own lunch from home. Baba brought me sliced fruitcake every evening to pack in my lunch box. I did, but felt no desire to eat it the following day. What I would have preferred was *kotkoti,* a special sweet sold by peddlars when they called at our house. In fact, they gave us those sweets in exchange for old shoes! Baba might think a fruitcake was the most delicious item in the world, but I didn't share that view. I at least had the freedom to decide what I would eat for my lunch, and what I wouldn't.

One day, during lunch break, I was standing by the railing on the corridor, my packed lunch ignored. There was nothing to look at except a patch of empty land that was really an old, disused pond, now covered with earth. Suddenly, to my complete astonishment, someone placed a hand on my back. It was Runi. I took a step back, then another, and a third. If I stood close to her, she might hear my beating heart and feel the thrill that surged through my pores. I had to put some distance between us. But Runi stepped forward, smiling as sweetly as ever, and said, "I'm going to stay at this school, in one of the teachers' quarters. Isn't that fun? Do you know Rebecca? She's the school doctor and my elder sister."

I stepped back even farther and stared at Runi from a safe distance, forgetting to answer her question. Her sudden arrival, like a comet in my lonely world, rendered me absolutely speechless. If one's love was true, only then could it bring the loved one close, before one's eyes. That was what I believed, anyway. Runi kept walking toward me, her arms outstretched, and I continued to move away until my back struck a wall and I could move no farther.

"Why are you so shy?" she asked, placing a hand on my shoulder. A tremor ran through my body. I didn't know what it was, I couldn't define it, but my breath was coming faster, so fast that I had to cover my face with my hands.

"Are you going on the picnic? Everyone in the school is being taken to a *zamindar's* house in Dhonbari for a picnic. It's quite far. I love going to places far away," said Runi.

Slowly, ever so slowly, I raised my eyes to look into hers. They held all the blue in the sky. I wanted to spread my wings and fly. Her beautiful body shook with laughter as she caught my half-open eye. Who but Runi could laugh like that? It was not surprising that I loved her; anyone would. But her love for *me* — was it love or just affection, or some kind of indulgence — embarrassed me very much. The more she tried to draw me out, the more I shrank within myself. If a big tree leaned over to greet a simple blade of grass, the smallness of the grass would be emphasized, more than anything else. When I felt Runi's love for me, I lost all sense of my own existence.

Runi left, but I stood rooted to the ground, as if I had reached my final destination in life, as if I had dreamed of arriving at this very spot for thousands of years. Suddenly, the shriveled old trees near the new school building seemed to come to life. The corridors appeared more lively. The hot, dusty wind felt like a cool, southerly breeze. The gray, barren land all around the school turned a lush green as soon as Runi stepped on it. I longed to rush out, barefoot, and stand on the grass.

To join the others on the picnic, I was required to pay ten takas. When I asked Baba for the money, he said calmly, "There's no need for you to go."

I couldn't let that happen. "I have to go," I replied.

"*Have* to?" Baba said irritably, "What do you mean by that? Who's forcing you to go? Picnics, is that one of the subjects you're studying? Will you get lower marks if you don't go?" Baba refused to part with a penny.

All the girls in my school were overjoyed at the thought of the picnic. I was the only one who fluttered about like a wounded bird. Eventually, a girl called Ayesha came to my rescue. "If you haven't got the money, why don't you borrow it from me?" she said casually and gave me ten takas. At last, my name was included in the list of those who were going. On the appointed day, we all climbed into a truck quite early and taken to Dhonbari. Runi went in a bus, together with the teachers and some senior students. Large pots and pans, cooking ingredients, plates, and glasses were loaded on the roof of the bus. Someone put on some music, switched on the speaker, and off they went, traveling with our truck. When we reached Dhonbari, I spent the whole day looking at Runi from a distance, admiring her beauty. If she turned left, I immediately turned right. If she turned right, I promptly went left. If she disappeared from sight, my eyes roamed restlessly, looking for her everywhere. When they found her, I just sat quietly in the shade of a tree or on the stairs.

By the time I got back home, it was dark. I found Baba waiting on the front veranda. "What took you so long today?" He leaped up and caught me as I walked in.

"I . . . I . . . went to the picnic!" I replied, picking my nails.

Baba dragged me to the courtyard, broke a branch from a jackfruit tree, and started beating me with it. I bent over mutely, offering up my back because it was understood that if either parent wanted to beat a child, the child had to take every blow passively. Baba struck me as many times as he wanted, until he was satisfied. Then he asked, "Who gave you the money?"

It was difficult to find my voice, but I had to speak somehow, since answering all questions Baba or Ma ever asked me was compulsory. "A girl in my class . . . she loaned me the money," I blurted out.

This time, Baba delivered a heavy slap to my cheek. "You *borrowed* money to go to the picnic? Why was this picnic so important? Well, I can tell you, my girl, I'll make bloody sure you never do it again!"

The following morning, before he left for work, Baba threw ten takas at me, together with the money that he paid me every day for the rickshaw. "If you disobey me just once more," he threatened, "I will break every branch of every tree on your back, I promise!"

Sometime after the picnic, my school began preparing for a cultural evening. Some of the girls sat in the common room and practiced their songs, accompanied by a harmonium. Others practiced dances, or recitations, or rehearsed a short play based on a long poem by Tagore. Arrangements were made for drawing on a blackboard in time with a song. Someone would sing "In this rice field today, the sun and shadows play hide-and-seek," while another girl would pick up a piece of chalk and draw the scene described in the song.

At first, I was a mere spectator. Then, one day, I found a Hawaiian guitar and played a song that I had secretly picked up from Chhotda: "If these songs, and this music stopped one day, you would forget me, my love." Those who heard me decided immediately that I must play the guitar on the stage. They would not take no for an answer.

My limbs trembled as I sat on the stage, fiddling with the guitar, but my performance brought applause from the audience. By this time, I was known in my new school as a good student. In our drawing class, I was called a genius. My English was judged to be excellent. The composition I had written for the entrance exam was also described as excellent. The teacher who taught Bengali said to me one day, "I say, you appear to be a poet!"

Soon after the cultural evening there was fresh excitement in my class. Girls were being selected to form a troop of Girl Guides, and I became one of them. We were taught physical exercises. Then I learned to play the drum, placing it round my neck. On Victory Day, the sixteenth of December, we went to the parade ground next to the Circuit House and did a garba dance.

I did all that, but still I could not overcome my shyness. Whatever I did, my eyes remained lowered, my gaze fixed on the ground. Jogesh Chandra, a dance teacher, arrived in our school one day to teach us "Chitrangada," one of Tagore's dance-dramas. He caught me at once and said, "Hey, you! Will you play Chitrangada?" I slipped out of his grasp and ran away. But that did not stop me from watching the rehearsals.

Excited by what I saw, I started rehearsing on my own, at home, with Yasmin for company. I was the princess Chitrangada, Yasmin my lady-in-waiting. We danced all over the field. Then I switched roles and became Arjun, Chitrangada's lover. I played Madan, the god of love, as well. The rehearsals in school continued. At home, I performed the whole play on the stage. My audience was Ma, Moni, Dada, Chhotda, and Poppy, the little dog.

11

Love

When Chhotda was in his second year of college, one day he made a request on behalf of a fellow student, a woman called Baby, who also attended Anandamohan College. She had nowhere to live — could she stay at our house? Her home was far away in a place called Netrakona.

Chhotda's request was granted. Baby arrived, suitcase in hand. She was to share my room, even sleep in my bed, but a separate table and chair were provided for her studies. Baby was dark and tall with very attractive eyes. She became one of the family in just a couple of days. No one outside the family had ever stayed in our house, and I had never had a complete stranger sleeping in my room. Baby's arrival created quite a ripple in my uneventful life.

When she talked about her family I could picture it all quite vividly — how her sister, Manjari, had once fallen from the topmost branch of a tree and broken her leg; how Baby traveled alone from Netrakona to Mymensingh to study in a college; how one of her brothers, who was mentally retarded, used to sit by the river all day, his legs immersed in the water. Baby's brother went missing one day and was never found. I could see the river where he sat, for it had become as familiar to me as the Brahmaputra. Manjari, I felt, was someone I had known all my life. Baby sat in the kitchen with Ma and went on talking. When her brother could not be found, her mother took to her bed. She refused to eat and began rapidly wasting away. One day she asked Baby to take her out to a pond and help her bathe. Baby did as she was told. Her mother returned home after her bath, draped herself in a white sari, and went back to bed. She did not get up again. Ma was deeply moved by this story. "You must look upon me as your mother," she said to Baby. "I had two daughters. Well, now I have three."

When Baba returned home, he asked Baby, "How about your studies? Do you think you'll get a first division?" Baby bowed her head and replied softly, "Yes, Uncle. I have every hope."

It didn't last long. Only three and a half months later, Baby had to pack her suitcase and leave. Ma had discovered Chhotda lying on his bed with Baby sitting by his side, running her fingers through his hair. "Baby!" Ma screamed, "I had no idea you had such evil plans! You made me think the two of you were like siblings, and you had *this* in mind? How dare you!"

Baby fell at Ma's feet, tears in her eyes. It was not what it seemed, she explained, Chhotda had a headache, and she had merely touched his forehead. She would never do it again. Could she please be forgiven?

Ma, not one to forgive easily, refused to relent.

The person who remained perfectly calm and apparently indifferent to Baby's departure was Chhotda.

It was nearly time to take the exam for the Higher Secondary School Certificate (H.S.C.). If Chhotda passed, he would get into medical college. It was Baba's long-cherished dream that one of his sons would become a doctor.

But one day Chhotda vanished. A couple of days passed, then a whole week — there was no sign of him. Baba went crazy looking for him. At the time, he was working as a civil surgeon, in charge of all the doctors who worked in the public health care centers in the city of Tangail. He had to leave at dawn to catch a bus to Tangail and returned quite late at night. Now, faced with a crisis at home, he applied for leave and spent all his time trying to find his son. Mymensingh was a small town. Eventually, Baba found Chhotda, but he was not the same person who had left home. He had married. Apparently, he had been in love with a Hindu girl in his class for a long time and he had now secretly married her, helped by one of his friends. It was in this friend's house that he was hiding with his wife.

Baba pressed the throbbing veins in his temples and said, "I . . . don't . . . believe . . . this! All my hopes, all my dreams . . . gone down the drain! How could he do this to me? Who gave him this idea? Only a few months from now he'd have sat for his H.S.C. Then he'd have started studying medicine. I would have been so proud of him! And now . . . how could he be so completely crazy and ruin his own future? I told him, didn't I, I told him a million times not to waste his time with his friends? I told him to pay attention to his studies, to become a proper man!"

Ma poured mug after mug of cold water over Baba's head. Ma didn't know it, but his high blood pressure was silently curling its black talons around Baba's heart.

Ma sobbed, "My poor boy . . . what a gem of a boy he is! Who knows where he is, who's feeding him! Someone must have put a spell on him. He's too young to be married. Why would he think of marriage unless he was under a spell? Allah, bring my son back to me!" Then, turning to Baba, who still appeared stunned, she asked, "Could . . . could it be just a rumor?"

Baba shook his head. No, what he had learned was true. The girl was called Geeta Mitra. A Hindu.

The whole house was sunk in gloom. No one bothered to cook. I lay in my room, staring at the ceiling. I felt quite lonely. Dada had gone to Dhaka to study at the university. Now if Chhotda did not come back, the house would really seem empty. Moni dozed on the veranda, the sunlight climbed down the stairs into the courtyard, but no one stepped out into the sun.

There was a time when Ma used to make us stand in the sun and rub mustard oil on our bodies, placing two tiny drops in our ears and one in our belly buttons. Chhotda was included in this ritual, although he was too old for it. He combed his hair in a special way, so that it looked wavy, he wore shoes with pointed toes, and smiled mischievously at Dolly Pal, the girl next door. But as soon as he stepped back into the house, he became Ma's stammering baby boy once more.

Sitting close to Baba's bed, Ma sighed again. "A Hindu girl . . . how could he marry a Hindu girl? She visited this house a few times. Frankly, I didn't like the way she behaved. At first she wanted to go to the cinema with Noman. When he refused, she started pestering Kamal. Chased every boy she could find — she's very clever, got her claws into my poor, simple son. I think . . . yes, Kamal did seem rather preoccupied the last few days. If only I had known! I could have tried to save him."

Ma sighed, leaning her elbow against the railing on Baba's bed, and continued, "Only Allah can help me get him back. Please, O Allah, please bring him back soon. Why, he was never meant to marry a Hindu girl! I could have chosen a bride for him . . . there would have been no dearth of good girls for my son, my jewel, . . . and we could have had a marvelous wedding. But . . . why did he do this? Why even think of marriage until you've finished your studies and gotten a good job! No. I am sure he will come back one day. He will realize what he has done. After all, anyone can make a mistake."

I remembered Geeta Mitra very well. She used to study at Vidyamoyee Girls School. Her face was round like a ball of tamarind, her eyes large and dark, like the eyes of a doe. She used to dance at various school functions. She met Chhotda when they enrolled at Anandamohan College. Her aunt, who was handicapped, used to teach us, which was why she sometimes came to our house and chatted with Yasmin and me. In fact, she was great fun to be with, or so I thought at the time. She offered to take us to the cinema secretly and teach us how to dance. Then she said she would get some custard apples for us, and she climbed straight up to the top branch of the tree. We were thrilled to find she was such a tomboy. Baby was different. She could cook and sew and was more of a homemaker. Geeta, the tomboy, won us over quite easily. But then, at the time, our hearts were so wide open to the whole world that one simply had to step into them to win them over. When it was time for Eid, Ma got some white satin to make dresses for us. Geeta took the material and said, "I can sew very well. I will make your dresses for you." Then she started visiting us every day — sometimes more than once — with a measuring tape in her hand to take our measurements.

She took thirteen days to make the two dresses, though her original promise was to finish three. She brought them around only on the morning of Eid. When I slipped mine on, I found it so tight across the chest that I thought it would burst; and it was so long that anyone would have thought I was wearing the kind of robe that the women in Amirullah's house wore. I had never worn such a strange garment.

It didn't end there. The whole day was ruined. Geeta helped me put the dress on, clapped her hands, grinned broadly, and said, "Oh, how sweet you look! Beautiful! Come with me, I will take you to a wonderful place."

The temptation proved too much. Lured by the prospect of visiting somewhere "wonderful" I got into a rickshaw with Geeta, and rode to the house of a judge, a rich man. One of the girls in that house, Ruhi, was Geeta's friend. The two were supposed to go out somewhere but Ruhi's mother had not yet given her permission. Ruhi — a girl with a very fair skin, but a body that was kind of flat — began badgering her mother. It took two hours for her mother to relent. Ruhi and Geeta spent the entire time whispering among themselves, and I sat on a sofa like a dressed-up doll.

Having finally obtained her mother's permission, Ruhi plastered her face with makeup, lined her eyes with kohl, and set off with us.

No one told me where this "wonderful" place was. The two older girls giggled throughout the journey while I sat like a wooden horse on Geeta's lap. Eventually, our rickshaw stopped outside a house in Gulkibari. There was a lawn in front. The man who emerged as we clambered out had a face like a fox. He let us in and then locked the front gate. I had never seen him before. The house was totally silent. When we went in, I realized that there was no one there except Fox-face. There were two rooms, one next to the other. Ruhi disappeared into the bedroom with the man. I sat in the other room on a sofa, but could see what Ruhi and the man were doing. The man sat very close to Ruhi on the bed, so close that I simply gaped. Then he lay down, pulling Ruhi onto his chest. A second later he jumped to his feet and came to the other room, carrying two bottles of Fanta. He thrust these into our hands and said, "Go on, Geeta, go and sit on the lawn." Then he vanished inside the bedroom once more, this time shutting the door.

Outside on the lawn, I asked, "Who is that man?" My voice trembled. Geeta smirked. "Khurram Bhai. He's very rich. He's got a car."

"But he took Ruhi in and shut the door!" I swallowed. "What's going to happen now? I feel very scared. Let's go home."

Geeta's teeth gleamed white on her dark face. "Don't worry. Sit here for a while. What do you want to go back for? We just came!"

The afternoon gave way to early evening. We were still sitting outside; I was still saying "Let's go home" every other minute, feeling extremely uncomfortable. Fox-face reappeared from time to time with a fresh bottle of Fanta. But that was no longer good enough. Hunger pangs were growing in my stomach. I walked up to the gate and said, now almost in tears, "Open this gate, please. I want to go. I don't like it here."

By now, Geeta herself was looking worried. She went back in, stood in front of the bedroom door, and shouted, "Khurram Bhai! She doesn't want to stay here anymore. Do let us go."

Fox-face reemerged. Above his fat lips was a thick mustache. Between his fingers he held a cigarette. His torso was bare, as were his feet. "Geeta, come and take some pictures. Come on in!" he invited. Geeta went in with him, while I stood at the door.

Ruhi was sitting in the center of the bed, her head bowed. Her hair, once tied in a ponytail, was now loose. She had been wearing lipstick when we came. Now it was gone. The kohl had spread around her eyes. I began to feel very sorry for Ruhi. Had the man stripped her? Had she been willing to take her clothes off or not? Had the man threatened her, or somehow frightened her into staying in his room? I couldn't work anything out. I saw the man pass a camera to Geeta and throw his arms around Ruhi. Geeta grinned and pressed the shutter. Then the man stretched himself across Ruhi's lap. Geeta clicked again. He placed his cheek against Ruhi's. Geeta obliged once more.

By the time we were allowed to leave, it was dark. Geeta dropped Ruhi home before taking me to mine. On the way she told me, "You must never tell anyone where you went!"

My parents were, quite understandably, livid. They had spent the day of Eid worrying about their missing daughter. Silently, and with a pale face, I bent over and offered my back to take the punishment I deserved.

That same mysterious Geeta who had given me that "wonderful" day was now Chhotda's wife! He was an accomplished guitar player, well known in our town, and he played at all the college functions. He provided the music, and Geeta Mitra danced. That was how their intimacy began. And now he was married! I remembered Baby saying, "You mustn't talk to Geeta. She's an awful girl." Geeta, on the other hand, warned me about Baby. "Baby's a bad girl. Make sure she never visits your house again."

Baba found his voice. "I shall disown that boy, completely! I brought him up, I did so much for him, and now he stabs me in the back!"

Ma stopped sobbing. Now her voice rose higher and higher. "What did Kamal do after all we did for him? Marry a witch! And what does her father do? Sell firewood. That Hindu firewood-seller is now the relative of a doctor! Do you know where the women in his house go to have a bath? To the tap by the roadside! They're bloody low class. And my son had to go and marry a girl from that family. My jewel married a dancer! *Chee chee!* Allah, how shall we ever show our faces to the people? Why did I give birth to a child like him?"

Ma wailed endlessly. We had never had to face such a difficult situation before. Baba sent for Grandma, Grandpa, Aunt Runu, and Uncle Hashem. Uncle Siddique came from Dhaka, as did Aunt Jhunu and Dada. Everyone was most concerned. They sat down for an emergency meeting from which Yasmin and I were excluded. We were not even allowed to peep in from behind the door. The meeting continued until midnight. Everyone spoke in such low tones that I heard nothing, even when I strained my ears. Only a few stray words wafted out, like cottonseeds, but it was impossible to tell which way the wind was blowing.

What happened the next day was terrible. Baba and Uncle Hashem captured Chhotda, brought him home, and tied him up with heavy iron chains in the living room. Shackles were placed on his arms and legs, their ends held in a padlock. The key remained in Baba's pocket. Baba roared, making the whole house tremble. Even the plants in the courtyard shook. I peered through the window and broke into a sweat. Yasmin fell on her bed, buried her face in pillow, and began to cry. Ma paced restlessly on the veranda, muttering under her breath, her prayer beads moving rapidly between her fingers.

"Will you leave Geeta, or not?" Baba shouted. "If you don't I will disown you officially."

"Do so, by all means," Chhotda replied coolly. "I am not going to leave her."

Baba's eyes began to bulge; his shirt, drenched with sweat, was clinging to his body. Arms akimbo, he stood breathing heavily. I could tell his blood pressure was rising.

"You will not leave this house, do you hear? The only place you'll go is to college. You'll sit for your exams. That's all."

Undaunted, Chhotda replied, raising his voice this time, "I did not want to come to this house. You tricked me into coming here. Look, I married Geeta. Let me go. I must return to her. I want nothing else from you."

"No. You will have to leave Geeta, or you'll die at my hands. I will whip you to death." Tongues of fire blazed from Baba's eyes. "I will give you two hours to think it over."

For the next two hours Chhotda sat in complete silence, his jaw set. Grandma, Aunt Runu, and Ma took turns trying to make him see reason. "Look, darling, you're a good boy. We all know that," they said. "At your age, many young boys make mistakes. Your father will forgive you if you come back home and go back to your studies. You'll become a doctor one day. Yes, you will. All right, so you're married, but, look, come back here and let your wife go back to her parents. Why don't you both finish your studies? When the time comes, your father will throw a big party, invite everyone, and accept your wife as his daughter-in-law. He will, we promise! How can you support your wife right now? You're only a student. What sort of a job do you think you'll get with what little you've learned? Do you want to end up as a coolie? Drive a rickshaw? Your father is a doctor, the whole town knows him. Please, please do as your father tells you. If he disowns you, you won't get a penny from him. Just think . . . you're an intelligent boy. Go and tell your wife to go back home. Your father has promised not to stand in your way, when the time comes. You are free to marry whomever you want, but now is not the right time, don't you see?"

Chhotda showed no sign of relenting. All he said was, "Take the chains off." No one obliged. Baba came back two hours later, whip in hand. He did not care if his son refused to change his mind. He was gambling his life away — how could Baba stand by and let him do it? He was his own son, after all. The same blood flowed through his veins; even his face resembled Baba's. Baba had worked hard to bring him up properly, give him the best opportunities. All his hopes and expectations were centered on Chhotda. He would bring him back, somehow.

"So — what have you decided? Will you do as you're told or not?" he demanded. His tone was quite impassive, neither harsh nor gentle.

Chhotda's jaw set even more firmly. "Let me go," he said.

"Yes, most certainly I will let you go. You are not to set foot outside this house unless I say so. You will not visit Geeta."

Chhotda spoke through clenched teeth: "I have only one thing to say. I will not live in this house. I will return to Geeta. Nothing will make me change my mind."

"What will you feed her? How will you take care of yourself?" Baba asked, swishing his whip.

"No one need worry about that," Chhotda replied. His jaw was still set, his teeth still clenched.

Had I been in Chhotda's shoes, I would probably have given in and accepted every condition Baba put forward. What's the use of putting up a fight if a tiger has you in its grasp? It was just stupid.

Now Baba's mouth set in a grim line. His eyes were bloodshot. His whip came down on Chhotda's body. A hungry tiger was attacking its prey. I felt as if the whip had lashed my own back, ripping open my flesh, exposing my bones as rivers of blood gushed forth. I closed my eyes. Eyes tightly shut, I waited for the whipping to stop. It did not.

Silently Ma, Grandma, Uncle Siddique, and Aunt Runu came out of the living room. One of them leaned against a pillar on the veranda and stared vacantly, unaware of what he was seeing. Another began walking aimlessly, not knowing where her feet were going. Ma stood clutching her hair, without realizing what she was doing. Each of them looked like a corpse that had come out of its grave, one that walked toward an unknown destination. Before their eyes stretched a thick curtain of darkness; in the depths of that darkness lay a forest; and from that forest came a single sound, the sound of a cracking whip.

Finally, Ma ran back into the living room. When she spoke, she had to raise her voice so that it wasn't drowned out by the sound of the swishing whip and Chhotda's screams. "Stop it!" Ma shouted. "He's going to die. Do you want to kill him? Tell me! You want to kill my son?"

Undeterred, Baba continued to cut open fresh wounds on Chhotda's back, and said, "Yes. Today I am going to finish him off. There is no need for a son like him to live."

"Let him go . . . let him go wherever he wants!" Ma sobbed. "What's the point in beating him? He's always been stubborn. Just look at him now. No one in his family is worth anything to him, it's that girl who matters, let him go back to her. Leave him alone!"

Chhotda was not allowed to leave. He was locked in his room. A new padlock was placed on his door and Baba put the key in his own shirt pocket. Chhotda was not to be fed even a morsel, Baba announced, nor was he to leave that room — even to answer calls of nature — until he came to his senses. Imprisoned in his own room, Chhotda tried to break open the door, and then the window. He failed. Both, made of solid iron, didn't even crack. The door was nine feet high, five feet wide.

All night he groaned. A number of creatures remained awake secretly that night in that house, which now appeared to be both old and haunted. I was one of them. In the dead of night — who knows how late it was — Yasmin said hoarsely, "I can't sleep!" I turned over on my side. "Neither can I!"

Our sighs rose into the room and formed a mist, turning everything hazy. The door, the windows, the furniture that caught some of the light from the lamp on the veranda outside — all became hazy. Darkness came sweeping down and settled on my hair, my eyes, my chin.

After four days of total starvation, Ma managed to pass some food to Chhotda through the iron bars on his window. Having fed him, she could finally bring herself to eat something. For four days she had starved with her son. Baba sat in his room, straining his ears for sounds of surrender from the locked room, surrender after the agonizing pain of hunger, of being kept in complete isolation. Not a single sound reached his ears. "No one may light the oven in the kitchen," he declared.

What! How would the others in the house survive? What would they eat?

"Let them eat a handful of chira with a glass of water, nothing else," Baba replied solemnly.

If anyone tried to pass items of food into Chhotda's room, he — or she — would be whipped as he was, we were told. Even so, edibles did slip into the prison when Baba wasn't looking. It was my belief, and I grew convinced of it, that Baba knew what was going on, but pretended not to have noticed. He extended his leave and waited for Chhotda's surrender. Chhotda lost a great deal of weight. Bones became prominent on his cheeks, chest and neck. A skeleton stood at the window, clutched its bars, and groaned all day.

Two ferocious tigers were fighting each other. The rest of us were mere spectators. A fortnight later, the battle came to an end.

Baba lost. Chhotda had to be released.

After he left, Baba clasped his daughters to his chest so tightly that I thought every bone in my body would be crushed. "Promise me!" Baba cried, "Promise me that the two of you will study hard and do well in life. Promise!"

We nodded vigorously. "Yes!"

"You girls will fulfill my dreams, won't you? Promise me you won't turn out like your brothers. Promise?"

We shook our heads. No, we wouldn't turn out like our brothers.

"I had cherished such dreams about Kamal. I did everything I could to bring my children up properly. Kamal was such a brilliant student. But now all my dreams are shattered. You are my last hope, my girls. You will make me proud of you, won't you? You will give me something to live for?" Baba's voice almost disappeared. Yasmin and I nodded again.

"I did not want to beat my son. You have no idea how much I suffered to see him like that, to starve him like that. I had to do it, one last desperate effort, to make him change his mind. I spoke to him with love, I tried to reason with him. He didn't listen to me, so I whipped him, but even that did not work, did it? You will listen to me, won't you?"

Once more, our heads bobbed up and down. Yes, we would listen to him.

Baba's tears drenched our clothes. That was the first time any of us had seen him cry.

But Baba was not the kind of man who would be happy with the word of two young girls. He said to Ma, "The whole atmosphere of this house is ruined. I bought a big house so that my children could all have their own rooms. There was never any noise, never any distractions. Each of them could study in peace in a healthy environment. I even tried to save them from bad influences in the neighborhood. But no . . . what I wanted just didn't happen." Baba sighed and stretched himself out on his bed. "What am I going to do with this house now? I shall sell it. Noman went behind my back, mixed with the wrong crowd, and ruined his career. Kamal has now left us, prefers to be with that girl. He's destroying his life as well. If these girls stay on in this house they won't get anywhere, either."

Ma said nothing. She watched, in total silence, the agony of a man who has suddenly slipped on the ladder of success. Every day after her namaz, Ma prayed for the return of her son, for his release from the clutches of a non-Muslim woman. May her son never forget his roots, his own religion, may he start doing his namaz, may he earn virtue. Ma's prayers failed to work. When Chhotda left the house he didn't look back once.

Two days after Chhotda's departure Baba packed our clothes and books in a couple of suitcases and deposited us in two different hostels. I was put in the girls' hostel at the Model School and Yasmin was sent to Bharateshwari Homes in Mirzapur. Neither of us had the courage to protest. Ma stood at the front gate, still as a statue. If anyone had shaken her she would have fallen to the ground, like the petal of an old, aging rose.

I had not yet turned thirteen. Never had I lived anywhere without Ma. It was she who brushed my hair, fed me, nursed me when I was ill, placing pieces of cloth soaked in cold water on my fevered brow, staying awake all night, if necessary. She put aside the biggest guava, the biggest mango, the biggest coconut or custard apple for her first daughter. She made all my clothes, my dresses with little puffed sleeves. If I couldn't sleep at night she patted my back gently and softly sang a lullaby: "Come, sleep, come to our house, come to this room, though there's nowhere for you to sit. Come and sit on my Raju's eyes. Come, sleep." Sometimes Ma affectionately called me Raju. But it didn't matter what she called me or how she felt. Now I had to leave my mother, my house, the squares I had drawn in our courtyard to play hopscotch, the playing field in front of the house where we played gollachhut. I had to leave everything that was old and familiar to sit huddled on my bed in the hostel, just because that was where Baba wanted me to be. The other girls looked at me in surprise and said, "Why are you in this hostel? Isn't your home in this town?"

I couldn't reply. All I could do was silently stare back at them. They smiled as if I was a new arrival in a zoo, a freak of nature for everyone to gape at.

I didn't feel like telling any one of them that in our house in Ishwarganj, where Yasmin was born, we often saw rows of black and red ants crawling up our wall. Chhotda used to pick out all the red ants and squash them between his fingers saying, "These are Hindu ants." Once I happened to kill a black ant. Chhotda was livid. He punched me in the back and said, "Why did you kill that black one? That was a Muslim ant. Get the red ones; you need to pick them out, one by one." The same Chhotda had now married a Hindu woman and left home. Left college. Left his parents and all of us. Our family was torn apart, forever.

A week later Ma came to my hostel and asked the superintendent to allow me go back home. Her request was not granted because Baba was my official guardian, and only his name had been entered in the records. Ma went away, crying.

The principal of the school, Wabaida Saad, lived on the first floor of the building. A handful of girls lived on the ground floor and made up the "hostel."

Baba came to visit almost every afternoon, carrying snacks and sweets. He would hand them over and ask, "How are your studies going?"

I kept my eyes fixed on the floor, and nodded to indicate that they were going well. Satisfied, he spoke gently, "There are other girls here, aren't there? Girls your own age?"

I nodded again.

"You will return here every evening after your classes, have a bath, something to eat, and get back to your books. You don't have anything else to do, do you? I have put you in a hostel for your own good. You may not understand that right now, but you will when you are older. A father always wants the best for his children. Isn't that right?"

"Yes."

My eyes filled with tears. I turned them skyward and fixed them on the sun, so that if Baba saw them he would think the sun was making my eyes water.

I didn't let Baba see how desperate I was to return home. No one was allowed to visit me except Baba. I was not allowed to see my mother if she came to the hostel. I felt like running away, but a hefty, heavily mustached *chowkidar* sat guarding the front gate. It was impossible to slip out unseen. The school doctor, Rebecca, had moved to the teachers' quarters at the medical school. Runi had therefore left the hostel and gone with her. Had she been around I might have suffered a lot less. But was that really true? I didn't know.

After classes, when we returned to the hostel, some girls went off to play badminton while others sat down to chat about the details of our teachers' personal lives: who had a husband, who was divorced, who lived alone, who was having an affair. I couldn't understand most of it. How did they know so much about what the teachers did at home, or what they thought about? I spent my afternoon either watching the girls who played badminton or listening to those who were chatting.

In the evening I had to sit down with my books. Our super came around to check whether we were studying or not. Tears dripped down onto my open book. Every night the letters slowly blurred before my eyes. Every night I would go to bed alone: no one sang a lullaby, no one implored sleep to come and sit on my eyes. What had I done to deserve this? Why had I been sent to exile? Chhotda had made a mistake, but I was the one paying for it. I believed that what Baba had done was totally wrong.

I had seen Dada fall in love, too, but his love was silent. Within three days of arriving at San Souci he fell for a girl called Anita. He was walking down a street when he saw a girl standing on the roof of her house. Her hair was long and thick and glossy, her eyes bright. That was all it took to make Dada fall in love. About six months later, Anita left for Calcutta with her family. Dada shed a few tears and took to writing poetry.

Then he met a girl called Sheela, who stemmed the flow of poetry for Anita. Dada had two friends, both called Farhad. One was referred to as Fat Farhad, the other Thin Farhad. Sheela was Thin Farhad's sister, tall, with an oval face. According to Dada, she looked exactly like the film star Olivia. He began cutting out Olivia's pictures from film magazines and filling his room with them. Inside his books and notebooks, under the tablecloth, under his pillow or the mattress on his bed — no matter where one looked, there was Olivia. If Yasmin or I found a picture of her anywhere, we passed it on to Dada. He spent hours staring at her pictures, saying things like, "Sheela's chin is exactly like that. Look at Olivia's nose, it's no different from Sheela's. And her eyes — why, someone could have taken Sheela's eyes and placed them on Olivia's face! When Sheela smiles, you can see a dimple on her left cheek, just like Olivia!"

After a while Dada began writing poetry with renewed vigor, filling the pages of a new notebook. He listened endlessly to love songs. He saved the money he was given for rickshaws and for lunch and bought a violin. Then he got Jamini Roy to teach him how to play it, and started playing slow, sad tunes while thinking of Sheela. Until then, his love was unrequited. Sheela had not fallen for him. Her heart would eventually be won, not by his music, but by his poetry. The doe would look into the dark eyes of her buck and say, "Where did you learn to write poetry? You write very well."

The buck would smile shyly.

Then the doe would say, "You keep walking up and down our street. My brother was asking me the other day, 'Why does Noman come to this area so often?' "

The buck would smile shyly.

The doe would go on, "Why should it matter to Farhad whether you come here or not? He doesn't own the whole street, does he? You have other friends here, so you could come every day to visit them!"

The buck would give another shy smile.

The doe would then say, "I can sew very well. I could make your sisters' clothes. If they have any fabric lying around, why don't you bring it over some day?"

The buck would nod.

"How hot it is! It must be far more pleasant up on the roof, if we could go and sit there. You must be feeling warm, too?"

The buck would nod.

Dada was pursuing a master's in psychology at the university in Dhaka. His heart, however, remained in Mymensingh. His study of psychology was suspended, as if it were no more than a bat or a monkey hanging from a branch of the peepal tree in the university compound. Dada returned home as often as he could.

One day, he found the doe, looking sad, under a silk-cotton tree. She said, "My father is trying to find a suitable boy for me. He'd like me to get married."

"Married? To whom?"

"Whoever, but not you."

"Oh."

"Baba is sick, perhaps he's afraid he might die, so he wants to see his daughter married. Then he can die in peace."

"What's wrong with your father?"

"Whatever it is, he wants to see me married."

"Oh."

"If your father speaks to mine, brings the proposal for our marriage, I don't think my baba will say no."

"Oh."

At this point, the doe would start to cry. The buck would ask, "Why are you crying?"

"Can't you see why?"

The buck would shake his head. No, he couldn't.

"You are a student of psychology, but you understand nothing about emotions, do you?"

The buck would look embarrassed and uncomfortable.

Dada raised the subject at home in a totally roundabout way. Sheela was a very good girl, he told Ma. She was about to get married, she would look very pretty in a red sari, she was a wonderful cook, and she could sew; Sheela would take very good care of her parents-in-law; she would give birth to beautiful babies.

Having heard him out, Ma said, "All right. Your friend's sister is pretty and good at several things. That's splendid news. Now tell me, what are you trying to say?"

Dada took several days to come to the point. He built up his case, bit by bit, and finally declared that he wanted to marry Sheela. Ma passed this on to Baba, speaking as gently and sweetly as she could. The sweetness was lost on Baba. At least, at first. He reacted as if he had been offered a bitter pill. However, Ma persevered and a few days later, Baba said, "Very well, I'd like to see this girl."

The buck then said to the doe, "You are invited to our house. My father wants to meet you."

The doe smiled shyly.

"I can't tell you how happy I am. You'll soon by my wife!"

The doe smiled shyly.

"Once he's met you, my father will visit your house and talk to your Baba."

The doe smiled shyly.

"Remember not to wear any jewelry, neither bangles nor earrings. And no makeup, either. My father doesn't like it. Tell him you got a first division when you did your matriculation exams. But . . . no, no, don't say that, he may catch you out. Just say that you're studying in college, you're working hard to get a first division in your final exam, and you'd like to continue your studies even after you're married. If he asks you what your goal is, tell him you want to teach in a college."

The doe smiled shyly.

Sheela came to our house. She sat in the living room, opposite Baba. Dada remained in his own room, his legs shaking, knees knocking against each other. He was too nervous to go into the living room. Ma made kheer with vermicelli in it and took it out to the living room, together with tea, biscuits, and sweets on a tray, placing it on the table in front of the settee. Baba talked to Sheela, occasionally helping himself to the food. A smile hovered on his lips.

When it was time for Sheela to go, Baba himself helped her into a rickshaw and saw her off. He stood at the gate and waved, still smiling.

Ma, wearing a new sari, her lips red with paan juice, heart dancing with joy, ran to join Baba. "That girl has such a pretty face, like the film star Madhubala's."

"Yes," Baba agreed.

"She's a very good girl, too."

"Right."

"Well, Noman is certainly of marriageable age. The sooner he gets married the better."

Baba, in a shirt and trousers and a tie and shoes, his curly hair falling over his face, simply said, "I will not have my son marry that girl."

Nothing could make him change his mind.

Two months later, Sheela was married off to a potbellied man with a mustache. He was five foot two, and older than Sheela by twenty-three years.

The doe was captured and thrown into a cage.

Aunt Jhunu cried too, but not silently, like Dada. The sound of her wailing had rocked the whole neighborhood. She didn't bathe or eat for days. She broke most of the china in the kitchen. In fact, she even tried to make a noose with her long scarf and hang herself from a beam in the ceiling, but failed. Uncle Hashem managed to break the door open and cut her down before it was too late.

An herbalist treated her, her head was massaged with special oil that was supposed to calm her nerves, and then a priest was called in to blow on her face in the hope that the holy air from his lungs would drive away the evil that had possessed her mind.

In spite of all this Aunt Jhunu did not recover. Eventually it was decided that she be sent to Dhaka to live with Uncle Siddique.

Runu and Jhunu were always very close. Everyone knew it. Even the chanachurwala, who came to sell his hot, savory snacks in the afternoons, stood outside the house and sang: "Dear Runu, dear Jhunu, where are you? Here's the hot chanachur, have some, do!" Runu and Jhunu laughed together, wept together, sang, danced, picked fruit, gathered flowers, and strung garlands, always in each other's company. Jhunu told Runu her deepest, darkest secrets. Runu divulged hers to Jhunu. The two sisters slept in the same room, in the same bed. Those who saw them said, "Look, they might have been twins!" One day, without a word to anyone, Runu vanished. The whole town was searched high and low, but she couldn't be found. Then came news of her whereabouts. She had eloped with Rashu and was now at Rashu's home in Begunbari. Jhunu broke into loud sobs as soon as she heard the news. She rolled on the ground, beating her chest. Why was she so upset?

Rashu was Jhunu's private tutor; he had nothing to do with Runu. Runu hadn't spent hours gazing into Rashu's eyes, listening to his heartbeat. Only Jhunu knew how Rashu's foot would find hers under the table; how his hand would come up secretly to touch hers and play with her fingers. Jhunu knew for whom her garlands were strung. She knew why she stood before the mirror every evening, lining her eyes with kohl, inspecting her face again and again. Everyone knew a young man came to teach Jhunu every day. No one knew how much time the tutor and his pupil spent on studies, and how much on other activities. No one was allowed to enter the room while lessons were in progress, and no one was allowed to talk outside or make any noise that might disturb them. Runu went into the room for a few moments with a cup of tea and biscuits for the tutor but this was the only disruption in their lesson. Now, if Rashu had gone and married not Jhunu but her sister, wasn't Jhunu justified in wanting to die with mortification and embarrassment?

Aunt Jhunu was convinced men were like animals. "If you believe what a man tells you, you're just inviting trouble," she announced a couple of days after the priest's ministrations. She was sitting by the pond, her legs immersed in water. "They are worse than pigs," she went on. "They will try to sample whomever they can find. They have no morals, no values. A man may tell you he loves you, then tomorrow he'll say the same thing to someone else."

Aunt Jhunu's hair rippled down her back to her hips, but it was all tangled. Her eyes had dark rings under them. Her pale yellow skin, which normally glowed like turmeric, now was dull, like dried grass.

Grandma's four daughters could be ranked thus: Aunt Fajli eighty out of a hundred, Aunt Jhunu fifty, Aunt Runu thirty, and Ma . . .

Dada used to do this. Like a schoolteacher he would grade Grandma's daughters' looks. "And how much would you give Ma?" At this, Dada shifted in his chair, moved his legs, bit his pencil, and said, "Ma gets zero, a round rasgolla."

Aunt Jhunu continued to speak. "See, Getu's Ma, you and I are in the same boat. You were tortured by a man, so was I. If there is a God, He will not tolerate this. He will judge these men as only He can." Aunt Jhunu, who had once been given fifty marks for her looks, spoke absently, as if she had just decided to renounce the world.

Grandma looked out of her window and saw her sitting close to

Getu's mother. "What is she whispering about?" she asked irritably. "Why speak to Getu's Ma? Jhunu can't keep anything to herself. Heaven knows what she'll spill!"

Getu's mother had her own woes to air. A deep, tremulous sigh escaped through her lips. "Allah is not just. He's very partial. Getu's father beat me, burned me, and threw me out, and then married someone else. Is he unhappy? No. He is quite all right. If anyone's unhappy, it's me. I haven't got a father, so I can't go back to him. My two brothers abuse me all the time and even say it's my fault that I was thrown out of my home!"

Her burned hand rested on the water. Aunt Jhunu placed her chin on her knees and said, "I don't want to live in this world anymore. But then, why should I be the only one to die? I should kill those two before I kill myself. If I am not happy, why should they be?"

Darkness crept up from the narrow, dingy alley and sneaked into Grandma's house. The half-moon slept in the pond wrapped in a blanket of leaves and water hyacinth. Getu's mother's burned hand slept under her torn anchal. Aunt Jhunu did not feel like leaving the spot where she was sitting; she wanted to sit by the pond all night, under the crooked date palm, dewdrops falling on her tangled hair. She would not gather white shiuli flowers from the damp grass when dawn broke. There was no longer any reason to make garlands; to get ready each evening by tying her hair with a red ribbon, lining her eyes with kohl, waiting for someone special.

Aunt Jhunu's whole life felt empty. She ran indoors and came back with a bundle of letters. They were all from Rashu. She had kept them safe in an old tin trunk in layers of old clothes. They smelt of naphthalene. While the half-moon slept and darkness hung from the branches of the date palm, Aunt Jhunu set fire to those letters.

"Come on, Getu's Ma. Let's sit by this fire. It's cold."

Bits of burned paper drifted against Aunt Jhunu's hair. Getu's mother's face started to turn red from the heat. The sight of a fire always made her want to cook — to put a pot of rice over the fire, to bend low over it and smell its heavenly scent. A dark cloud came swooping down on Getu's mother like a bat.

"Why do we take all this abuse from men?" asked Getu's mother. "Because we women are hungry. When you are hungry, you do not think of love. I never got a chance to give my heart to anyone. Love is not for us, it is for rich people. A poor woman doesn't have a heart, she has only an empty stomach. If someone gives her food, she calls him 'husband.' ' "

Getu's mother's tales of hunger did not appeal to Aunt Jhunu. For several days, she herself had had no appetite at all. She felt sick each time she lifted a handful of rice to her mouth. It seemed as if her heart had been replaced by an empty, desolate plain. If she had been able to spend her life with Rashu, she could have lived quite happily under a tree. If she could just gaze into his eyes, she would need nothing else to survive. Even if she and Rashu were to drown together, she would have been far, far happier than she was.

The fire went out before the last letter was fully destroyed. Aunt Jhunu sat in the dark with the half-burned letter in her hand. She longed to read it. It might just be the same letter in which Rashu had written that he loved her more than his life.

Before she left for Dhaka, Aunt Jhunu did something that only she and I knew about. One day, we climbed out of a rickshaw outside a yellow, two-story house in Jublighat near the river. It had the words DAK BUNGALOW on it. I followed her. When we stopped outside room number 12 Aunt Jhunu knocked on the door, I noticed that little beads of perspiration had gathered on the tip of her nose. The man who opened the door was thin, with a long mustache that drooped down to his chin. He looked like a spook. I had seen him a few times before. His name was Zafar Iqbal, and his own house was a couple of houses away from Grandma's. He pulled her into the room and shut the door. I stood in the corridor outside, staring at the Brahmaputra River.

I spent all evening watching the glittering waves rise and fall, and heard the *bhatiali* songs the boatmen were singing. When the western sky turned red and the sun — a deep shade of golden yellow, like the yolk of an egg — began slipping into the Brahmaputra, I remained rooted to the spot, because that was where Aunt Jhunu had asked me to wait.

She emerged from the room as the sun set. She stroked my cheeks gently and said, "Listen, if anyone asks you where you went, tell them I took you with me to visit a friend."

As we were climbing into a rickshaw to return home, Aunt Jhunu spoke again. "And if they ask you which friend, what's her name, where does she live . . ."

I waited, looking impassively at Aunt Jhunu's face for further instructions. She said, "Tell them her name is Fatema; she lives in Kalibari. No, no, not Kalibari. Say you went to visit Fatema in Brahmopolli, all right?"

It might have been all right, or it might not. I said nothing. Aunt Jhunu looked at my silent figure and knew that her secret was safe. I didn't open my mouth easily. I wouldn't open it now.

⌐··· 12 ···⌐

Return I

Four months after I moved to the hostel, Ma brought me home. It wasn't easy, but eventually I was handed over to my mother, the same woman who was not supposed to see me even briefly. It turned out that Ma met the superintendent periodically, wept, and said, "My husband wants to have a second wife. That's why he has sent our daughter away. It's all a big conspiracy. He wants to sell the house and live in a new one with his new wife. Please let me take my daughter back home. Neither of my sons lives with me anymore, but if I have my daughter, maybe I can stop him from marrying again. If she's at home, how could he sell the house?"

After a while, the super's heart melted. She agreed to reunite mother and daughter. The daughter returned home.

Yasmin, too, had been brought back from Mirzapur. Ma sat with her daughters by her side, alert and tense.

When Baba saw us, he acted as if he had seen a pair of ghosts. His eyes grew red. His jaw set, his teeth clenched. I shrank with fear. Yasmin tried hiding behind Ma.

"Well, I gave birth to these girls, didn't I?" asked Ma, speaking softly. "Don't I have any rights?"

She threw the words out into the air — to strike whomever was listening.

Baba didn't say a word in reply. But the next day he stopped buying food for us. Ma brought packaged food from Grandpa's restaurant and flung more words into the air every day:

"He wants to get married again, and he thought he could do it just by getting rid of you girls! I would never have let that happen, not on my life! What did he have when he first came to the town? Just a torn blanket. It was my father who gave him money, kept him from starving."

Ma threw her words in the air while walking. Naturally, her real target was Baba, but she didn't face him or look him in the eye when she spoke. Her words were cast in the air from the room next to Baba's, or from the passage outside. We all knew he could hear her easily.

Baba stopped giving us money to pay for the rickshaw to school. We stayed at home all day. Ma said, "All right, let's see how long this will continue." It was her belief that when it came to schooling Baba couldn't remain indifferent.

Three days later, after watching us miss school, Baba finally broke his silence. On the fourth morning he had a cold shower, got dressed, and called for me. Then he coughed, as if a lot of phlegm had collected in his throat, and said, "What is going on? Don't you think there's any need to get on with your studies?"

I remained silent. It was Baba who was going to decide whether or not I needed to go back to school. I was not allowed to make any decisions for myself.

"If you think there's no need," Baba continued, keeping his eyes fixed on the ceiling, "then please say so now. I won't need to worry about you anymore. Your brothers have told me quite frankly that they aren't going to study. I send money every month to Noman, but he says he's not going to take his exams this year, that he'll give it a try next year. And that other brother of yours . . . well, his life is finished. If you and Yasmin wish to follow in his footsteps, kindly tell me so that I don't waste my money on school tuition."

Maintaining my silence, I looked out and let my gaze sweep indifferently over the tall, overgrown grass in the courtyard, the mossy ground near the tap, the tail of a crow sitting on the guava tree. I was not in the habit of opening my mouth in Baba's presence. The longer my silence, the better. The fewer my movements, the better. Baba was a lot more reassured if I could be both quiet and still.

This was the accepted practice: Baba would rant, say what he liked; I listened without a word, my head bowed. Baba might choose to stroke my cheek with affection, or land a tight slap on it — I would have to accept it without protest. I knew he didn't really mean what he had just said about following in Chhotda's footsteps. If I were to believe him and actually say that was what I wanted to do, not go back to school, he would never accept it. If anything, he would then try to skin me alive.

"Why have you stopped going to school?" Baba shouted suddenly at the top of his voice. My whole body shuddered at this unexpected attack. I shifted my gaze from the crow's tail back into the room. If Baba was roaring, it meant that this time I was required to reply. He knew very well why I had stopped going to school, but I had to tell him what he already knew. To point out that it was his fault, not mine. So I raised my voice as high as I possibly could in his presence and said, "I haven't got the rickshaw fare."

"Why not? If your mother can feed you, why can't she find the rickshaw fare?"

Baba threw two coins at me. They landed, facedown, on the floor. Never mind, I told myself, let them lie there. But Baba continued to fume and, in the face of his rage, I had to give in, bend down, and pick the coins up. Only once was Baba defeated in a battle — with Chhotda. In my case, it was difficult to say whether he thought of it as defeat, but he did accept the situation. He could have packed me — and Yasmin — off to our respective hostels once more, but he didn't.

We were allowed to remain at home but it was turned into a dark prison. The windows that overlooked the street were permanently blocked. Baba called in builders and masons, bought cartloads of bricks and cement, and raised the compound wall so that it was now twice as high. We were totally cut off from our neighborhood. Going up to the roof was forbidden. If either of us was caught there, not only were we dragged down but we were also threatened with the possibility of a broken leg if we went up again.

The roof was where we danced in the rain. We had a pretend-house there, and we cooked in its pretend-kitchen. I often leaned against its railing and read books I was not supposed to. From there, I could observe the intimate details of our neighbors' lives. It was a wonderful place, but now it was now forbidden territory. For the life of me I couldn't understand why my movements were being curtailed so drastically. I was just beginning to get acquainted with the outside world. When I walked up on the roof in a fresh breeze, words would sometimes begin to form. Like a fine drizzle, they fell into my mind, little droplets scattering everywhere. I picked them up and strung them into garlands.

Because I was now banished from the roof, I wanted to be there all the time. I ran up there the minute Baba left the house. When the black front gate creaked to announce his return, I rushed down like a sweeping hurricane and sat down at my desk, my face as innocent as a child's. The narrower the confines became, the stronger my urge to crash through them. It drove me mad. I could now recognize two distinct people within myself, one quiet and indifferent, the other deeply curious.

It took me a few months to grasp why Baba wanted to turn me into a prisoner. I realized that he was afraid that one day I, too, would fall in love with a man who was completely unsuitable and would run off with him, ignoring my studies and my entire future.

My life remained suspended between home and school. Just for a few days, though, the arrival of Ratan swept me up in a wave of joy and fun. Ratan came from the village Elenga in Tangail district. He slept in Dada's room and, in the evenings, played cops-and-robbers with us. This involved the use of paper and pen. The words "thief," "police," and "bandit" were written on three pieces of paper, each of which was then folded in an identical manner. Ratan threw them up in the air, and each of us had to pick up one when they fell. If I happened to get the one marked "police," I had to guess which of the others was the thief and the bandit. If my guess turned out to be wrong, Ratan would yell at the top of his voice: "Dabba!" That was how he referred to zero.

Ratan's father was a doctor Baba knew. Long ago, before I was born, Baba went through a very rough patch when he had virtually no money. Ratan's father came to his rescue, generously providing whatever help was required. Hence a warm welcome always awaited Ratan when he visited us. He was two years older than me. He smiled mischievously and romped around the house, hair and shirt blowing in the wind. He was like one of the family, or at least that's how he behaved. Usually, soon after his arrival, he would grab a towel and disappear for a bath. When he emerged his fair skin glowed even brighter. He would brush his hair stylishly and make his way to the kitchen, saying, "Come on, Aunt, what have you cooked today? I'm starving!"

Ma was very fond of his mother. "Does Bulbul still look the same?" she would ask every time she saw Ratan. According to Ma, Bulbul was extraordinarily beautiful. I had never heard Ma gush over another woman's beauty the way she did over Bulbul's.

Ratan played *Ludo* and cops-and-robbers with us, and showed us card tricks, thereby considerably reducing the pain of not being able to go to the roof. But this time, just before he left, he placed a folded piece of paper on my desk, tapped my head as he always did, and said, "Be good. Good-bye."

Ratan then flew out of the room. He never walked. There was an irrepressible force within him. When he left, I unfolded the paper and realized that it was a letter. In it Ratan told me that he loved me very much. If I didn't love him back, his life would lose all meaning, totally and absolutely.

My heart started trembling as I read his words. My mouth and throat felt parched. I clutched the folded piece of paper in my hand and locked myself in the bathroom to read it again. The paper was now damp from my sweating palm. I stared hungrily at the word *love*. A tremor ran through my body when I remembered that the letter was addressed to me. When Ratan gave me that letter, had anyone been secretly watching? If yes, there would be hell to pay. Things would be much worse. No matter what I did or where I went, disaster would follow. The safest thing was to tear it up and put my anxiety to rest, but I couldn't bring myself to do it. Let it be, my heart said. Let it stay inside the pages of my history book or under my pillow; in some secret spot known only to me, let it live. I went about guarding that crumpled piece of paper but felt no surge of love for Ratan. If anything, I loved the letter.

Baba discovered it in just a few days. While I was in school, he decided to go through my books to see how far I had read, whether the pages read had been marked, and how I did my sums. He found Ratan's letter. He said nothing to me. All he did was write to his friend in Tangail to tell him that Ratan was no longer welcome in our house and must never be seen anywhere near it.

So what if Ratan never comes here again? I said to myself. *Who cares?* Then I began feeling sorry for Ratan's father, a man I had never met, for he would no doubt be offended by Baba's letter. Suddenly I started feeling extremely guilty, as if I was responsible for Ratan's action. As if the whole business was entirely my fault.

About the time that Baba was engrossed in hatching a variety of complex plots to save me from downfall he said, sounding extremely concerned, "Prices are going up. From now on, you will eat rice only once a day. If you have it for lunch, you must eat bread for dinner."

Bread? Instead of rice? What did this mean? Was it a new game Baba wanted to play? Ma remarked, sounding cross, "Perhaps he's taken a new wife. He has to feed her, you see, so he's trying to save some money by starving us!"

Ma was wrong. She misread the whole situation. On my way to school I saw hundreds of beggars walking along the roadside. "People from villages are flooding the towns," my rickshaw driver informed me, "They're all here because there are no crops this year. They're starving in the villages."

Curious, I watched all the beggars and refugees from my rickshaw. They carried bowls in their hands, bowls that were empty. I saw them running toward Notun Bazar. Their eyes bulged and their ribs looked as if they would burst through their skin; it looked like a procession of skeletons. Some had fallen behind, gasping by the side of drains; others were standing outside large houses, clamoring for rice.

There were people outside our own front gate. Each wanted a handful of rice. It could be stale, it could be rotten, it could be left over from two nights earlier, they didn't mind. Even uncooked rice would do.

When I returned from school, fully fed, the sight of so many people made me run to our storeroom. Surely a couple of handfuls of rice would be easy enough to spare? All our rice was stored in a large drum. I found it locked. Who had done that? Baba. The lock was large, heavy, and strong. There was no question of unlocking it without asking him.

"Ma!" I called anxiously, "give these people something to eat. I don't think they've eaten anything for days!"

Ma was doing her namaz. She finished her prayers, kissed her hand, rolled up her prayer mat, and replied wanly, "There isn't any rice."

Never before had I seen her turn a beggar away. Finding a handful of rice was no problem at all. Potfuls of cooked rice were often thrown away, since it went bad easily in the hot weather. Occasionally beggars were fed leftover rice, soaked overnight. Today even that was not available.

That afternoon I finished the food on my plate and, licking my fingers, said to Ma, "Give me some more rice, please."

This, coming from me, was a most unusual demand. Normally, even as a small child, I was reluctant to eat much. Ma fed me, talking incessantly, telling stories to distract me, often playing little games to trick me into eating more. She would mix the rice on my plate with fish curry, arrange it like a garland, then break off little bits from it and say, "Look, this one's a tiger, and this is a lion, that one's an elephant, and here's a bear. Let's see if you can eat the bear . . . come on, open your mouth! See, the bear's frightened of you. It knows you'll swallow it. Now try the elephant!" Thus entertained, I did as I was told and ate my food.

Now, here I was in 1974, licking my fingers and saying, "Can I have some more?" But Ma said, "There isn't any more."

Had we suddenly become poor? No one had ever been refused a handful of rice, not in our house. It was extraordinary. Every beggar was being turned away. Why?

Baba ate bread for lunch as well as for dinner. So did Ma, and so did our servants. Rice was cooked only for Yasmin and me and what was stored in the big drum was slowly running out.

Baba pressed his temples and said, "There's a famine in our country."

The number of beggars on the streets swelled. They went from door to door, begging for the leftover rice water. They were happy with just that. One day a live skeleton turned up at our door. It was a small boy, perhaps seven or eight years old. I saw him and turned my eyes away. He didn't ask for anything, neither rice nor its water. He couldn't speak. I called Ma and told her to give him something to eat, for I didn't mind if my share of rice went to him.

Ma gave him some rice. I saw him lift his hand, the bones jutting out from under his skin, and put the rice in his mouth. All of us watched the young boy, starving to death, so exhausted that he was finding it difficult to swallow. I had seen poverty before, but never had I seen starvation turn someone into a living skeleton. In the past, we had thrown away a lot of food that was eventually eaten by stray dogs and cats, or pecked at by crows. Now, before our eyes, here were human beings dying because there was nothing to eat.

That night, over dinner, Ma said, chewing her bread, "When I was small, there was a famine. Food was dropped from airplanes, packets of food. We had to run to collect them as they fell. None of us ate any rice for days on end."

Even Baba broke his silence to say, "How could you? There was no rice anywhere. People had money, but there wasn't a grain of rice in the shops. Millions starved to death. In Calcutta, I have heard, corpses lined the streets. Do you know how we survived? We ate a portion of plantain — the white bit that's inside — that's all we could find. In our village, so many sold their own daughters, husbands sold their wives, just for a handful of rice." After a pause, Baba added with a sigh, "Who knows if this famine will turn out to be just as terrible!"

What would happen now, I wondered, when we ran out of all our stored rice? Would we never get to eat again? Turn into skeletons as well, like that boy Israil? The thought made my limbs go numb.

This had happened to me before, when people from Amirullah's family spread the news that a dojjal was being dispatched by Allah to test our virtue. This avenging angel was huge, his appearance grotesque, and he had an ax in his hand. He would chop the head off anyone who didn't believe in Allah and cut the body into five pieces. Every time I closed my eyes I would see the massive, naked body of the dojjal — huge as a mountain — standing with all his ugly teeth bared in a horrific grin, hacking off heads in our courtyard. There was blood everywhere. I was screaming, dying painfully, but the dojjal was still laughing uproariously. When that image rose in my mind I clenched my teeth and tried with all the strength in my body to bring virtue to myself.

What *was* virtue, anyway? Ma said it simply meant believing that Allah was one and that Muhammad was his Prophet. I repeated these words to myself, again and again, to gain virtue. This business of "belief" was still a bit hazy and mysterious to me, for I was supposed to believe everything Ma told me. Without seeing. Without under-standing. It was no different than believing in ghosts or jinns, or a creature like Fo-ting-ting, who spoke through his feet. I had never seen this creature, but I had heard of him. If this Fo-ting-ting had the power to send a dojjal to chop people's heads off, I would have had to chant *his* name: Fo-ting-ting! Fo-ting-ting!

If I was given the power to choose, I didn't think I would believe *everything* I was expected to. In school, I was told to believe that there were gases in the atmosphere. I had to accept it. If someone told me, with enough force, that I had seen a horse fly, I probably would have. Now, faced with the possibility of starvation, I could quite clearly see my own body turn into a skeleton.

I heard Ma's voice, "Haven't I told you every day not to waste food? If you drop a single grain of rice on the floor, Allah gets cross.

You've seen how expensive it's become. People are dying everywhere because they can't get it."

She leaned her elbow on the arm of the sofa, hand on her cheek, and added, "Who knows what's happening to my sons? Maybe they're starving."

"I send Noman enough money regularly, don't worry," Baba comforted her.

But Ma was actually thinking of Chhotda. No one sent him any money. None of us knew where he was, how he was. Ma thought of her missing son and broke into tears.

"It's quite late. Go to bed now!" Baba threw the words at her and went back to his own room.

With the dawn, a crowd had gathered outside our front gate. Ma saved the water from our boiled rice and gave it to them. In the evening, the same thin boy, Israil, came back. He was again given some rice to eat.

A procession went past our house, shouting:

> We want food, we want clothes, yes we do!
> We wish to live as we were meant to!

It was a march led by the Communist Party. They were going into every house and holding out a red sheet, saying, "Give us some rice. Save the poor. They're starving." They came to our house, too, red scarves tied around their heads. One of them said to me, "Go inside and call a grown-up. Tell him we must have some rice." My hair stood on end in excitement. I ran back inside and said to Ma, "Ma, bring some rice out. There are people here collecting it. We've got to give them some!"

Ma snapped at me, "What! I don't have to give anyone anything just because they're asking for it. What will you eat if they take our rice?"

"But others have already given so much — they've got a sheet filled with rice. Come and have a look!" I pulled her by her hand. Ma went and stood behind the front door and asked, "What do you want?"

One of the young men stepped forward to answer her. "We'd like some rice, Ma. People are starving to death. So we — we're all students — are collecting rice from every house to feed the poor and hungry. Please give us whatever you can."

The men behind him chanted,

> Some will eat, and others won't
> Do we want that? No, we don't!

I was trembling all over. "Go on," I nudged Ma, "break that lock and take out some rice."

"Your father will kill me!" Ma muttered.

"Let him. Let him do what he wants. Come, let's go." I felt reckless.

Ma looked at the crowd gathered in the field outside and felt nervous. "If we had sent word to your father somehow, that would have helped. How am I going to manage this chaos on my own?"

The front gate was wide open. Some of the local boys had turned up to see what was going on. Still Ma hesitated. Excited, I picked up a brick from the courtyard and struck the padlock with it. One, two, three times. Then, on my fourth attempt, it finally cracked into two. It was Baba's padlock — very big, very strong.

The drum was half full. I scooped up whatever I could in a towel and ran back to the field. Ma watched me without a word.

Having gotten their rice, the men left, singing a song. Enchanted, I stared after them, feeling a great surge of pure joy. From within my being, a new person was struggling to get out — strong, defiant, determined. Incredibly brave. A dreamer. I looked at my own new self and was amazed. Was it really me, or was it just a young adolescent girl, momentarily dazzled by a group of young men?

Ma replaced the bolt on the gate and went back inside. Her face looked pale. "Your father will break every bone in your body," she told me.

I smiled. "Baba beats me every day; that's nothing new."

Ma had led me to believe that the Communists were bad. If they were, why were they collecting rice for the poor? Surely saving them from dying was not bad? They didn't believe in Allah, but they were not committing a sin, were they, by taking care of the needy? They were going to feed hundreds like Israil, weak and gasping by the roadside. I felt like joining those men, going from house to house, singing and collecting rice. I felt like starving myself, not eating my share of the food, until the famine was over. But I was not to do what I wanted. I could hardly cross the boundaries that had been set for me. All I could do now was wait to be whipped by Baba. The whip he had bought for Chhotda was still under his mattress.

Baba returned in the evening and went straight to the drum containing the rice, just as I had anticipated. The broken padlock was still hanging around its clasp. I expected Baba to pick it up and go through the house, roaring like a tiger. He did exactly that. I sat in my room, holding my breath, fearing that at any minute Baba would lift his mattress and get the whip out. It would then cut into my back, leaving bleeding welts. Almost as if on cue it arched like a bow. A sharp pain shot down my spine in anticipation of the first blow. The whole house would tremble under Baba's roars. My body was ice cold. In the sockets of my face sat not a pair of eyes but two hard stones. Before me stretched a room full of darkness, nothing more. I was floating, floating away like a feather. Where was I going? I didn't know. I had no family, no friends. I was completely alone, as if I was no longer part of this world. It was of no use to me. I had attained nirvana.

The entire house had fallen silent, as if no one else lived in it, as if no one ever had. Everyone crept into their own hiding hole. I waited to be called to the bridge, the same bridge that would take me to the other world. Today it would be decided, once and for all, just how much I had sinned. A new realization began taking shape in my mind: I had committed no sin. For the first time in my life I had discovered a belief, all by myself. Trying to straighten my arched back, stiffening all my muscles, I did my best to bring honor and virtue to myself. My lips started moving, rehearsing the lines I was going to speak in my own defense: "The books I have read all say, 'Feed the hungry.' So when those men came and asked for rice, I gave."

Ma spoke before I could. I heard her voice clearly. "Why are you shouting? Can't you speak softly? I broke that padlock. The two girls were crying with hunger."

"Crying with hunger? Why? Didn't you cook today? Didn't they eat?"

Ma's voice sounded shrill as she spoke from the veranda outside the kitchen. "That little rice I cooked wasn't enough. You just left about enough for the two girls, didn't you? Well, I got sick of eating bread so I had some rice from their share."

"Really? So you decided you had the right to break my padlock? How dare you! Why didn't you call me?" Baba was still shouting.

"Call you? How? Who's at home, tell me, who could I send to inform you?" Ma sounded cross.

Baba stopped roaring. All of a sudden. The silent house slowly roused itself, as if stretching after a long sleep. People started climbing out of their holes, emerging into the light. I could hear the sound of plates and glasses in the kitchen. Ma walked by on the passage outside.

When Baba left the house, I saw Ma slip out, go past the woodapple tree, and out of the black front gate. Her stomach bulged under her burkha.

This had started happening frequently. Ma would sneak out of the house, pass the woodapple tree, and vanish from sight. Her stomach always bulged under her burkha. One day, like a shadow, I followed and saw her silently open the gate. Then she got into a rickshaw. The rickshaw turned left. The road to Amirullah's house, as well as Grandma's, stretched to the right. Who was Ma visiting?

"Where did you go, Ma? I saw the rickshaw turn left. Who lives there?" I asked her when she got back, my eyes narrowed.

Ma pursed her lips. "Oil in your machine, girl. Don't ask so many questions." She always did this. If she didn't like what I said she didn't answer my question. Sometimes she lost her temper completely. Once I asked her, "What did you take in that bundle the other day when you went to visit Amirullah?" and she struck me so hard that I spun around and banged my head against the metal bars on a window.

That day Ma didn't reveal where she had gone but a few days later, she asked, "Do you want to see where I go?"

"Yes!" I jumped to my feet.

Together we walked the whole way, going past Golpukur Par and Mrityunjay School. Then into an alley in front of the school, where people lived in a slum. In that slum, in a room that measured six feet on a side, we found Chhotda and Geeta Mitra. Ma lifted her burkha and disclosed what she had smuggled out of our house: a few jars and containers. The largest of these contained rice. I stared speechlessly.

"*No one* must know of this!" Ma warned.

I swallowed. "I'm not going to tell anyone," I said.

"Afroza, you can start cooking now. You've got some dal, haven't you?" Ma asked, arranging the containers.

"Who's Afroza?"

"Geeta has become a Muslim, you see. Now her name is Afroza," Ma said happily.

Afroza was sitting, her head covered with her sari. Chhotda was sitting by her side, looking morose. Apart from that cot, only a small clay oven and a few utensils rested on the room's uncemented floor.

Where was the young man with a trendy hairstyle who used to whistle? Here he was, living in a poky little hut. The look on his long face made my heart ache. Suddenly I felt guilty. When he was being tortured and tormented, I had done nothing to protest, had not spoken a single word. It was as if my lips had been sealed. Who had ever heard of such outrage in this day and age, a man being tied up with heavy chains and beaten? Only Baba could do a thing like that. None of us had been able to do anything for Chhotda except secretly shed tears for him.

"Chhotda, there's a lot of mail for you back at home," I informed him.

"Hmm," he said, lighting the oven.

"I met Kotonda the other day, he was going past our house. He said, 'Where's Kamal?' I didn't say anything." I raised my voice slightly this time.

Chhotda made no reply. Silently he placed a pan full of water on the oven. It began boiling. Then he pushed a few pieces of wood into the fire, somewhat clumsily. It was clear that he was not used to living like this. To me, such a scene was totally new. Chhotda, I noticed, seemed not at all interested in either his mail or in what Kotonda, his guitar teacher, had to say. He had changed a lot in the last few months. I watched him leaning over the containers Ma had brought, opening them and inspecting their contents: rice, cooking oil, spices, even chicken curry in one, ready-cooked.

Chhotda pressed his lips to hide his joy and continued to push fuel into the fire as if, at that moment, there was no job on earth that was more important. Perhaps he was very hungry. He must have felt hungry before, when he was living at home, but he was hardly regular with his meals. Often, a plate of food would wait on the dinner table while he spent time chatting with his friends.

I couldn't stop staring at Chhotda. I hadn't seen him for so long! Like Edward VIII, who had given up the English throne for love, Chhotda had left — voluntarily — the comfort of his warm, soft bed and chosen to sleep on the cold, hard floor. This small room, I was convinced, was packed with enormous wealth. It might not have much to do with the material world, but the wealth he and his wife possessed was of a different kind altogether. After all, not everyone was capable of giving up creature comforts or the lure of money. Once, Chhotda had written to Dolly Pal, telling her that he was prepared to spend his life living under a tree if he could be with her. He had made a similar promise to Geeta Mitra, in a letter that ran to thirty-two pages. Living in a small room in a slum was really no different than living under a tree. How brave Chhotda was, how easily he took risks! Now he was truly a free man. No one could control or exploit him; no one was going to tell him when he should return home, or whether he should sit down with his books. I, too, wanted to be free like him, free of the invisible shackles that were holding me back, shackles very much like the ones Chhotda had been tied with.

Once secret contact with Ma was established, Chhotda began to visit us in the afternoons when Baba was at the hospital, safely out of the way. Geeta Mitra followed him in, walking stealthily, her head covered as before. Ma locked the front door so that no one — not even the birds on the trees — could see what was going on, and fed them. When they left, she would give them bags filled with rice, dal, oil, and onion.

We two sisters remained on the alert, listening for any unexpected noise that might herald Baba's arrival. Chhotda crept about like a cat, touching various objects: a radio, a clock, the record player. Sometimes he was heard muttering, "I need this one," before he moved on, acting as if there was something special he was looking for. He looked under the mattress, in the table drawers, on the bookshelves, behaving as if he was new to the house. He rummaged through everything, open wonder in his eyes.

It gave me great pleasure to have him back in the house. I wanted to see him living with us again, falling asleep at his desk as he used to, drooling over an open page. I wanted to see him standing again in the sun in our courtyard, scrubbing himself with a brush before his bath. I wanted to hear him knock on the door at night, every night, his hair blowing in the wind, a guitar slung across his shoulder. I wanted to hear him whistling again.

Slowly, Chhotda began removing his belongings — his guitar, his clothes, his tin trunk. One day I saw that the wall clock in the living room was missing. The next day the radio disappeared. I pretended not to notice and placed heaps of paper and a number of old books on the table where the radio used to be. It filled the empty space. I hung a colorful calendar where the clock used to be. Yasmin, like me, ignored the disappearance of various objects. Ma began asking me the time in a different way. "What time is it on your wristwatch?" she would say, quietly giving up her old habit of glancing at the wall clock.

The three of us kept up the act as if we had all gone blind. None of us asked any questions and hoped silently that Baba would never want to hear the news on the radio or check the time on the clock. Should he start looking for the missing objects, I thought I would say something about its being the work of a petty thief. They were in and out of people's houses all the time. It seemed to me that Ma and Yasmin were preparing similar answers. One day I returned from school to find Chhotda wrapping our record player with a sofa cover. Again, I pretended not to have seen, turning my eyes away to look at the calendar and humming softly. But Ma came swiftly into the room and said in a low voice, "Don't take this one. Your father will be absolutely furious."

"But it doesn't work properly anymore. Let me take it to the repair shop," Chhotda replied, his tone cold.

None of us could bring ourselves to stop him. When overwhelmed by regret and compassion, it is easy to feel put out at times by the object of that compassion, but it was impossible to get really angry with Chhotda. We watched silently as he carried the record player out, bending under its weight.

One day slipped into another. Nothing was repaired, not a single item came back to the house. We didn't mind. If it gave Chhotda any happiness to remove the things he liked the best, so be it. It gave us the opportunity to atone for our sins.

Then one day our worst fears were confirmed. Baba returned home unexpectedly. I froze. Chhotda and his wife slipped into the nearest room and bolted the door from the inside. The sound of the bolt being pushed into place was as loud as an explosion. What if Baba heard an unfamiliar noise? How far would he go to trace its source? My limbs went numb. Ma stood by the closed door, trying to look as if it was she who had shut it. The room was empty. No one was in it, no one was supposed to be. When she spoke, what she said was meaningless, something like, "Why haven't you washed your hands? Don't you want to eat?" I had, in fact, returned from school some time ago and had already had a meal. Then she said, "It's getting late for my magreb namaz." It wasn't late at all. The afternoon was hardly over.

On other days, if Baba returned earlier than expected, he simply checked whether I was doing my homework. Had any of us been on the roof? Were the doors and windows all closed? If everything was all right, he would stand by my desk, rattle off lines spoken by great and wise men, and go off to see his patients. On this particular day he went through the same motions but seemed to be taking much longer than usual. Every moment seemed to last an entire decade.

As he finished inspecting the other rooms in his squeaky shoes, he approached the room in which Chhotda was hiding, Ma said to him, "Are you hungry? Shall I get you something to eat?" Like her other remarks, this question was quite irrelevant, for it was time neither for lunch nor dinner, and no one would want to eat at such an hour. Baba made no reply and pushed the door. It didn't open. Every member of his household was present, clearly visible. Who, then, was inside? It was a perfectly valid question. Yet it seemed to me that such a question was most unfair. What business was it of Baba's if someone wanted to stay in that room? What if I had locked the door from inside and come out by magic? Magicians pulled such tricks all the time. P. C. Sarkar did. So did Houdini, who was tied up and locked in a box. The box remained where it was, but the magician emerged; no one knew how.

Baba pushed the door again. "Who's in there?" he shouted.

Ma silently removed herself from the scene. There was nothing left for her to guard. My cold and numb body suddenly awoke, wanting urgently to answer a call of nature. The smell of burned food began wafting out of the kitchen. Yasmin bent over her books and, like a statue, neither moved nor breathed. There was no one around to dissuade Baba from going further into the matter of the locked door. He would see it through to the end now that his suspicions were aroused. He was like that, never able to let things be. But no one bothered or was even prepared to answer his question. "Who's inside?" he asked again, looking at us, then just flinging the words into the air.

Where was the need to worry about a stupid door? His daughters and animals were where they should be — the two girls at their desks, the dog and the cat on the veranda. No one was walking on the roof; all the doors and windows were shut. Even Ma was at home — it wasn't as if she had left us alone and gone off to visit Amirullah. Everyone was in place, so there was no reason at all to suspect that something was amiss. But Baba wouldn't stop.

"Who is in there?" he went on asking. I was bent over my geometry book as if a most difficult problem was claiming all my attention and I was totally deaf to Baba's shouts. Slowly I rose and began walking toward the bathroom, still pretending that I knew nothing about the locked door or was concerned in any way with the drama that was taking place. It was geometry that was addling my brain, and I had to pour cold water over my head to cool it down.

I shut the bathroom door and heaved a sigh. I realized that I had neither the strength nor the imagination to picture what might happen now. Whatever it was, I had no wish to see it. But no, why should I be allowed to escape anything? A hand started banging on the door. "Open the door! Open it quickly!" As soon as I stepped out of the bathroom, Baba caught me like a cheetah catching its prey. "Who's in that room?" he demanded.

The fury on his face made me catch my breath. I stood mutely, as if I was a criminal, as if whatever had happened was somehow my fault, as if only I knew the secret behind the closed door, and only I was responsible. Baba stomped around the veranda, holding me tightly and demanding an immediate answer. If he was not given one, he would do something terrible.

Eventually, it was Ma who appeared — Ma, my savior, with her thin, limp hair, with her dark skin and blunt nose. She snatched me out of Baba's grasp and said, her voice icy, "It's Kamal. He's come with his wife. She's become a Muslim."

"Who? What did you say? Who is here?" Baba shrieked, his voice creaking.

"Kamal. He's come to visit us," Ma repeated.

"Who's Kamal? I don't know anyone by that name," Baba said, and raced to the closed door. When he spoke, his voice shook the whole house. "Tell them to get out of my house. Now. At once!"

I was still standing on the veranda. My arms and legs had started to go numb again. Baba's finger was still raised and pointing at the front gate.

Chhotda slipped out of the back door and began running toward the gate, holding his wife by the hand.

~~ 13 ~~

Blood

One day as I returned from school I took my uniform off and I saw that my white salwar had turned red with blood. How? Had I cut myself? How could I have done that? I wasn't in pain, so what was wrong with me?

Ma was in our kitchen garden, collecting cauliflower. I ran to her, buried my face in her lap, and wailed loudly. "Ma, Ma, there's a deep cut somewhere. Look," I pointed below my abdomen, "I'm bleeding!"

Ma stroked my head. "Don't cry," she said, wiping my streaming cheeks.

Ma smiled. "There's nothing to cry about, I promise. You'll be all right."

Blood was spurting out of my body, and yet Ma didn't seem worried at all. She went back inside with a couple of cauliflowers in her hand. For the first time, she made no attempt to grab the bottle of Dettol and dress my wound. On the contrary, she calmly shook the dirt off the cauliflower and said with a slight smile, "You're a big girl now. Big girls get this."

"Get this? What do you mean? Get what?" I asked, looking with considerable disgust at the smile that was still hovering on Ma's lips.

"All this bleeding. It's called menstruation. We call it *hayez*. It happens every month to all grown-up women, even me." Ma continued to smile.

"And Yasmin as well?" I asked anxiously.

"No, not yet. But it'll start when she is grown up like you."

So I grew up one evening, all of a sudden, just like that. Ma said to me, "Remember, you are not a little girl anymore. You cannot play or go outside as you used to. You must remain in the house, as all grown women do. And don't prance around everywhere. Learn to sit quietly. Don't go near the men."

Then she tore off a few strips from an old sari, folded them, and passed them to me with a cord normally used to hold a salwar in place. When she spoke, she sounded serious. The smile had gone. "Tie this cord tightly around your stomach. Then put these pieces of cloth between your legs and make sure the ends are held in place by the cord. After that, just sit quietly. You'll bleed for three days, or maybe four or five. Don't be afraid. It happens to all girls, and it's perfectly natural. When this pad gets wet, wash it and wear another. But make sure no one sees anything. It's all quite embarrassing, so you mustn't speak about it."

This frightened me all the more. Not only was I going to bleed, but I was going to bleed *every month*? Why didn't it happen to men? Why were only women chosen for this? Why did it have to be *me*? Was nature as unfair as Allah?

All at once I felt as if I had grown up like Ma and my aunts, that I could no longer sit around and play with my dolls. Now I would have to wear a sari like the adults, cook like them, walk slowly, speak softly. It was as if someone had physically pushed me off the playing field, off the squares I had drawn to play hopscotch. In no time at all, what little freedom I enjoyed had vanished, like cotton in a strong wind. Why couldn't I just wake up and find that nothing had changed, that all was as before? I wished with all my heart for the whole thing to be no more than an accident, sudden bleeding from some secret injury within my body.

I banged my head on the wall of the bathroom, but felt no pain. My body had become only a carrier — I carried a bleeding heart within it. The torn pieces of cloth were still in my hands. I was holding my destiny in my hands — a destiny that was mean, unjust, and unfair.

Ma knocked on the door and spoke softly, "Why are you taking so long? What's wrong? Come on, do as I told you, and come out quickly."

Why couldn't Ma at least leave me alone to cry? I was furious with her and everyone else in the house, as if they had all conspired against me. Only *I* would smell foul. If anyone was heading for disaster, it was me. How was I going to keep this obnoxious event a secret from everyone? How could I walk in front of everybody, knowing that under my salwar was a pad made of torn cloth, drenched with blood? What if people guessed? I hated myself. I spat on myself in revulsion. I was now like a clown in a circus. I was different from everyone else. I was ugly and rotten. Inside my body lay hidden a serious sickness. With no cure.

Was this what growing up amounted to? I noticed that nothing I had thought or felt before had changed. I still enjoyed running across the field to play gollachhut, but Ma's instructions in this matter were quite clear: "You mustn't jump or run. You're not a child anymore." If she found me standing in the field, she snapped, "Come inside at once. I can see men staring at you from their roofs."

"So what? Why does it matter if someone looks at me?" I protested faintly.

"You have grown up. That's what matters."

Why was that a problem? I never got a clear-cut answer from Ma. Men from outside my family were quickly banned from my life. Ma became completely absorbed in the business of keeping me out of sight. If any of her brothers came over, accompanied by their friends, Ma pushed me out of the living room. I was slowly becoming both invisible and untouchable.

One day, while looking for a bunch of keys, I happened to touch the Koran. Ma saw this and came running. "Never touch the Koran with an impure body."

"*Impure* body? What do you mean?" I asked bitterly.

"You are impure while you are having menstruation. When that happens you are not to touch the book of Allah, or do namaz."

I had heard Ma call a dog "unholy" and "impure." So women could also be impure at times? The act of washing one's hands and feet before doing namaz was supposed to cleanse one of all impurities. Anyone could do namaz, except women who were menstruating. I felt as if I had been thrown into a pool of stinking, stagnant water. From head to toe, I was immersed in filth. It made me sick. I started to hate myself. Every time I had to wash my bloodstained pads I wanted to throw up. It would have been better if a jinn had possessed me, I thought. But I had to stow my revulsion and pain into a dark recess of my mind, bury it underground in a secret spot where no one ever set foot.

Nor was this the end. Something else was causing me embarrassment. I could no longer take my dress off, even if it was boiling hot in the afternoon. My breasts were growing bigger. Sad and depressed, all I could do was lie on my bed.

Three days later, exhausted and devastated by constant bleeding, I was found by Baba as I lay in bed, still as a corpse. He came charging in like a wild buffalo. "What is this? Why are you in bed at this time? Get up, start working. At your desk. *Now!*"

I pulled myself to my feet and dragged my poor body to my desk. Baba shouted again, "Why are you moving so slowly? Don't you eat enough? Where's your strength gone?"

Ma appeared, once more my savior. She called Baba out and took him to the next room to explain. A few sounds pierced the wall and came through — faint whispers; I couldn't make out the words. My ears burned as if an invisible fire surrounded every single word. The letters in the open book became blurred. Slowly, that fire began to devour my books, my pens, pencils, notebooks, every object on my desk. A wave of heat rose from it and hit my face.

Baba emerged from the other room and quietly came back to where I was sitting. I could feel him place something on my shoulder — was it his hand, or his whip? He said, "If you want to rest for a while, do. You can do your lessons later. Go, back to bed. The body needs rest, too. But that doesn't mean that you should be lazy and sleep all day! You have a lazy brother, don't you? Noman. He's never done well because he's so idle. He is studying psychology! What a subject! Only madmen can choose this kind of subject. I have no hopes left."

Baba pulled me from my chair and helped me lie down. Then he stroked my hair and said, "I have only two children left now, Yasmin and you. You know that, don't you? You are my only hope; you are all I live for. If I can bring you up properly, see you well settled in life, I will find peace. If you cause me pain and disappointment, I will have no choice but to kill myself. All right, if you are tired, take a few minutes off. Then, when you feel rested, go back to your studies. I have never spared any expense in giving you good food and every comfort. Why? So that you will be free to spend all your time on your studies. You are a student. Your only mission should be learning. Then it will be time to work, to earn a living. And after that, time for retirement.

Every phase in your life is run by a set of rules, and there is a particular time for every phase. Do you see?"

Baba's hard, dry fingers pushed my hair away from my face, tucking it behind my ears. I had noticed him do this before. His idea of caressing me was to remove every strand of hair from my face. He wore his own hair firmly brushed back. He couldn't bear to see loose strands falling over anyone's face. Oh, how rough his hand was! I couldn't believe it. His rough, coarse fingers ran all over my back. It was far from a gentle stroke. I felt as if Baba was removing all the dead skin from my back with a pumice stone.

I simply couldn't bring myself to accept the situation. Why should I leave my games and sit at home with a long face just because I had started to menstruate? How I had longed to grow up, to grow so tall that I'd be able to reach the bolt on top of the door! I could reach that bolt if I stood on tiptoe, but this business of bleeding put an end to my childhood so quickly and placed such a high barrier between me and the world that it frightened me. When I turned eleven, Ma had made me long salwars that replaced my shorts forever. A year later, after my twelfth birthday, she had said I would have to wear an urna because my legs were now longer and my chest was getting bigger. If I didn't hide these behind an urna, people would call me shameless and brazen. No one in our society liked shameless girls. Those who are shy, who behaved modestly, found good husbands. Ma hoped fervently that I would succeed in making a good marriage. Mamata, the bookworm in my class, had been married off some time ago. I asked her, "Do you know the man you're marrying?" Mamata had shaken her head. No, she had never met him. The groom arrived on an elephant. The whole town watched his arrival. He had demanded — and received — an enormous dowry, consisting of seventy grams of gold, thirty thousand takas in cash, a radio, and a wristwatch. After the wedding Mamata, too, rode on the elephant to her new home. From that moment on, she would spend her life looking after her husband's family. Her studies had come to an end. That man who went about riding an elephant would make sure to destroy Mamata's passion for novels.

I had hardly come to terms with the idea — and inconvenience — of menstruation when a supposedly important man in our village turned up one day with a large fish and told Baba that he wanted to see his son married to Baba's elder daughter. Baba heard these words, returned the fish, and promptly pointed at the front gate. He wished to hear not another word, he said. Would the man just leave?

Ma was quite put out by this. "What did you do that for?" she complained. "Don't you want our girls to marry? Nasrin has grown up. This is the right time for marriage, I think."

Baba stopped her at once. "*I* know when my daughter should, or should not, be married. You don't have to poke your nose into this, all right? She is studying now. One day she will be a doctor. Not just an MBBS like me — she'll be an FRCS.* I wish to hear no more about her marriage. Is that clear?"

I pricked my ears and listened carefully to these words. Suddenly, all my anger at Baba melted. I wanted to get up and make him a glass of lemonade. Maybe he was thirsty. But I had learned not to go anywhere near Baba, had learned not to give him anything unless he asked for it. It was impossible to crash through the barrier imposed by habit.

I noticed Ma was quite excited by my growing up. She bought a black burkha one day and said to me, "Look, I got this for you. Why don't you try it on?"

My face went red with mortification. "What! You're asking me to wear a burkha?"

"Yes, most certainly I am. Aren't you grown up now? A grown woman must wear a burkha," Ma replied, measuring its length.

"I won't!" I said firmly.

"Aren't you a Muslim? Allah Himself has said that all Muslim women should cover themselves and be modest." Ma spoke gently.

"Yes, Allah may have said that, but I'm not going to wear it."

"Haven't you seen Fajli's daughters? They wear burkhas, such good girls. You're good, too, aren't you? If you wear a burkha, people will say what a nice girl you are!"

Ma began stroking my back. Normally her soft, warm touch broke down all my defenses. But I wasn't going to let that happen today. I had to say no. I braced myself to utter that word.

"No!"

"*No?* You mean you're really not going to? . . ."

"I already told you, didn't I?" I replied, quickly moving away from Ma. But she grabbed me and hit my back with the same hand that had

---

*Fellowship of Royal College of Surgery, a degree that must be obtained in England. Doctors on the Indian subcontinent dream of getting this degree.

stroked me before. "You'll go to hell!" she warned. "I am telling you, my child, you *will* go to hell. You didn't turn out right after all. I took you to Noumahal so many times, but even that didn't open your eyes. Didn't you see those girls? Some the same age as you, others even younger, but they were all draped in burkhas. They looked beautiful. And they do their namaz and observe roja. You've given all that up, haven't you? Yes, hell is where you'll end up, I can see."

Let Ma hit me as hard as she liked, I would never wear a burkha. I went and sat down at my desk. A book lay open before me, but I only stared at the pages. The letters were blurred, as if hidden under the wings of a vulture.

I could hear Ma walking along the hall outside my room. She was still talking, loud enough for me to hear: "She might seem meek and docile, but underneath that she's a devil. She answers me back! No one else does that. They don't dare. If I could whip her the way her father does she'd listen to me. Well, if she goes on being difficult, I will have to act accordingly."

When Ma decided to act "accordingly," she changed completely. She wasn't my mother anymore; she turned into a witch. She looked so ugly! I found it difficult to believe that she was the same woman who once fed me lovingly, taught me rhymes, and stayed awake night after night if I happened to be ill. I became like dust on the floor, but deep inside a blind rage began to gather force, as sharp as a sparkling diamond.

I felt like swallowing poison and ending it all. The world was such a cruel place — better to die than live in it as a woman. I had read in a magazine that, somewhere in the world, a girl had become a boy. I longed to wake up one day and find that something similar had happened to me, that I had turned into a boy. That there were no unseemly mounds of flesh on my chest. That I could wear a thin, transparent shirt and roam all over town. That when I returned home late at night after having seen a film and smoked a cigarette with my friends, Ma would serve me the biggest piece of fish just because I was a boy, her son, the one who would carry forward the family name. No matter what I did, Ma would forgive me. No one would order me to cover my chest with an urna, wear a veil, wear a burkha, or stop me from standing at a window or going up on the roof.

But who was going to turn me into a boy? I couldn't do it myself. Who could I ask? Allah, Allah was the only one I could pray to. If only there was someone else, someone in addition to Allah! Hindus had millions of gods and goddesses, but why should they hear my prayer? I wasn't a Hindu. I had prayed to Allah before, but He hadn't granted a single prayer. So I prayed to no one. I simply told *myself* what I wanted: to either die or become a boy. I repeated those words again and again. Baba had often told me that I could get what I wanted if I had a strong enough will. So I willed myself, with every fiber of my being. I poured my mind, my heart, my thoughts, my feelings, my virtues, my sins into that simple act.

I just willed myself.

~ 14 ~

Phulbahari

$\mathcal{I}$ lost my overwhelming desire to become a boy the day I saw Phulbahari's mother arrive in San Souci. She was as thin as a rake. She had been very ill, her whole body was yellow, and she said that only the blessings of peers and fakirs had helped her survive. No one wanted her to work for them anymore. So she now went from door to door, begging for food. She collapsed on the veranda attached to our kitchen and clutched a pillar for support when she rose; it seemed as if she was so tired that she could no longer carry the weight of her life. It made me think about life in general. Perhaps, sometimes, it simply alights and perches on one's shoulders. The poor body and mind, no longer strong enough, can't carry it forward.

This same woman once used to grind spices in Grandma's kitchen with a funny scraping noise: *ghosh-ghosh, ghosh-h-h; ghosh-ghosh, ghosh-h-h*. When she left our house, dragging her feet past the woodapple tree, I heard that noise again. Who knows where she went. I didn't run after her to see where she was going or where in this big, wide world she could possibly go.

The memory of that funny grinding sound took me right back to the broken threshold in Grandma's kitchen where I used to sit and watch Phulbahari's mother crouched over the grinding stone, her body rocking as she moved her arms. She would start quite early in the morning, not finishing until early afternoon. She had to crush and grind different spices: turmeric, black pepper, cumin, coriander. She had to grate onions, garlic, and ginger. A man from Grandpa's restaurant used to come take it all away in a big bowl. But Phulbahari's mother's work was not done. She would come back in the afternoon to grind more spices, spending the whole afternoon. I felt like grinding spices, moving my body backward and forward. Once I said to her, "Will you give me a few spices to grind?"

Phulbahari's mother stopped, looked at me, and smiled, revealing her dark, paan-stained teeth. "No, Apa," she said. "You couldn't do it. It's a very difficult job."

Phulbahari's mother was the same age as my own mother, yet she called me Apa, older sister, because I was her master's granddaughter. Grinding spices was not my job. Only someone from a lower class could do it, dirtying their hands at this difficult and messy task. I learned at the age of three to distinguish between upper and lower classes. Phulbahari's mother might be a grown-up, but it was all right to look down on her because she came from a lower class. I was not supposed to touch anyone from that class, or climb into their laps, or eat anything they might have cooked. They were not given the right to sit on our sofas and chairs. If they had to, they would sit on the floor, even sleep there if need be. If we called out to them, they were expected to answer at once, then come running and do what they were told to do without question. That was the rule for every member of the lower class.

"What's your name, Phulbahari's Ma?" I asked, looking at her dark teeth.

She made no reply. Maybe my question was crushed under the noise of her grinding and she could not hear. In the afternoon, when all the adults had stretched themselves out on their beds after lunch and a stray cat had stolen in to sleep by the oven, I repeated my question, raising my voice this time: "What's your name?"

Phulbahari's mother stopped her grinding and looked at me. Her forehead was damp, as were her nose and chin. According to Aunt Jhunu, if the tip of a woman's nose became wet with perspiration, her husband loved her. Phulbahari's mother's husband had died many years ago, so who was going to give her any love? My question clearly amused her, but she didn't reveal her dark teeth this time. Instead, she pouted, thrusting out her thick bottom lip and puffing up her cheeks. Then she met my curious eyes with her own quiet ones and said, "I have no name. People call me Phulbahari's Ma."

I laughed and asked in a voice that implied that I knew she was being silly, "What were you called before Phulbahari was born?"

She wiped her face with her sari and repeated, "I had no name."

"Then what did people call you? What did your parents call you?"

Phulbahari's mother sighed deeply. "My parents? They're no more. They died years ago."

"All right, but didn't they give you a name before they died? Look, I have a name. I am called Nasrin," I said, speaking like a school-teacher.

Phulabhari's mother resumed her grinding. "No," she said firmly, "I didn't have a name. Ever. If someone wanted to call me, they simply said, 'You, gal!' or 'Oy, you monkey!' or things like that."

I stared in amazement at her rocking body. I could hear that scraping noise, not on the grinding stone, but inside my head.

Later, I shared this news with Ma. "Guess what, Ma — Phulbahari's mother doesn't have a name of her own!"

"Hmm," Ma replied, not in the least surprised to hear that a woman who was the same age as her didn't possess a name. I couldn't understand how she could be so indifferent.

"How can a human being not have a name?" I asked, lifting my eyes from my book.

"Oh, don't go on about it!" Ma snapped. "Just read your book. Come on, read loudly."

Like an obedient child, I began reading aloud, moving my body backward and forward: One becomes great only when others call one so. Giving oneself airs does not achieve greatness . . .

"He who studies hard gets to ride a motorcar . . .

"Always tell the truth."

A little later, Phulbahari came into the room. I stopped reading for a minute to tell her in a low voice, "Phulbahari, did you know your mother doesn't have a name?"

Like Ma, Phulbahari took this revelation perfectly calmly, as if it was absolutely natural for her mother not to have a name. But she did give me a piercing look, as if she wanted to know whether there was some secret reason behind my sudden interest in her mother's name.

"So what if she doesn't have a name? What would she do with one? What does it matter whether a poor woman has a name or not?" she asked, her jaw set firmly.

Ma often said that Phulbahari had a sharp tongue. She hadn't learned to mince words. What she said gave me food for thought. Could it be true that a poor person didn't need a name? Perhaps she was right. The poor didn't have to go to school, so they were not required to register their names in the school attendance book. The poor had no property, so there was no need for a name to be put on documents. That meant it was entirely possible to live without a name, but only if you were poor. But then, the poor had to make do without so many other things — blankets and quilts, fish and meat, shoes and sandals, fancy clothes, hair oil, soap, cream, powder — they lived without any of these. My heart ached for Phulbahari as well as her nameless mother.

Now Phulbahari was mopping the floor, crouching over it as she moved from one end of the room to the other, occasionally dipping a piece of rag into a bucket of water. A bidi was tucked behind her ear. She would light it when her work was done. No one objected to her smoking bidis. Women from lower classes could smoke, but not those from the upper class. Never. A man, however, was free to do what he wanted, eat what he liked, even smoke what he fancied, regardless of his class. Phulbahari's tall, dark figure, her pockmarked face, and the bidi tucked behind her ear were all very familiar to me. She took a moment to squat on the floor and light her bidi, quickly blowing out the smoke. When she did this, I noticed, she seemed happier than at any other time.

"Don't you know the alphabet?" I asked her. Phulbahari resumed mopping the floor. "No," she shook her head. I quickly wrote an "A" on a piece of paper and showed it to her. "Look, that's the first letter. It's A. Say it, A." Phulbahari repeated after me: "A." She had stopped her mopping, and she had a curious expression in her eyes.

"And look, here's your name, Phulbahari," I said, writing the word down on the same piece of paper and holding it before her.

She stared in wonder at her name, as if it was a picture of some distant, unfamiliar land she couldn't recognize. Thank goodness Ma wasn't around, or she would definitely have complained that Phulbahari was not doing her work. It was only because Ma was absent that Phulbahari could sit properly on the floor and look so attentively at her own name. "Is that really my name, Aunt?" she asked. The spirited woman with a sharp tongue was smiling like a little girl. I wanted to teach her to read, teach her the whole alphabet, all the vowels and consonants so that she could write her name herself.

"Tell me, Phulbahari, why do you call me aunt? I am so much younger than you!"

Phulbahari turned puzzled eyes on me. "Why, what else can I call you?" she asked. "You are rich, you're from a different class. So what if you're younger? I have to call a newborn baby aunt if she is from a rich family. I cannot call anyone by their name, not if they are richer and better than me. That's the destiny of the poor. It's all written here." She tapped her forehead.

I laughed and touched my own forehead. "Look, my forehead is no different than yours. You mean the poor have foreheads that are crooked or something? Deformed?"

Phulbahari couldn't help laughing at that. She sounded like an innocent child. "No, no, that's not what I meant. When I said 'forehead' I meant destiny, luck."

She dipped the rag in the bucket once more, sighed, and finished mopping what remained, including the threshold. Then she said, "When my father died, things became so much worse for us. I have to work as a servant now, in people's houses. How can I learn to read and write?"

"Your father died? How? What happened to him?"

Phulbahari spoke without raising her eyes. "He caught the wind," she replied, "and he died."

"Wind? What wind? How can anyone 'catch' a wind and die?" I craned my neck in amazement.

"It was an evil wind, Aunt. The work of a jinn. My father lost the use of his arms and legs one day, just like that, and took to his bed. He never left it. He died." Phulbahari wiped the threshold and sighed again. I noticed that her thick cotton sari was slightly torn near her knees. She had only one other sari, which was green and torn in several places. Again, my heart ached for her.

Having finished her work, Phulbahari left. I stared dumbly after her, my mind in turmoil over the cause of her father's death. Catching an evil wind? Was that possible? Later, when I asked Ma, she said, "Yes, a jinn can tamper with wind, make it evil. If you catch it, your limbs can go numb, and you may never recover. That's true enough."

That puzzled me even more. Jinns and ghosts and spooks . . . it was all so mystifying. Uncle Sharaf frequently saw ghosts, but I had never seen any. I had tried, at times, to catch a glimpse of a female spook who was supposed to be able to flash in the dark, like lightning. But I didn't succeed, not even when I stared at the dark bamboo grove through a crack in our window.

Barely a week after my conversation with Phulbahari, little Getu caught the evil wind, made evil by some jinn, and his right leg became numb and quite useless. His mother went nearly insane with anxiety and grief, but Getu's father wouldn't let her see her own son. She went as far as their courtyard, but he shooed her out. After their divorce, she no longer had any rights, not even to see her son.

Getu's mother returned to Grandma's house, wailing loudly. Everyone in the house heard and watched her in silence, some standing by the door, some sitting in the shade of the mango tree, others by the hand-pump. Aunt Jhunu said, "Tch, tch!" in sympathy, then vanished inside the house, swinging her long braids. Grandma continued, mutely, to fill paan leaves with spices. Suddenly Uncle Tutu gave a furious roar, ordering Getu's mother to take herself away. He couldn't stand the sight of a woman wailing and moaning.

Getu's mother stuffed a corner of her sari into her mouth to stifle her sobs and left the house. No one saw me following her. I should have been afraid to walk through the bamboo grove, but I wasn't. I should have remembered that I, too, might catch the evil wind and lose the use of my arms and legs, but I forgot. I was a thoughtless, irresponsible, ill-mannered, impudent girl. Getu's mother walked toward the railroad tracks. So did I, following her like a shadow. She sat on the tracks and cried. I collected pebbles and threw them: clang, clang, clang, clang! Getu's mother stopped crying, turned around, and saw me, my uncombed hair, my dusty legs, my unbrushed teeth. I said, "Don't cry, Getu's Ma. Move away from those tracks; a train might come soon. One day, I'm sure Getu will chop his father to bits and come back to you. You just wait and see."

I had heard Ma threaten to chop people to pieces with her kitchen knife. Phulbahari had been threatened thus when she forgot to watch the fish curry that was cooking and fell asleep. When she woke, it was burned black. Then when Ma found a love letter from Razia Begum in Baba's shirt pocket, she made a similar threat. I had never seen Razia Begum, but could somehow picture her looking a little like Aunt Jhunu. I felt sorry for her, too.

What I found easier to imagine was Getu killing his father. My body didn't tremble at the thought of their courtyard being splattered with blood, just as it hadn't trembled when I passed through the bamboo grove, following in Getu's mother's footsteps.

About five days after Getu died, someone else caught the evil wind. It was the man who ran the local sweets shop. Everyone called him Thanda's father. Anyway, when he caught this wind, he closed his shop and took to his bed. His limbs were fine, but he kept bringing up blood when he coughed. A maulvi came to blow on him, and special holy water was brought from a peer in Shorshina. Thanda's father drank the water but it did nothing to stop the blood. People who were hit by the evil wind never lived long. All the relatives and friends of Thanda's father waited patiently for his death.

After a few days Baba heard the news. "What's the matter with him? Let me have a look," he said, turning up at the house of the stricken man. He checked his pulse, pulled his eyelids down, told him to put his tongue out, and eventually asked Thanda to get some medicine from the pharmacist. Thanda's father took the tablets and capsules and recovered from tuberculosis after a while. To everyone's complete amazement, a victim of the jinn's evil wind not only had survived but also in less than a week had reopened his shop!

Having witnessed this miracle with my own eyes, I began to be convinced that the evil wind was not, after all, as powerful as it was made out to be. Baba certainly didn't seem at all surprised that his patient had recovered. It was as if Thanda's father was meant to recover all along. I couldn't help thinking that, had he so wished, Baba could have saved Getu's life as well.

Thanda's father was a distant relative of Phulbahari's, some sort of a cousin of her mother's; not that he ever acknowledged that relationship. One day, Phulbahari told me, smoking her bidi, "He's got a shop, he's got money, and he doesn't want people to know we're related. Do you know why? It's because we work as servants. Even the poor have differences."

Thanda's mother had told everyone that it was the holy water that had saved her husband's life, but Phulbahari was of a different opinion. "It was your father's medicines that did the trick. I've heard it said that no one can survive if they catch the jinn's wind. Well, Thanda's father recovered, didn't he?" It was clear that she had little faith in what people said. When she spoke, she always looked up, keeping her dark neck straight.

After Uncle Hashem, Grandma had had two sons who had died as a result of the evil wind. Ma recalled those times after she heard about Thanda's father. Each time the baby had diarrhea, it stopped feeding at its mother's breast. The local herbalist came, blew on the child, and told Grandma that a jinn lived in the jamun tree in Shahabuddin's house. The same jinn had put evil in the wind.

Grandma was told to keep a piece of leather and a piece of iron with her at all times. Jinns, it was said, were averse to both. Every time she left her room — even when she went to the kitchen or even the bath-room — Grandma carried small pieces of leather and iron in her hand. But that was not all. There was every danger that the jinn might, through a cunning trick, climb on her shoulder and gain entry to her room. Grandma, therefore, kept a low fire burning at the entrance to her room, which she stepped over. Then she brushed her-self thoroughly with a broom, in case the harmful jinn was hiding within the folds of her clothes. That was the only way to get rid of it. Sadly, despite these precautions, her two sons didn't live.

When Ma gave birth to her own children, Grandma made similar arrangements. A small fire burned in Ma's room; and if Ma happened to leave it Grandma waited for her return with a broom in hand. When Ma came back, Grandma told her to step over the fire and brushed her down. Baba saw her do this after I was born. "What the hell are you doing?" he asked.

"I have to do this," Ma replied, "to protect my baby from the jinn. If it decides to put evil in the wind, and my baby catches it, she will stop feeding, get dysentery, and die."

All four of her children were still alive. None of us stopped feeding, and even when we got dysentery, we survived. No one caught the evil wind produced by the jinn. But then, it could be argued, Ma had a powerful chant (that, too, in Arabic) with which she could keep every ailment at bay. So she told everyone, including Baba, that what she chanted was *alhamdu lillahillayi khalakas samawati wal arda was jayalaz zulumatay wannur, chhummallayeena kafaru birabbihim yadilun.* Baba heard her claim but pretended he hadn't.

After Thanda's father's recovery, instances of people catching the evil wind were fewer and farther between. Those who seemed afflicted came to Baba. He either treated and cured them himself or sent them to the hospital. Everyone made a full recovery and went back home.

After Phulbahari lost her job in our house, we heard one day that she was down with fever. No one blamed the jinn this time. The imam of the local mosque came to see Thanda's father, tied an amulet around his arm, and said, "I hear Phulbahari is ill. At last, Allah has done something really useful. That woman was totally shameless. She never walked, did she? She went stomping around everywhere. O Allah, kill her with this fever!"

When I heard about Phulbahari's illness, I said I wanted to go and see her. Ma tweaked my ear painfully and said, "What! This girl just doesn't want to stay at home. Are you just looking for an excuse to go gallivanting?" I couldn't visit Phulbahari during her illness, but she recovered. After she did, one day we suddenly heard that she was to marry an old man who lived in the same slum. He was seventy, most of his teeth were missing, and he already had three wives. Phulbahari's mother came to ask us for money. After all, a wedding was an expensive business. I saw Grandma untie the knot in her sari and remove five takas. Two or three other families helped as well. With the money raised, a red sari was bought for Phulbahari, and her husband was given a dowry of two hundred takas.

Phulbahari seemed suddenly to have grown quite distant from the rest of us. I would never see her smoking outside our kitchen on lazy afternoons; nor would she chat with me. She would now stop working as a servant in other people's houses. She would cook for her husband, and cover her head with her sari when she went to the pond, pitcher under her arm, to fetch water. Somehow I couldn't imagine Phulbahari in such a role. It just didn't suit her. She looked far better when she was stomping around. On one memorable occasion, a group of local boys had followed her, calling her names. One called her a "motherfucker," at which I saw Phulbahari stop, turn around, and slap the boy's face. I witnessed this scene and was completely enchanted. The balloon I was holding escaped and blew away, high in the sky. I didn't notice.

Today, however, it was not Phulbahari but her mother who had come to our house. By the time she left, dusk had fallen. She made her way to the front gate, past the woodapple tree, slowly fading into the twilight. I could hear the words she spoke before she disappeared: "Phulbahari's husband killed her. Throttled her to death. But I do not cry. What good will it do? Will a few tears bring her back? Allah has seen it all. He will punish him one day."

I felt as if a huge python had escaped from a gypsy woman's basket and swallowed me whole. A silent, devastating grief began to tear me apart, crushing my whole being on a grinding stone. I could hear the noise as my heart crumbled: *ghosh-ghosh, ghosh-ghosh-h-h!*

~•• 15 ••~

The World of Poetry

In this hungry world, the earth is harsh,
the full moon like a burned bun.

$\mathcal{U}$ncle Siddique had uttered these words while standing in Grandma's moonlit courtyard. At the time, Uncle Kana, seated on a low stool, was telling us the story of the two warriors, Sohrab and Rustam. Uncle Siddique's words made him stop and smile. "Who wants to eat a bun? Who's that hungry?" he asked.

"Thousands of poor people starve to death!" Uncle Siddique replied, his wooden clogs striking on the floor as he walked.

I said softly, so that no one could hear me:

Get me that moon-bun,
Someone, do.
Some I shall eat,
The rest I'll give the slum dwellers, too.

Uncle Kana heard me. His ears were very sharp. "What is this? Has everyone here turned into a poet? Who just mentioned the slum dwellers?"

I didn't reply. Silently, I covered my face with my hands.

This was one of my many bad habits. I often made up little rhymes that were parodies of popular and well-known poems. If I were asked to recite a poem in school, I forgot the real one. Instead, what sprang to my lips were the funny ones I'd made up. There was one that began:

Busy bee, busy bee, are you on a buzzing spree?
Stop a while and chat with me.

I'm off collecting nectar, my friend,
Time's slipping by,
Cannot stop and chat,
I have got to fly.

One evening, as I was sitting in Grandma's house, reading aloud from a book of rhymes, I spotted Uncle Kana crossing the courtyard. Instead of "Busy bee, busy bee," I said to him:

Uncle Kana, Uncle Kana, where are you off to?
Stop a while and chat with me, oh please do.

I'm off looking for all the kids,
Got no time to chat.
I have lovely tales to tell
Both of this and of that.

Ma heard me from inside and shouted, "Oy, what's all this? You're getting into a very bad habit. Stop making fun of old rhymes!"

On New Year's Day, naughty and impertinent girls in my school hung up on the notice board a list of nicknames given to certain students. No one could ever figure out who thought up the names or who put them up, but everyone crowded around to read the list. On one occasion, I found the words "a burst melon" next to my own name. In fact, there was more than one list. On a different wall, someone wrote of me, "butter wouldn't melt in her mouth."

The most beautiful girl in my class, Dilruba, had "slut" next to her name. "What does it mean?" I asked her. Tears sprang to Dilruba's eyes. She didn't reply. I felt very sorry for her. So I sat beside her, gently placing my hand on her back. I had heard the word before because Ma used that word when she lost her temper with any of our maids and began abusing them. But no one had ever told me its meaning. We were not close friends, but from the time I reached out to her, we were drawn to each other. Slowly, just as the first rays of dawn wipe out the darkness of night, Dilruba began to influence me, and I blossomed like a lotus.

Once our friendship was formed, Dilruba began telling me stories. She told me about her brothers and sisters, Lata, Pata, Tona, and Tuni.

Based on her stories, my imagination took flight and they began living in my mind. Later, I met them in Dilruba's house, even exchanged a few words with them; but somehow, the people in Dilruba's stories seemed more real to me than those in real life. When I met Lata after her illness, I didn't ask her how she was. Instead, I asked Dilruba when we were alone, "What happened to her?" She replied, "Lata didn't recover. A number of doctors saw her, a number of medicines were given to her, but Lata kept shrinking until she became as thin as a thread. That thread simply hung in her room. Some said it should be dropped into a river; some said it should be held in a close embrace. Then someone did come along, held her close, kissed her, and Lata opened her eyes. She smiled, and we all thought she would live again."

When Dilruba told me these stories, she seemed to inhabit a different world. Even when she looked at me, it was as if she was looking at something else. Once my anxiety about Lata's health was over, Dilruba showed me a notebook. It was full of her poetry. I began reading, then stopped suddenly at a page:

> Grassflower,
> will you take me? Will you?
> All my days I have spent here and there.
> Finally, to you — my haven — I say,
> take everything I have;
> take me in your arms;
> touch me;
> touch me softly.
> I have come to you so late,
> if you reject me,
> then make me drown in nowhere,
> I will struggle up the bank
> to return to you once more.
> If you throw me nowhere again,
> still I will try to reach you.
> Grassflower, take me, will you?

"Dilruba, will you teach me how to write poetry?" I asked, bending over the page.

Her lips were soft and pink, flawless as the rest of her face. She had masses of thick curly hair tied into a knot behind her head. A few unruly strands escaped from it and hung over her forehead and neck, some touching her chin. Looking at her, I suddenly had a strong feeling of déjà vu. This whole scene had taken place before — I, asking to be taught to write poetry, Dilruba, saying nothing in reply. I had sat beside another girl, who had looked exactly like Dilruba. We were before an open notebook, by an open window, beyond which was an open field. The sky rolled down to meet the field where it ended.

Dilruba was even quieter and shyer than me. When all the other girls ran and skipped all over the playing field, she sat quietly by a window, staring at the distant sky.

"No one can be taught to write poetry. If you look at the sky, you will be moved to tears. If you can cry, really cry with all your heart, you will be able to write," Dilruba told me. Her voice held a gentle warmth.

Quite often she was punished for not paying attention in class, and she was made to stand holding her ears with both hands. Sometimes she was even told to leave the classroom. She did not seem to mind at all. She remained outside the door, standing on one leg, her eyes fixed on the sky, with which she seemed to have a strange rapport. When I looked at her, I felt as if someone had cast a spell on me. I walked by her side, talked to her, placed a hand on her shoulder, all in a sort of trance.

I tried looking at the sky as well, but, unlike Dilruba, my eyes did not fill with tears. However, one day I found a torn, empty paper bag in our courtyard and, thinking of Dilruba, found myself writing a poem on it:

> Let's play, Dilruba.
> Do you know how to play gollachhut?
> Let's get lost.
> Let's go somewhere,
> far away,
> across seven seas,
> thirteen rivers;
> Dilruba, let's go.

Dilruba smiled sweetly when she read the poem. I had never seen such a sweet smile. Runi's smile had been like this . . . but no, it wasn't wholly like Dilruba's; it was slightly different. "Anyone who has an attractive smile has no need to talk," Rabindranath had once said, and he was right. I had felt very shy in Runi's presence, but not in Dilruba's. We built a different world together, one in which we simply played with words. Dilruba wrote in her notebook:

> Wherever you want me to go, I will.
> I will melt into you, I promise.
> In return, you must come close to me
> And say only, "I love you."
> Nothing else.
> Wherever you want me to go, I will!

That was all I had learned to do: love. Our love grew deeper. We left home and traveled to distant lands, like princes did in fairy tales, across seven seas and thirteen rivers. Only in our imagination of course. Neither of us could do anything to step out of the real world.

I thought Dilruba was very much like the poetry she wrote — quiet, like a still, deep pool in a forest, its water the same shade of blue as the sky. Just occasionally, one or two leaves dropped into it and floated on its surface, like rafts. They were rafts Dilruba had made just for herself, to sail away on.

One day, the same Dilruba shocked me profoundly by announcing that she was about to get married. Her father had made all the arrangements.

"No!" I exclaimed, gazing at her pale face and gray eyes. "You must refuse. Tell your father you won't do it."

Dilruba gave me a wan smile. Only someone burning with a high fever, ailing for many days, would smile like that. The very next day she stopped coming to school. I was totally alone. Even after the school day was over, I sat by the window for a long time, staring at the sky, feeling intensely her absence. Where was she? Had she turned her face away from everyone in hurt and pain and vanished into the sky? I tried very hard to find her there. Now, for the first time, looking at the sky brought tears to my eyes.

Two days before her wedding Dilruba came to our house, to San Souci. This time she came to run away from home, to escape to a dense, lonely forest, to a land of dreams far, far away from this cruel world, where girls whose hearts were sad could fly up to the sky and play hide-and-seek with the fairies hidden in the clouds. She opened our black front gate and stepped in. I happened to be standing at a window from which the gate was visible. Mesmerized, I looked at her beautiful face and saw her move toward the house. It seemed to me as if she was not walking, but floating.

She didn't get very far. Through the same window I watched her leave. Baba had refused to let her enter. She was turned away from the front door. Baba had asked her who she was, where she lived, why she was at our house, and then decided that there was no reason for a young girl to ignore her studies in the late afternoon to visit anyone. He had simply looked furious and pointed at the gate. "Get out. You've come just to a chat? Wasting everyone's time! Bad girl! Get out at once!"

The "bad girl," the "slut," had left without a word. I didn't know it then but I would never see her again. I didn't know that she would be married off to a total stranger, a much older man. Her notebook of poems would be burned, and she would be forced into a life of peeling, cleaning, grinding, cooking, and serving, as well as bearing a child almost every year.

And what would happen to me? Would I continue to watch the sky on her behalf and feel tears welling up in my eyes? Would I go on writing poetry? I would hate our society and the rules it imposed; would feel the invisible shackles placed on my hands and feet, realize that my wings had been chopped off, and that I was to be thrust into a strong cage where I would remain for eternity.

Or — perhaps — it was the other way around. Perhaps there was a cage inside my own being that confined me and pulled me back into its depths each time I wanted to spread my wings and soar in the sky.

~ 16 ~

Lying Cold on a White Bed

One Thursday night, Aunt Fajli's daughter died quite unexpectedly, much to the amazement of her family. Although not close, Mubashwera and I had played together whenever she came to visit our house, or whenever I went to Amirullah's. We had built a pretend-kitchen on our roof and cooked imaginary meals. Since such games were not allowed in her own home, she pretended to be Hassan, her brother Muhammad Hussain, and they beat up Yazid and Mabia in the imaginary battlefield of Karbala. No one wanted to be Yazid and Mabia, so they remained invisible. Hassan and Hussain threw punches in the air and kicked vigorously, each kick aimed at figures they couldn't see. I was the only witness to this war game.

I was never close to any of Aunt Fajli's children. They were quite distant. None of them spoke the way we did. Their tone was distinctly different, and they spoke more like people from India. The girls started doing namaz at the age of five and wearing burkhas at age ten. They didn't go to school or run about freely in a playing field or step out of the house unaccompanied, because the grown-ups had told them that this would anger Allah.

When Mubashwera was about fifteen, the steel factory once owned by Abu Bakar became Amirullah's property. He gave it to Amirullah, transferring all the relevant documents to his name. That was what Allah wanted. The crowds swelled in Amirullah's meetings; people queued up, like ants crawling in a row. Amirullah made his selection from those hopefuls and offered jobs in the factory only to those who were known for their devotion to Allah.

Uncle Tutu and Uncle Sharaf had by this time said good-bye to their studies and become followers of the peer. Aunt Fajli was delighted — she had succeeded in bringing her brothers onto the right path, away from the world of the flesh. Uncle Tutu and Uncle Sharaf both stopped wearing trousers and shirts. They now dressed in panjabis, placed round caps on their heads, and stopped shaving. In order to remove the last traces of the mundane world, Humaira, Sufaira, and Mubashwera took them to the little rooms, newly built, and offered naseehat. That is to say, they offered advice and guidance on how to walk on the path shown by Allah. After all, Allah was the master of the universe. One day I inadvertently stepped into the room where Uncle Tutu was receiving instruction and guidance from Humaira. He yelled at me and told me to get out at once. He was lying in bed and Humaira was stroking his chest as she spoke.

This was how naseehat had to be given, in complete privacy, in a dark room, stroking the chest of the recipient. That was what Ma told me.

Mubashwera was chosen to offer naseehat to Uncle Sharaf. It was all right, for Uncle Sharaf was her own uncle, not someone from the outside world. It was while she was giving advice that, one day, a jinn possessed her. This jinn was different from any other. It made its victim sit alone under a tree and weep. She told no one why she was weeping. She lost her appetite, complained she was feeling nauseous, gave up doing her namaz. All she did was look for a suitable tree to sit under. The naseehat sessions began to be ignored.

Eventually that vivacious girl, the player of war games, took to her bed. Even before steps could be taken to get rid of the jinn, she burned with unbearable fever. She was given holy water to drink, prayers were muttered, and various people blew on her, but the fever didn't abate. Aunt Fajli sat with her daughter's head in her lap, placing cold compresses on Mubashwera's forehead. The wet cloth dried in no time, letting off steam from the heat in her body. Mubashwera became breathless.

"I can't stand this anymore!" said Aunt Fajli at last. "Call a doctor."

"A doctor?" asked Musa, her husband, son of Peer Amirullah. "You think a doctor will succeed where our holy water has failed?"

"He might not, but what's the harm in trying? Allah will cure her, if she is to be cured at all. But Allah may route His cure through the doctor's medicines, who knows!"

Baba was sent for. He left for the peer's house clutching his medical bag. It was half-past midnight.

The patient was lying on a white sheet. Ailing for a whole week, she was exhausted. Her tongue was white, her eyes pale, her nails colorless. The doctor checked her pulse, took her blood pressure, listened to her heart. Then he told everyone to leave the room for ten minutes. He gave his patient an injection. A deep crease appeared between his brows. It got deeper, and he said, "Let's just wait and see."

He didn't expect a fee, because he treated his relatives free of charge.

In the morning, Mubashwera was found lying cold and dead in her bed. Aunt Fajli broke into loud sobs. In her house, if someone died, the others were not allowed to cry loudly. It was time for the dead person to go, so he — or she — had gone. Death simply meant returning to Allah, so there was no reason for anyone to cry or display their grief in public. If tears were shed for the dead, it might displease Allah. So, bid farewell with a smile on your lips.

As soon as Aunt Fajli began sobbing, Zohra, Amirullah's eldest daughter, leaped up and placed her hand over Aunt Fajli's mouth. "Sh-sh, what do you think you're doing? Your daughter has gone back to Allah. Pray for her. Look at her, her face so bright. She will definitely go to heaven. Allah has taken back what belonged to Him. It is a sin to cry over that. If you must weep, do so, but, for heaven's sake, don't make any noise!"

Wailing and giving free expression to grief in this house was considered sin, as bad as kabira. Aunt Fajli had to bow before the rules. She stuffed her veil into her mouth and gulped down her sobs.

When Ma returned home in the evening, her eyes were full of tears. "Mubashwera died," she said to Baba when he got home.

"She might have been saved if they had consulted a doctor earlier," Baba said. "By the time I saw her, it was too late."

Ma wiped her eyes and nose with her left hand and sighed. "Her time was up. Allah didn't allow her any extra time — how could she have lived? She must have gone to heaven. She was saying 'Allah! Allah!' before she died."

Baba took off his shoes and placed them under his bed. Then his socks came off, and he stuffed them into his shoes. There was a frown on his face. He started unbuttoning his shirt.

"She was pregnant," he said.

"Who was pregnant?"

I was straining my ears in the next room to hear this conversation; my ears started ringing at Baba's words.

"Who do you think? Your sister's daughter. What's her name . . . Muba . . . Mubashwera!"

Baba placed his damp shirt on a hanger.

"She wasn't married. How could she have been pregnant? How can you utter such foul words about a sweet, innocent girl? Your tongue will drop off, I'm telling you!" Again, Ma began weeping.

Baba slipped a lungi over his trousers, holding a corner of the top end between his teeth. Then he took his trousers off, hung them on a rack, released the lungi, and used his free hands to tie a knot over his stomach.

Ma was pacing in the room. From the next room I could see her feet as well as Baba's. She took five steps forward, then turned around and retraced them. She did this a few times, then began moving toward Baba. Her feet were bare and so were Baba's. Ma's were dark and soft, and the nail on one of her big toes was damaged. Baba's feet were fair, rather pale from always being covered by socks. His feet were dangling from the bed, the toes clustered together. The dark, unsteady feet with a damaged toenail went past the pale nails, then returned once more.

"She must have tried to get rid of the fetus using the root of some plant, perhaps. The whole thing got infected. Septicemia." Baba's voice sounded cold.

"No! Lies, you're just telling me a pack of lies! You'll be punished for this. Allah won't spare you for slinging mud on a poor, virtuous girl." Fire dripped from Ma's voice. The door slammed.

The sound of voices still floated into my room, but now the words were fragmented. I couldn't put the broken bits together and make a single whole sentence.

Death, it seemed to me, could come quite easily. Today, I was alive. Tomorrow I might be lying cold on a white bed. Today, I could move my limbs, tomorrow, they might be stiff and lifeless. Tonight, I might dream, tomorrow, I might not. Death would finish everything. According to Ma, it was the soul that flew up to Allah — the body stayed behind. The soul was the all-important thing. How did it fly? Like a white dove? Ma maintained that it was invisible, that it couldn't be seen. There were so many things on earth that remained hidden from our eyes!

After Mubashwera died, Uncle Sharaf turned away from the path of Allah, because there was no one left now to offer him naseehat. He went back to wearing shirts and trousers and living his life in the world of the flesh.

Only for a little while did he store a few memories in his trunk — pieces of bloodstained rags.

Return II

𝒟ada gave up his studies at the university in Dhaka, found a job in a foreign pharmaceutical company, and returned to Mymensingh.

"I have taken this job purely for Ma," he said. "There's no one to look after her. No one gives her any money. I don't want her to suffer anymore."

With his first month's salary, he bought four saris for Ma and ordered a pair of gold bracelets.

Ma fell on her saris and wept. She had, in fact, given up wearing them. But now she picked up one that Dada had bought and put it on, still sobbing as she made the pleats. She looked beautiful. Flinging her arms around her son, she said, "No, you needn't buy me anything else. I don't need anything more. You must save your money. Think of your own future."

The same woman who had once looked crushed and beaten now walked with her head held high, her back straight. Her own son was now earning; she no longer had to depend on a man who had been chasing another woman. I had never seen Ma so lively, so vivacious. Since it was a sin to maintain relations with a kafir, Aunt Fajli had once taken Ma to court to arrange a divorce with Baba. Ma had even signed the divorce papers in court. But later, when those papers reached Baba, he said, "To hell with it!" and tore them apart. Ma loathed having to live under the same roof with a kafir. But although she had often wanted to leave his house, she had never been able to do so. What I could not fathom was why she had not left. Was it because she had nowhere to go, or was it because she felt a strange attachment to the house, the people who lived in it, and the trees she had planted herself?

"My son has returned from the university with a bachelor of science degree. Oh, I am absolutely *delighted!*"

Baba uttered those words, speaking through clenched teeth, as soon as Dada came back from Dhaka. As a matter of fact, when he went to Dhaka, Dada already had his degree. Baba had sent him there in the hope that he would obtain a master's. However, two years later, Dada had come back, still carrying in his pocket the certificate he had acquired from his college in Mymensingh. "*I* would much rather have died with shame!" Baba exclaimed.

Dada sat in his room and heard Baba's comments in silence, his eyes as expressionless as those of a dead fish. Shortly afterward, he settled down and rearranged the furniture in his room. The first thing he did was remove Chhotda's bed and stand it up outside on the veranda. Surprisingly, this simple act seemed to upset Baba enormously. "Put this bed back where it was. At once!" he shouted. "If the person who once used that bed comes back one day, where do you think he's going to sleep? Put it back, and make his bed, just as you found it. Do it now!"

Ma sighed. "Kamal is never going to come back. I've heard he's left town, gone to Islampur, or some such place. Who knows how he's doing, whether he gets enough to eat?"

Baba hit the roof once more. "Why should *I* be concerned with what he eats, or how much he eats? Let him starve to death. Let him suffer. I don't care. *You* are responsible. You spoiled the children rotten."

Ma stepped forward and looked Baba in the eye, holding herself ramrod straight. "Why shouldn't I talk?" she asked, raising her chin. "How long will you keep me quiet? What do you do for me, anyway? Now my son looks after me, gives me money, buys me clothes and whatever else I need. I don't have to depend on any other man. How brutally you beat that poor boy, and then threw him out. Now what's the point in making a bed for him? What's the use?"

The use, Baba told her firmly, was purely Baba's business. Ma need not concern herself with it at all.

Dada bought some books by Rabindranath Tagore. He read aloud from them at times in his deep voice. Sometimes he asked me to read a few lines. I read poem after poem. Dada listened, corrected my pronunciation, told me about the degree of emotion I should display, where I should read slowly, where the tempo must be faster. "If you can't pour your heart into it, you should never read poetry," he said.

Some evenings were wholly dedicated to reciting poetry. The two of us took turns reading and listening. Only Dada was the judge. A new phase in my life began under Dada's supervision. He gave me a red notebook that had the name of his company printed on it. I began writing two or three poems in it every day. Dada read them and pronounced his verdict. Some, he said, were good; some were very good; others were "shit, just shit, nothing else, not poetry at all."

That red notebook started making its rounds among the girls in my class. When one finished reading it, another took it home. It was nearly a month before I got it back. Dada read a poem called "A Free Bird" and said, "Oh, if only I still had that magazine *Pata*! I would have published this poem of yours."

It was not just poetry that we read in the evenings. Sometimes we read short stories as well. Dada would read one, then I would read another. At times, Dada was so impressed by a few lines that he exclaimed, "Aha! Aha!" and read them all over again. I learned to do it, too. Our sessions remained quite lively — till Baba returned.

Songs were included as well. If asked to sing, I tried a couple of lines in my tuneless voice, then gave up. Dada couldn't sing either. He sounded like a mooing cow! Only Yasmin could sing well, so we included her in our music sessions. Dada thought of buying her a harmonium.

He bought a record player, and spent some evenings simply listening to songs. One day, after he had finished playing the song "The Days Gone By Keep Calling Me Back," I saw him crying. He did not know that I had quietly slipped into the room.

"Dada! Are you crying?" I asked.

"No!" Dada denied, hastily wiping his eyes. "Why should I cry? It was just . . . oh, it's nothing."

But I knew he had been crying. Was it for Sheela?

I could not forget this. It made me realize Dada had some secret sorrow. Sitting alone in the privacy of his room he shed tears for someone who had once been close, in days that had gone by.

I went and sat next to him by the window. The lilies in our garden were spreading a sweet smell. Dulal passed our house, playing his mouth organ. He walked so fast that he always appeared to be running, and he played his mouth organ all the time. Morning, afternoon, evening, or midnight — the sound of his playing would tell everyone he was there. He never spoke to anyone, or stopped on the way. He just kept running, as if he was on his way to some important mission. The truth was that he did not work at all. People said he was mad.

"Is Dulal really mad?" I asked Dada.

"No, I don't think so," Dada replied. Then he sighed and stood up. A smile appeared on his face, as if heavy clouds had parted to let the sun shine through them.

"Go, go and get the chessboard out. Let's see who wins today," he said. That smile instantly made me feel better. I brought the board and placed the chessmen on it. Dada had taught me to play, but now I could beat him anytime. He cheated endlessly, and changed the positions of the chessmen when I wasn't looking. So I said before we started, "Look, you must promise not to cheat." Yet twice I caught him out; and then, within an hour, I took his king and said "Check!" At once, Dada turned the board over.

"You lost, you lost!" I yelled.

"When?" Dada looked at me innocently. "How did I lose? You just did. Okay, tell me how I lost." He continued to look innocent, and refused to admit that I had beaten him. Why, then, did he turn the board over? It was because I had made a false move, and he couldn't bear to see me play so badly, he said. Not once did he acknowledge that I had learned to play very well indeed, and that I had won.

I came to be known in my school as a good student. In my class I always managed to secure one of the top three positions. However, that was still not good enough for Baba. He was convinced that I neglected my studies, otherwise why didn't I stand first? He was as irritable as before.

Ma, of late, had started to spend most of her time pleasing Dada. She cooked all his favorite dishes. He only had to say the word and it was ready: hot savories, spicy khichuri, fried hilsa, whatever he wanted. Ma's visits to Amirullah's house became irregular.

Dada had become an important man, now that he was earning. He took us to Chitrarupa, our local studio, and had a family photo taken. Then he had several photos taken of himself, from different angles, striking different poses. He even had a few of those enlarged and framed.

"Look!" he said. "Don't I look like a film hero?"

Yes, I had to admit that he did. He *was* a good-looking man.

I had drawn two portraits, one of Tagore and the other of Nazrul. Dada had those framed as well, and put them up on the wall. He pointed them out to all our visitors, and said, "My sister drew those." Then he bought me paints and brushes and told me to paint more pictures. Perhaps I would go to an art school, I thought. A long time ago one of my teachers had said that I would grow up to be a well-known artist. Now, no matter what I drew, Dada seemed to be just as impressed. "I am so glad I taught you how to draw when you were little!" he told me. "How else could you have drawn these lovely pictures?"

I told Dada about my secret dream, of going to an art school to study, so that I might improve my skills. Dada made a face. "If Baba hears of this," he said, "he will kill you. He'll never let you become an artist. He'll say there's no money in art."

Dada bought new clothes and shoes not just for Ma, but for Yasmin and me as well. He also took us to the cinema. I wanted to go back there, again and again, and pestered him every day to take me to see another film. At times Dada said to me, "Very well, send me a written application. I will consider the matter and see if your request might be granted."

I wrote out a formal application, starting with "Dear Sir" and ending with "Your most obedient servant." I copied it from my grammar book, which had examples of how to write an application. The page I consulted said, "write to your manager asking for a loan."

I substituted "going to the cinema" for "loan."

Dada, however, refused to make a quick decision, even after the application was submitted. I grew restless. He noticed this and said, "Look, why don't you have any patience? I hate people who get impatient easily."

I loved Dada, but I envied him, too. He was free to go where he liked, to do whatever he wanted. He bought a motorcycle and roamed all over town, sometimes going out of Mymensingh, to Tangail, Jamalpur, and Netrakona. I longed to go with him, to step out of the boundaries set for me. "I will take you one day to look at the mountain," Dada said.

I waited every day for him to let me join him. My agitation grew. But he kept postponing it from one month to the next. Still I lived in hope: that one morning, just as dawn broke, before anyone else woke up, I would go to see a mountain, far, far away, stand against its stillness and seclusion, and watch the dewdrops drip slowly.

A few months after Dada's return, Baba was transferred to the Mitford Hospital in Dhaka. He got more and more irritable each time he was transferred. This time he left Dada in charge of the household. He took a train from Dhaka every two days, reaching Mymensingh in the dead of night. Then he had to leave again the following morning, almost at the crack of dawn. He was now a professor in the jurisprudence department of the hospital. He taught medical students, and slit his knife through cadavers. The person who felt the happiest about Baba's transfer was me. It was time for me to spread my wings; I was at that age.

One evening I felt like walking by the side of the Brahmaputra, dipping my feet in its water. The river was close to our house, but I was never allowed to go near it. When I was small, I was told I must not go so far on my own because there were kidnappers who would stuff me into a sack and carry me away. Besides, there was also that creature Fo-ting-ting who spoke through his feet. He might gobble me up. Now that I was much older, I was told that it was not safe, nor seemly, for a grown-up girl to be seen walking by herself.

So I snuck out of the house without telling anyone, taking Yasmin with me. Ma was asleep, Dada out, Baba in Dhaka — there was no one to stop us. I was no longer afraid of Fo-ting-ting. Why shouldn't I go to the river? It was a dream I had cherished for many years, building it up bit by bit, drop by drop, to make it as long as the river itself — the dream to walk freely on the bank of the Brahmaputra, going where I liked, sitting by its side, soaking my feet in the water.

We got to the river and began walking. The wind was fresh, blowing my hair, lifting the hem of my dress, whistling softly in my ears. The gentle evening sun fell on the sandy bank, making it glisten. Just at this moment, just as my heart was full of joy, a man walked toward us from the opposite direction. I said nothing to him, did nothing to provoke his action, but when he was close enough to touch me he suddenly reached out and pinched my breasts and my buttocks painfully. Then he walked off, laughing. His friends stood at some distance and clapped and laughed with him. As if my body was not my own but was a toy they were free to play with.

The Brahmaputra belonged to everyone, including me. I had as much right to walk next to it as anyone else. But what right did those men have to humiliate me like that? I clenched my fists. I wanted to whip each one of those men, cutting open his flesh. But I couldn't. I couldn't take another step forward.

"Bubu, let's go back home. I'm scared!" said Yasmin. Her voice trembled.

We returned home, seething with rage, to find Uncle Aman and Ma sitting very close together.

"Here you are, dear. How are you?" Uncle Aman asked me.

I gave him a sharp glance and went to my room without speaking a word. Then I shut the door and burst into tears. But I did not let anyone else see my tears. No one knew that a whirlpool of pain was pulling me, dragging me down, farther and farther, into its depths.

Later, I asked Ma, "Why did Uncle Aman come to our house?"

Ma smiled sweetly. "He wants to turn to Allah. I was offering him naseehat."

"Don't overdo it, Ma. It was giving naseehat that killed Mubashwera. You saw that for yourself, didn't you?"

I did utter those words, but my voice was so faint that Ma didn't hear what I said. Or it could be that she was so preoccupied with her own thoughts that she did not even try to hear me.

Uncle Aman came every evening. He sat in Ma's room and the two of them whispered together. Ma kept her door ajar at such times. One day, I happened to push the door open and go into her room. I saw Uncle Aman jump off the bed. Ma was still under the mosquito net.

"Why is the room so dark, Ma? What are you doing here?" I asked.

"Well," Ma replied, "you see, Aman is having a few problems with his wife. He's very sad, so he comes to me sometimes to talk, to share his sorrow. It makes him feel better. I keep telling him to think of Allah."

"I am hungry. Give me something to eat!" I said, quite unnecessarily. If I wanted something to eat, it would have been sufficient to tell Moni. She would have brought me a plate of food.

This time when Ma spoke, she sounded annoyed. "I have a headache. I was trying to lie down for a while. Why won't you let me rest in peace?"

I left her room and went to stand on the front veranda. I took deep breaths. The sight of Uncle Aman and Ma sitting so intimately had brought a tightness to my chest. I was finding it difficult to breathe. When I was seven years old that man had stripped me naked. Now, I was afraid that he might do the same to Ma, in her dark room.

Even Dada noticed Uncle Aman's arrival at odd hours, darting uneasy glances everywhere.

~ 18 ~

The House of Termites

(M)a had a wooden cupboard. One shelf was packed with books, the other shelves were crammed with clothes tossed in any which way, not a single one neatly folded. Among the books were some by Maksudul Momenin, the Neamul Koran, a book of poems by Amirullah called *Minar, Tajkeratul Aulia,* and a book he had written in English called *Who Am I?* So Amirullah knew English, too! Ma had often enough said to me, "Huzur is most knowledgeable. He speaks fluent English!" When she uttered these words, her eyes would light up.

Did that mean he studied things that might make him think of worldly pleasures? The question rose to my lips but I swallowed it before it could slip out. Ma would no doubt have found it impertinent. The truth was that in the matter of Allah and the Prophet, logic and reason had no meaning whatsoever for Ma. The same applied to Amirullah. If I simply went along with whatever she said, making appropriate noises, she was happy. Since I was her child it was my duty to make her happy, or at least, that was what I had been brought up to believe. Besides, if I could make her happy I was spared her slaps and punches and when I sat down to eat she served me pieces of meat. To gain her affection I kept my lips together, sealed with invisible glue. Those who did not follow the Koran and the hadith were not Muslims; Ma was very clear about that. They would burn in hell: No one would be spared. It was as simple as that. The basic rules were all very simple: The fire in hell would roast you alive if you did not do your namaz or observe roja; if you went out without draping on a burkha; if you talked to a man who was not your relative; if you laughed too loudly or cried noisily. No matter what you did, there could be no escape from that fire. Fire,

fire, and fire. I wanted to ask Ma why everyone was so afraid of fire, especially in this day and age. Why, in cold countries people lit fires in all their rooms! And what about the circus? So many of their exciting shows involved playing with fire. Minor burns were easily treatable nowadays. Why did Allah have to terrorize everyone with the threat of fire? There were so many other ways of hurting people. Surprisingly, Allah did not seem interested in any of them. Wicked people enjoy causing physical pain. However, those with real cunning enjoy causing mental anguish. A battered mind is so much harder to bear than a battered body. But Allah, it seemed to me, was more wicked than cunning. No different from Getu's father. Or, at times, very much like Baba, who did not hesitate to thrash me black and blue if I did not obey his every command. The difference between him and Allah was simply that he wanted to give me an education in this mundane world, so that I could be successful in life, and Allah wanted me to study the Koran and hadith.

To me Baba was as distant as Allah. I felt a lot happier when he was not around, and any mention of Allah — formless and shapeless as He was, poor thing — also caused me much discomfort. The truth was that I wanted both of them to stay away from me. They pushed me in two different directions, so much so that I ceased to have an existence of my own. All that remained was a corpse, divided in two, lying in a morgue. If Baba was pleased with me he brought me large boxes of sweets, telling me to help myself to the best pieces of fish at dinner. Allah, I heard, behaved in a similar fashion. If *He* was pleased with anyone, the best food was provided in abundance — the flesh of exotic birds, grapes, wine, and many other things. Beautiful pink women, their skin glowing, poured wine into men's glasses. Grandpa, having returned from hajj, was convinced that he would go straight to heaven. And there, after a good heavenly meal, when he belched, he would emit a wonderful smell. I couldn't stand anyone belching, wonderful smell or not. What would happen to less fortunate people, I wondered, who might be denied such a meal? Would they simply stand around and smell someone else's belching? In my mind, I cast Getu's father in the role of the unlucky man, Grandpa the fortunate one. I placed the hadith on my right, and put the two men on my left. One continued to belch, the other continued to smell. I felt part of the scene, too; at the same time, however, I was not.

There was a nest of termites in the hadith. Our house was damp. Termites often attacked our books if they were not regularly aired and their pages turned. The sight of a fat termite made me cross. As I was sitting on the floor, I placed a black shoe within reach. I pressed the shoe on the hadith and smashed some termites. One of my eyes remained fixed on the dead termites, the other read the half-eaten words in the holy book. Some of them had been arranged to proclaim the following:

> Everything in the world is for enjoyment. The best thing to enjoy is the virtuous wife.
>
> Whatever you see in this world is for consumption by pleasure-seekers. The most precious thing in the world is a virtuous woman.

I was half reclining on the floor, one hand under my chin, the other clutching the book.

> If I were to order anyone to bow, I would certainly order all women to do so for their husbands.
>
> If a wife ever tells her husband that she is dissatisfied with whatever he does, she will lose all the virtue she may have gained over a period of time, even as long as seventy years. She may have kept roja during the day, and done her namaz at night, but every virtue earned thereby will be lost.
>
> A husband has the right to beat his wife in four different cases: 1. he tells her to dress well and come to him and she disobeys his command; 2. she rejects his invitation to have sexual intercourse; 3. she ignores her duties, and fails to do her namaz; and 4. she visits someone's house without her husband's permission.
>
> Women who do not get jealous when their husbands take a second wife, but accept it with patience and fortitude, are treated as martyrs by Allah and are sent to heaven.
>
> If pus and blood are oozing from a man's body and his wife licks it all up, it is still not enough to pay him back what he deserves.

The man with the lowest rank in the heaven, even he will have eighty thousand servants and seventy-two wives.

If a husband orders his wife to do something, she is bound to follow the order of her husband, even if she is running from one mountain to another.

Some insects left the book and began crawling toward me. Were they going to eat me as well? This house was being taken over by termites and woodworms. At night, the worms ate through the woodwork, making clicking noises. The termites devoured our books in absolute silence. They even ate the words of the great Prophet Muhammad. Were these termites Muslims? No, they couldn't possibly have a specified religion. They seemed to enjoy the complete works of Saradindu Bandopadhyay, a Hindu writer, as much as the holy Koran.

After Dilruba's departure, books became my only companions. I had finished most of what our school library had to offer — books by Bankimchandra, Saratchandra, Bibhutibhushan Bandopadhyay, Rabindranath Tagore. Whatever I could lay my hands on. I took to the roof or sat on the stairs, or read at my desk and even at times in bed. When Baba came home, I hid these "unsuitable" books behind my schoolbooks, holding the latter in front of me without reading a word. When everyone went to sleep at night, I lit a lamp under my mosquito net and read every word of the "unsuitable" ones. Yasmin lay next to me, fast asleep.

Ma sometimes said to me, "What rubbish do you read all the time? Mubashwera died. You saw that, so you should think of Allah now. We all have to die, haven't we?"

I made no reply. Ma's commands and instructions hung over my head like the sun in June — waiting, as if to burn me to a cinder. Many times I was warned that if I did not follow the precepts laid down in the Koran and the hadith there would be hell to pay on the day of judgment. However, until now, I had no idea what *hadith* meant. Now that I knew, I did not wish to delve any deeper. I knew that it was useless to search for pearls or diamonds in a pot of shit. I closed the termite-ridden book. It seemed to move under my hands, as if it was belching; as if it, too, had eaten some food served in heaven. The sound of Ma's footsteps made me spring back and quickly replace the book on her shelf. She had no idea that termites were silently eating away at the hadith. She was busy doing naseehat with Uncle Aman. Every night I could hear whispers from her room, also suppressed laughter. I said nothing to her about the termites. If they were hungry, let them eat what they could. Why should I try to kill them?

What I couldn't understand was why I was supposed to turn to Allah because Mubashwera was dead. I had no wish to think of Allah. All that business about Allah was just made up. I thought that the Koran was written by a greedy, selfish man like Uncle Sharaf, or the man who grabbed my breasts by the river. If the hadith was the words of Prophet Muhammad, then he was definitely like Getu's father: nasty, cruel, an abuser, insane. I could not find any difference between Allah and Muhammad.

Even after I had put the book back, millions of termites remained deep inside me, silently eating away all the letters and words in my head, and who knows what else.

Getu's mother arrived in the evening. It took me a while to recognize her, although she spoke in her usual hoarse voice. Ma was sitting in a chair on the veranda, listening attentively. At the same time, her prayer beads were moving in her hand. For the beads to move, it was necessary to recite the *darood,* the holy Arabic verses, carefully. How could Ma do that *and* listen to Getu's mother? Perhaps she had two minds, one focused on Allah, the other on this world. Ma's world, in particular, was quite small. It was possible to go around it twice a day quite easily.

Suddenly Getu's mother stopped talking and lifted her sari. Ma's fingers were pushing the beads much faster now. The sari moved and so did the beads, one in rhythm with the other. Getu's mother exposed her leg. The whole leg, from thigh to foot, was burned. Ma gave a horrified gasp. This time it was not Getu's father who had done this but a man called Safar Ali. About two years ago Safar Ali had married Getu's mother. It was he who had attacked her with a burning log. Why? A voice piped up inside my head: Because he was her husband, and every husband has the right to do whatever he likes with his wife. But both Ma and Getu's mother were of the view that Safar Ali was a low-down, third-rate character.

I felt like telling Ma that Safar Ali obviously followed what was written in the Koran and the hadith. That was why he had beaten his wife. The words trembled on my lips, but then I thought better and gulped them down. Would my words also be eaten by termites? Who knew?

Getu's mother had come to look for a job in our house. Now, with a charred body, she could never hope to marry again. No man would be prepared to feed her. The prayer beads moved more slowly in Ma's hands. "But I already have a maid to do all my work," she said. "I don't need anyone else."

Ma's legs moved as she spoke, in keeping with an unheard rhythm. Perhaps she could hear some music deep within her heart. Perhaps a peacock danced in her mind. Ma kept her feathers tightly folded during the day, unfurling them at night. I sat on the threshold and, through the gap between Ma's legs, watched the darkness of the evening falling on Getu's mother's face. On the veranda, the blue beads in Ma's hand glinted like a cat's eyes.

Although Ma refused to offer her a job, she did say, "Don't go without eating something. Take some rice and dal."

This time, I had to speak. Without moving, but turning my eyes away from Getu's mother's burned legs, I blurted out, "Why can't you give her a job? Surely the world won't come to an end if you do?"

Ma simply shrugged and said, "It is going to anyway."

Getu's mother continued to sit on the veranda, still and lifeless, like the tree stump. A swarm of mosquitoes moved over her head, going around and around, settling on her arms and legs — a solid, dark, and hungry mass greedy for nourishment, as if they were visiting a restaurant with free meals. She did not drive them away, perhaps because her burned skin had lost all sensation. The only feeling left in her was in her stomach, pangs of hunger. That's what happened to the poor. They lost everything — family, friends, property, wealth. What never left them was hunger.

What would I have done had I been Getu's mother? I put myself in her place and saw myself get up and start walking away without waiting to be fed. I would have passed the woodapple tree and gone out our front gate. I would have walked very quickly, faster than the wind, a bit like the mad boy Dulal. I didn't have a mouth organ, but what I did have frozen inside me were screams I had never uttered. I needed no musical instrument. Waves of heat emanated from my body, but they could no longer hurt me. My mind had been reduced to ashes a long time ago; nothing was left in my body that was not already burned. Yet sparks would fly out of my charred body as I walked. I would soon reach Safar Ali's house. When I reached it, he would be amazed to see me and would promptly grab a red-hot log to strike me. But before he could touch me flames would shoot out of his own body — hissing, fuming, blinding, raging flames. With arms raised high, they would encircle Safar Ali and dance a merry dance, slowly consuming him and the burning log in his hand. I would watch until there was nothing left but charred remains. Only then would my hunger be appeased.

The same fire they had kept locked within me all these years would now burst forth, its strength magnified tenfold, its fury immeasurable. I would start walking again, speeding before the wind, not really caring where I was going. But the fire within me would become a shining beacon, one that would show me the way to Getu's father's house, back to his courtyard where I would hear the sound of my own wailing. It was the same me who had been beaten, crushed, and finally given talaq, a divorce, in the presence of a large audience who had filled the courtyard. The breeze would still carry the sound of my sobbing.

Having thought thus far, I stopped for a while. Getu's mother was still sitting like a statue, the mosquitoes swarming around her. I looked at her crumpled body and decided not to be her anymore. Instead, without moving an inch from the threshold, I became the new wife Getu's father had taken, a girl so young that she still played hide-and-seek with other children. When I became her, Getu's father picked up a sickle and struck me with it. I fell down in the courtyard, bleeding and moaning, in front of all those who had gathered to watch the spectacle in silence, some with their hands on their elbows or resting their heads on their hands, as if they were simply waiting for the final scene in a film. Suddenly, I startled everyone by springing to my feet and snatching the sickle from Getu's father. I slashed his skin to ribbons and sprinkled salt all over him. Everyone from the crowd shouted, "Mad, you are totally mad!"

Yes, so I was. Perfectly insane.

Once, when Moni had failed to clean some prawns properly, Ma threatened to skin her alive and sprinkle salt on her wounds. Uncle Aman had asked for prawn curry, but because they were not properly cleaned, he had been sick afterward. Ma was absolutely livid. Moni had taken the threat quite seriously. So had I.

"What happens if someone sprinkles salt on wounds?" I asked her.

"It causes enormous pain," Moni replied, looking as white as a sheet. I started to wipe her tears, then recalled those nights when I had played with her body. I moved my hand away from her face.

Go away from here, Moni, I said to her in my mind, *forget those days, Moni. Leave this house, go with your mother and sister and build the home of your dreams somewhere near a green rice field. If you can find a river, try to see how the sun sets in its waters. How beautiful it is, how gorgeous the colors of the sky! You'll feel a lot better. I promise.*

In the end, Moni was not skinned alive nor was any salt sprinkled on her. Even today, however, I use that method in my mind to punish people. I punished Uncle Sharaf and Uncle Aman. Today, I wanted to cause a great deal of pain to Getu's father but all I could do was imagine hurting him, nothing more. Here I was, just a young girl, so thin that a strong gust of wind would have blown me over. How could I possibly have the strength to protest, to rebel?

But then again — it did occur to me sometimes — at least I had the will. Surely that counted for something?

~ 19 ~

After the War

Some of the Hindus were returning to their empty houses. They were back from the refugee camps in Calcutta, back in their own country, their abandoned homes. Their houses had been looted. Stray dogs, which could be seen lying stretched out in most courtyards, had been the only occupants of those vacated houses. Now the houses were full of people once more. I stood on the roof, resting my chin on the railing, and watched the return of my neighbors. It seemed as if a fresh new tide had risen, rushing into a dry, sluggish Brahmaputra. A dead garden was suddenly full of colorful blossoms. No one expressed regret about stolen goods. They were simply happy to have found their homes intact. Already, the sound of *keertan*, Hindu chanting, could be heard from some houses. The women were lighting lamps every evening, and ululating. A silent graveyard had shaken itself awake.

One day, about a week after the Hindus' return, a group of freedom fighters opened our black front gate and walked into our house. They were all carrying rifles. Behind them were more than a dozen of the newly returned people. We knew them only by sight. I invited them in with a smile but their faces remained grim, as if they were visiting a sworn enemy. The armed men moved from one room to the other, saying, "Why, where's the stuff that was looted? Come on, people, grab what you think you've lost!"

Our neighbors, people we knew only by sight, stepped forward and began taking things away. They took our bronze plates, glasses and bowls, brass pitchers, even tables and chairs. At that moment, Ma happened to be pouring machine oil into her sewing machine.

The container remained clutched in her hand while a man picked up her sewing machine and placed it on his shoulder. I stared speechlessly, as did Ma.

When the men left, taking most of our belongings, Ma remarked, "You must pay for your sins, mustn't you? Serves him right."

Her words were meant for Baba; I could guess that. Upon our return from the village, when we thought the war was over, we had noticed a few objects in the house that were not there before. Ma had said to Baba, "What's all this? Did you buy this stuff? Why couldn't you buy new things? Look at those drums — they're old and rotting away! I suppose they are used for storing gur, but how long will they last? What will you do with them?"

Baba was engaged in taking off his socks and placing them inside his shoes. He did not reply.

"Or . . ." Ma wrinkled her nose, "did you bring those in from some Hindu household?"

Those old drums of gur surprised me as well. I found it difficult to believe that Baba had taken them from someone else's house without their knowledge. Baba had offered his protection to a Hindu boy, Pradeep, who had to change his name to a Muslim one, Alam, during the war. He was allowed to stay in our house and even handled all the cash in Baba's pharmacy once the war was over. Could the same Baba who had placed so much trust in a Hindu have been tempted to take some of the possessions the Hindus had left behind? But no, in 1971 people from Madarinagar were staying in our house — my grandfather and my uncles, Riazuddin and Iman Ali. Maybe taking those drums was their idea!

Since I did not have the courage to ask Baba directly, I went and asked my grandfather. "Did you loot things that belonged to the Hindus?"

My grandfather — whom I called Boro dada — was sitting on a metal chair watching our ducks and hens roaming in the courtyard. He appeared to be giving them all his attention, as if no other creature on earth was as worthy and important as the ducks and hens, as if a human being standing by his side asking questions did not deserve an answer at all. I had to give him a little push and repeat my question before he came out of his reverie.

"It was the Biharis!" he said. "Well, they were the ones who had thrown things out on the streets and were burning them. So we . . . we just picked a few things up and brought them home, that's all."

"*Who* brought them home? Baba? Was Baba involved in this?" I persisted.

Boro dada began throwing grains of wheat at the hens. "We did it. It was us," he told me. It was us. That was all I learned, but the answer was far from satisfactory.

When he returned home and saw that our house had been looted, Baba said nothing. He simply stood on the veranda, his arms folded across his chest. Was he regretting his behavior? It gave me considerable pleasure to think that he was. I longed to look at his remorseful face. All I had seen so far in my life was his arrogance; all I had heard were his roars. Such a lot of arrogance, I thought, could well turn a man into a devil.

When Dada came back home I said to him, "Some people came today to take back their looted stuff."

An eerie silence gripped our house. Baba continued to stand on the veranda, his arms intertwined.

It was Ma who broke the silence. She stood at a distance from Baba, but close enough to make sure he heard every word. When she spoke, her voice sounded brittle. "Where was the need to steal a few old and rusted drums? Allah always punishes sinners. But I have been punished too, through no fault of my own. They took my sewing machine. I bought it myself, with the money I'd saved."

It is true that misfortunes never come singly. The day after our house was looted — the very next day — Dada was picked up on the street and arrested by the security forces. A special band of men, the Rokshi Bahini, had been appointed by Sheikh Mujib to combat terrorism. They built camps in various places, and had started arresting anyone who struck them as suspicious. All suspects were tied up and beaten, even Dada, who had never hurt a fly. Baba went to get him released, but had to return alone. The Bahini kept him for two weeks, beat him regularly, and then, when he still showed no sign of being a terrorist, they let him go.

After Dada returned from the camp he turned violently against Mujib. He went around saying, "We were better off with the

Pakistanis. At least our roads were safe then." A lot of other people who once supported Mujib had also started saying, "What kind of a government is this? Appointing a special task force to harass poor, innocent citizens!"

People's dissatisfaction with the Mujib regime grew steadily over the next few years. Sheikh Mujib had formed a political party, Bakshal, and placed a ban on every other group.

"What sort of a government have we got? There's a raging famine now and people are starving to death!" Baba commented.

A number of bearded men emerged from nowhere, wearing caps on their heads. "This isn't independence at all!" they shrieked. "It's all so meaningless. We'll have to build another Pakistan."

Uncle Siddique sighed and said, "I just cannot imagine what's going to happen to this country. What this government is doing is something even the Pakistani government had never done. They celebrated shab-e-baraat with such pomp and show in Bongo Bhavan. No one did that in the Pakistani regime. Mujib went to attend Islamic conferences. What a lot of help we got from Russia during the war! And now Mujib's government wants Bangladesh to be recognized as a purely Muslim nation. They even dare to speak against India! Could they ever have gotten their independence if the Indian army hadn't come along to help?"

I understood very little of politics. All I knew was that whenever I heard Sheikh Mujib's speech of March 7 broadcast on the radio I felt a strange thrill. All my hair stood on end. "Our struggle this time is a struggle for independence! This battle is for our freedom!" These words were not mere slogans, they were like poetry — moving, inspiring, passionate. They made my heart tremble. In my school, I sang, "Joy Bangla! Banglar joy!" But it was not just a song; it was much more than that.

In our neighborhood we had frequent entertainment programs. I ran to watch the moment I heard the music on loudspeakers. Groups of boys and girls played the harmonium and sang; some danced to those songs. How wonderful they looked! Their songs made my heart beat faster. A similar thing happened when I heard songs about Khudiram. Uncle Kana used to tell us stories about Khudiram. He was a young boy who had thrown a bomb at the viceroy in an attempt to free his country from British rule. He was hung by the British. I wanted to be like Khudiram. Brave like him, and reckless.

One day the entire town appeared tense. Little groups gathered on street corners to talk in whispers, as if the world would be destroyed in just a couple of minutes. Some men were holding transistor radios to their ears. Their faces were white, their eyes round. What had happened? What was the matter now? We had already been through all this in 1971. The days of listening intently to the radio were over. Four years had passed since then. We had dealt with a famine in that period and were getting our damaged roads and blown-up bridges repaired and rebuilt. So what could be the matter? What had gone wrong?

Whenever there was a serious problem that seemed to affect the whole nation, people turned to the BBC. No one had faith in the local news. In our house, Baba did the same. He told me to turn the knob on the radio and find the BBC. I felt quite proud to be given this important task, since Baba usually never asked me to do anything except study. I was seldom included in any activity. If a knob had to be turned on a radio, it would normally be done by either Dada or Chhotda. I was supposed to stand at a distance and gape in silence. But today Dada was not at home. He had gone to Sherpur for a couple of days. In my brothers' absence I was given the responsibility of turning the knob.

As soon as the needle got close to the BBC, Baba said, "Stop! Stop!" A few words came wafting across on the ether; the sound broke up from time to time, destroying sentences.

Sheikh Mujib had been killed.

But that was not all. The killers had murdered virtually everyone in his family at the house where they lived. What! How was it possible? Baba clutched the veins throbbing at his temples and sat mutely. Had Chhotda been around, he would have pursed his lips and gone out to sit on the veranda. Dada would probably have said, "Mujib's two sons, Sheikh Kamal and Sheikh Jamal, were driving everyone mad at the university in Dhaka. Each went around with a gun in his pocket. Honestly, they were crossing all boundaries. How long could people take it without protest?"

Ma paced restlessly, saying from time to time, "How could they be so cruel? They killed his sons, their wives, even his youngest son,

Russell. He was only a child! What did any of his family do to deserve this? How can anyone be so completely ruthless? How?"

"Will our country go back to being another Pakistan?"

I threw the question at Baba. There was no reply. He was still sitting silently, clutching his head.

"Ma, why doesn't anyone tell me? Will this country turn into another Pakistan?"

I spoke as if my parents had answers to all my questions. That, obviously, was not the case. All Ma could say was, "The whole family . . . wiped out, in the middle of the night, just like that! Allah is our judge. He will punish them."

Even now, Baba did not speak a word. A little later, although it was still quite early, two men came to visit Baba. They were Makhanlal Lahiri and M. A. Kahhar. They sat in the living room, drank tea, and spoke harshly about the future of our nation. I listened at the door and understood some of what was said, but not all of it. None of the grown-ups included me in their discussions. Whether it was because I was not old enough, or because I was a girl, I could not tell.

I looked at the picture of Sheikh Mujib that hung in my room and felt very, very sorry for him. There he was, his finger raised, talking. He had been here on this earth just yesterday. But today he was no more. I could not believe it. When I switched on the radio again, the song "Joy Bangla" was not being played. I began to feel afraid. My nightmares returned. What if another war started? What if we had to get into a cart and run away again? What if guns boomed in the streets again and people were killed? Anyone could be killed, without any questions being asked. And what if a flashlight fell on my body again, a cold, wriggly snake slithered into my flesh, into my blood, into the very marrow in my bones?

Things had changed overnight. We were no longer supposed to speak Sheikh Mujib's name, or say "Joy Bangla!" I felt suffocated. Baba kept saying, "What about the future? What's going to happen now?" His words crawled out of the living room and slipped into the inner part of the house.

He repeated those words the next day when he discovered that Abu Ali, his right-hand man at the pharmacy, had stolen two hundred thousand takas and run away with it.

"A miser," Ma proclaimed, "can never enjoy his wealth, especially if he saves it by neglecting his wife and children. He always loses his money somehow or other. When my mother lost all her money — and wasn't it looted from this house? — I said to you so many times, please help my mother. But you didn't lift a finger to help her. Now, haven't you had all your money taken from you? Allah sees all, it is His punishment."

The whole country was still charged with tension, but Riazuddin and Iman Ali continued to travel from Madarinagar and Baba gave them a great deal of money to buy more land. Ma made them sit in the kitchen and fed them rice in large bowls, with only a little dal poured on one side, and dried roasted chilies. They crushed the chilies, mixed them with their rice, and ate the lot. Ma made beds for them on the floor, but did not bother to give them mosquito nets. Their faces turned blotchy and red from mosquito bites.

Baba got back home late at night and asked, "Have you fed them?"

"What do you think?" Ma retorted sharply. "They've had their fill!"

I continued with my studies, still reading a lot, hiding "unsuitable" books under "suitable" ones. Baba continued to dream: One day his daughter would finish her studies, be a brilliant success, and stand on her own feet.

I still crept up to the roof, in secret. I liked looking at the boys who walked past our house — the wavy hair of one, the dimple on another's cheek, or the laughter in his eyes. When it got dark I would call it a day and go back to my room. From inside my room it was impossible to know if there was a moon in the sky or whether the sky was dark. For a long time now I had not walked with the moon.

Ma continued to visit Amirullah, and Uncle Aman continued visiting Ma, always arriving after dark. Ma continued giving him naseehat, pouring her heart into the task. She had packed herself a suitcase, which remained tucked away under her bed. Soon she would leave for Mecca, traveling in the vehicle that Allah would send. She still begged Amirullah to include her name in the first batch of people who would go. I no longer felt, as I did when I was young, that if Ma died, so would I.

Baba was transferred from the Mitford Hospital in Dhaka back to Mymensingh. He taught at the medical college, trying to drive some sense into a lot of senseless heads. In the evenings he sat in his pharmacy behind a door marked DOCTOR and examined his patients. The number of his patients grew every day.

Razia Begum divorced Chakladar and began sending messages to Baba.

None of us knew what had happened to Chhotda, whether he was dead or alive. Baba still kept his bed ready for him, in the hope that one day he might return. Dada started making new furniture for his room, and looking all over town for a pretty girl with an oval face to marry.

And I, in my corner, I continued to grow.

GLOSSARY

Abbaji father.

akika Muslim ceremony during which a child is officially named.

Amma "mother"; can be used for any woman to whom someone wishes to show respect as well as a certain kind of affection.

anchal sari end.

annas pennies.

Apa term of respect for an older sister or any woman older than the speaker or to whom the speaker wishes to show deference in Muslim society. Bear in mind that Bengali custom forbids the use of the proper names of one's elders or social superiors. Apa eventually becomes part of a name when one addresses a woman in the context of a respectful but close relationship.

ayah child's nurse.

Baba father.

Bajan a close equivalent of Bhai saab.

Bhai saab term of respect for addressing an elder brother or any man of a certain age or social status.

bidi a small cigarette that is rolled in a tobacco leaf rather than paper.

Bihari a Bengali term designating Indian Muslims, the majority of whom come from the province of Bihar and who, following the Partition in 1947, opted for Pakistan and chose to take refuge in East Bengal, which was nearer than western Pakistan. They do not speak Bengali but a language closer to Urdu. During the events of 1971 they supported the Pakistan army, which allowed them to occupy the properties of Bengal Hindus who had fled to India or were hiding in the countryside.

Borobu term of respect for the oldest sister-in-law in a Bengali household.

Bubu a very informal term for the oldest sister.

burkha a long veil worn by Muslim women over their clothes that covers the entire body.

chanachur a snack food made from chickpeas, lentil noodles, and other ingredients; it is generally quite spicy.

Chhotda commonly designates the youngest of elder brothers; this is what Taslima calls her second brother, because it violates Bengali tradition for younger family members to address their older siblings by name.

chira puffed rice.

chum sweets.

Dada eldest brother; this is what Taslima calls her oldest brother, whose name is Noman. It may also be used when addressing a man who is older or of higher social status than the speaker as a term of respect and affection.

dak bungalow an official dwelling for the use of government administrators when traveling to provincial towns.

dal generic name for members of the legume family, such as lentils, and all the various dishes prepared from them.

dhoti the traditional clothing of Bengali Hindu men that consists of a long piece of high-quality cotton worn knotted about the waist so that it covers the legs.

Dula-bhai a term of respect for a brother-in-law.

Eid name of two Muslim festivals. A distinction is made between the small Eid (Eid alfitr) that marks the end of the monthlong fast of Ramadan and the large Eid (Eid al-Adha) that commemorates the sacrifice of Abraham.

garam masala a blend of spices that includes cloves, cardamom, and cinnamon.

gur a brown sweet made from date palms.

jalebis a sweet made of a light pastry that is deep-fried in a ring or pretzel shape then dipped in a thick sweet syrup.

kalia a culinary preparation that involves the use of thick spicy sauces.

kazi a judge who specializes in Islamic law; he presides over marriages and all family matters that have legal standing.

korma a heavily spiced roasted meat dish.

lungi a kind of long cotton apron or loincloth worn knotted around the waist. It is the sole lower garment of by poor men, who may wear a T-shirt with it to cover the torso. Men of the middle and leisure classes wear this as a garment to relax in when at home.

maulvi a professor and specialist in Islamic tradition and Koranic studies.

Miabhai a term used to address the eldest brother or any man when one wishes to show great deference and respect.

neem a tree whose small fibrous branches, which are very bitter and astringent, are used to clean the teeth. In country villages the leaves are used as a medication.

pajama fine-quality cotton pants, white for men and colored for women, that billow out at the waist with different leg sizes according to the style of various regions in India.

puja Hindu religious rite consisting of offerings, prayer, and ritual gestures addressed to a particular deity.

pulao a spiced rice dish accompanied by meat.

Punjabis what Bengalis most often called Pakistanis, because the majority of the soldiers in the Pakistan army were natives of this region of West Pakistan.

rasgolla the favorite sweet of the Bengalis; it is a ball of cheese and flour cooked to a spongy consistency, which is then dipped in sweet syrup.

sahib designates foreigners in general, particularly whites. Added to the name, this term becomes an honorific that more or less corresponds to the English *mister*.

salwar-kamiz a woman's garment originating in Punjab and other regions of northwestern India and Pakistan, where it is the traditional garb of Muslim women. The salwar-kamiz is a suit of several garments, consisting of a kind of large pajamas tied at the ankles and a long tunic.

shiuli name of both the bush and its very aromatic flowers.

taka the monetary unit of Bangladesh.

zamindar a large landowner.